Breaking the Silence

Breaking the Silence

Lessons of Democracy and Social
Justice from the World War II
Honouliuli Internment and POW
Camp in Hawai'i

Social Process in Hawai'i
Volume 45

Suzanne Falgout
Linda Nishigaya
Guest Editors

Department of Sociology
University of Hawai'i at Mānoa

Social Process in Hawai'i

Executive Editor
D. William Wood

Volume 45
**Breaking the Silence:
Lessons of Democracy and Social Justice
from the World War II Honouliuli Internment
and POW Camp in Hawai'i**

Guest Editors
Suzanne Falgout
Linda Nishigaya

Copyright © 2014
Department of Sociology
University of Hawai'i at Mānoa

21 20 19 18 17 16   7 6 5 4 3 2

Cover photographs by R. H. Lodge,
courtesy of Hawai'i's Plantation Village

Manufactured in the United States of America.

Distributed by
University of Hawai'i Press
2840 Kolowalu Street
Honolulu, Hawai'i 96822-1888

ISSN 0737-6871-45
ISBN 978-0-8248-4733-3

Contents

Preface

A sheltered valley forged by Pele's fires opens its mouth to the shimmering waters of Puʻuloa below. On days, it seems Pele's fires still burn in the gulch and ravine. Absent cooling breezes, searing heat from the earth's red soil rises toward the skies, but the valley's steep walls box in the air, forming a stratigraphy of radiant thermals. Puʻuloa's cooling waters tease the thirst that is the valley called by Pele's children Honouliuli or "dark bay."

Puʻuloa forms another bay, so coveted by the United States that in 1873 its war secretary, W. W. Belknap, secretly dispatched two generals to survey the harbor for its commercial and military value. After a two-month stay, the agents reported to Washington that Pearl Harbor, so-named by foreigners, constituted excellent plunder for US imperialism in the Pacific. Hawaiians stoutly resisted an erosion of their sovereignty despite considerable sentiment by influential white sugar planters to cede Puʻuloa to the United States in exchange for trade reciprocity. Both bays, the dark ravine and militarized waters after the illegal US takeover of the kingdom, would form correspondences after December 7, 1941.

Japan's attack on the US installation at Pearl Harbor, as the studies in this remarkable collection document, connected the liquid with the landed bay. War with Japan, as was planned by the United States decades before 1941, led to martial law in Hawaiʻi, forced removals, and the detention of aliens and citizens alike. Puʻuloa was the site of Japan's attack; Honouliuli became the place of "custodial detention" after the closure of Sand Island concentration camp in March 1943. Honouliuli for Japanese Americans confined in the ravine was a descent into Jigoku Dani or "Hell Valley."

Those related acts of imperialism abroad and segregation at home centered spatially at Puʻuloa and Honouliuli reveal US history at work. Those themes of US expansion and conquest and the absorption and segregation of those annexations of empire constitute a central spine of the nation's past in the alienation of "free" land from American Indians. Manifest destiny furthered the course of the US empire, which snatched Mexico's northern territories and its peoples, Mexicans and American Indians, and splashed into waters to capture islands in the Caribbean and Pacific. Hawaiians were engulfed along with the native peoples of Puerto Rico, Guam, and for a time the Philippines and Sāmoa. Prior to and during those periods of expansion, America's plantations employed and expired Africans and Asians in the slave and coolie systems of labor.

Despite their conquest and thus containment within the nation, "persons of color," according to the US Supreme Court ruling in *Dred Scott v. Sandford* (1857), were "not included in the word citizens." Since the nation's founding, the court reasoned, citizenship and therewith membership within the nation were reserved for "free white persons" per the Naturalization Act (1790). That segregation between white and nonwhite, the "citizen race" and "persons of color" stood for nearly one hundred years. The Thirteenth (1865), Fourteenth (1868), and Fifteenth (1870) Amendments to the US Constitution finally allowed the African American citizen and thereby transformed the complexion of the Constitution's "We, the people." Still, the rule of Jim Crow persisted to *Brown v. Board of Education* (1954) and beyond.

The extinction of Hawaiian sovereignty and expropriation of land throughout the eighteenth and nineteenth centuries, accordingly, was neither original nor novel, and the forced removal and detention of Japanese Americans was not an aberration and act of wartime hysteria. Pu'uoloa and Honouliuli are extensions of US settler and colonial history. As a consequence, I hold, this collection of essays remembering Honouliuli as a place of confinement for US aliens and citizens, women and men, and US prisoners of war, soldiers and civilians alike, marks a signal occasion for the nation's historical consciousness.

This collection reminds us of the pattern in US history slighted by standard narratives of nation. Those histories, these essays reveal, are purposeful creations in the constitution of a nation and people, and they uncover how exclusions can operate to install hierarchies of power. Memorializing that past in words and as a place and pilgrimage of remembrance, by contrast, calls to mind vigilance as a requirement of democracy. It is in that sense and spirit of commemoration I urge a close reading of the accounts contained herein, an appreciation of the labor exerted to locate, excavate, and preserve this site and history, and a commitment to right past wrongs and to advance the cause of freedom.

Gary Y. Okihiro

Acknowledgments

I n spring of 2009, University of Hawaiʻi–West Oʻahu (UHWO) faculty received an e-mail from Jim Bayman, then president of the Society of Hawaiian Archaeology, inviting our students to volunteer for a field archaeology project spearheaded by archaeologists Jeff Burton and Mary Farrell and the Japanese Cultural Center of Hawaiʻi (JCCH). The project's site, Honouliuli, lies in close proximity to the UHWO campus and thus was ideal in its location and opportunity for experiential learning in the field. At the end of this short project, UHWO faculty also visited the site and we were encouraged to begin in-depth research on this important story of World War II in Hawaiʻi. This special issue of *Social Process in Hawaiʻi* is the culmination of several years of intensive research, writing, review, and perseverance of dedicated scholars and practitioners who seized the opportunity to uncover the little-known history of World War II internment and imprisonment in the Honouliuli Internment and POW Camp in Central Oʻahu, Hawaiʻi.

Over the course of our study, grants from the National Park Service's Japanese American Confinement Sites program and Valor in the Pacific National Monument, Pacific Hawaiʻi Parks, UHWO, the University of Hawaiʻi Foundation, and the Wo Foundation helped to fund various stages of our research. We were especially fortunate to travel to the US National Archives II where Eric Van Slander was extremely skillful in guiding us through the archival maze and helping us to access age-old materials. Other librarians and archivists assisted us in finding information from scattered and diverse sources: Jane Kurahara and Betsy Young from JCCH, Sherman Seki from the Hawaiʻi War Records Depository, Toni Palermo from the King Kamehameha V Judiciary History Center, and others from the Bishop Museum, Fort Shafter, Schofield Barracks, Fort DeRussey, Kilauea Military Camp, and the Buddhist Study Center.

We are very grateful to the individuals who generously allowed us to interview them about family members who were interned as well as their own experiences and memories of World War II in Hawaiʻi. We conducted 27 interviews that included 38 participants who shared their stories.

Our research also benefited from a number of others who gave their assistance in this project. Ronald Beckwith served as a volunteer field archaeologist, teaching students the basics of Total Station mapping. Ross Brown, who at times was accompanied by other volunteers from the O'ahu community, instructed students in the use of the metal detector. Student research assistants—Mary Grace Busto, Tracey Imper, Felicia Wun, and April Iliff—worked tirelessly to transfer our interviews to CDs, make careful transcriptions of them, and organize and manage our collected and donated archival materials. Mariko Miho of UH Foundation added her significant talents in highlighting our work within various sectors of the local Hawai'i community. And, we are especially grateful to Gary Okihiro, who served as the 2012 UHWO Distinguished Visiting Scholar and an important source of inspiration to our authors.

We owe special and sincere thanks to those whose excellent work has resulted in the production of this volume for *Social Process in Hawai'i*. For the articles contained in this volume, more than 20 local, national, and international experts offered their time, keen insights, and peer evaluations. We are also very thankful to Kiyoshi Ikeda, Kalei Kanuha, and D. William Wood (*SPH* editors), Stuart Robson (copy editor and proofreader), Mark Nakamura (layout specialist and designer), and Lucille Aono (University of Hawai'i Press).

The research and preservation efforts of all who have been involved in this special issue are continuing. We have only touched the surface of what might be discovered and preserved. With the publication, we hope to shatter the silence that surrounds internment and imprisonment in Hawai'i and at Honouliuli Camp. We also hope that this special issue will be in some measure a tangible thank-you to all those who helped in our work, as well as a memorial to those who were interned and imprisoned at Honouliuli Camp during World War II.

Linda Nishigaya
Suzanne Falgout
Guest Editors

Background and Introduction

SUZANNE FALGOUT
LINDA NISHIGAYA
TONI PALERMO

The bombing of Pearl Harbor in Hawai'i marked the beginning of American involvement in World War II, and over the years since this Hawai'i site has become a major symbol of the war itself. However, until very recently, very little has been known about Hawai'i's detention of more than 2,000 of its local residents and its imprisonment of nearly 17,000 enemy nationals captured during the war.

Hidden deep within a gulch located just a few miles inland from the famed World War II site of Pearl Harbor, lies the Honouliuli Internment and Prisoner of War Camp. The US Army's Honouliuli Camp that opened in March 1943 was the largest and longest lasting of at least 13 internment sites and 13 POW compounds found throughout the islands of Hawai'i. Articles in this volume focus on the Honouliuli Camp and the very important role Hawai'i played in the wartime activities of internment and imprisonment.

To aid readers' understanding of the articles that follow, we begin with a brief background on Honouliuli within the context of Hawaiian history, from ancient times up through the beginning of the war. We will see that in addition to the prominence of this area during World War II, Honouliuli has held a deep significance throughout Hawaiian history.

Suzanne Falgout, Professor of Anthropology, University of Hawai'i–West O'ahu, 91-1001 Farrington Highway, Kapolei, HI 96707; Linda Nishigaya, Professor Emeritus of Sociology, University of Hawai'i–West O'ahu, 91-1001 Farrington Highway, Kapolei, HI 96707; Toni Palermo, Program Specialist, King Kamehameha V Judiciary History Center, 417 S. King St., Honolulu, HI 96813. This material is based upon work assisted by a grant from the Department of the Interior, National Park Service. Any opinions, findings, and conclusions or recommendations expressed in this material are those of the authors and do not necessarily reflect the views of the Department of the Interior.

Honouliuli's Prewar Significance

The wider Honouliuli area is an ancient Hawaiian ahupua'a (land division), one of 13 within the moku (district) of 'Ewa. It consists of mostly arid, yet very fertile, lands located in the leeward portion of West O'ahu that stretch from the oceanfront up into the slopes of the Wai'anae Mountains. The indigenous Hawaiian term, Honouliuli, translates as "blue harbor" or "dark bay," with the area taking its name from the beauty and bounty of that oceanfront region. This is an area with its own unique traditional history, as told in numerous stories and songs, and holding a number of significant Native Hawaiian cultural sites (Sterling and Summers 1978).

During ancient times, all land had been managed by Hawai'i's ali'i (high chiefs) who granted use rights to their subjects. Western contact beginning in the late eighteenth century led to the unification of a Hawaiian kingdom under Kamehameha I and the islands' entrance into the world economy—first as a major Pacific port of call and then with the development of agricultural plantations, particularly for sugarcane. Later heirs to the throne worked to enact the Great Mahele ("to divide or portion"); by 1848 the land could be split into parcels owned or leased by Hawaiians and various settlers to the islands (Merry 2000). During the decades that followed, plantations imported contract laborers, particularly from China, Japan, Okinawa, and the Philippines (Takaki 1983).

By the late nineteenth century, much of the Honouliuli area was included in the extensive landholdings of the Oahu Sugar Company on Campbell Estate property headquartered in the town of Auali'i (today known as Waipahu, "gushing water," referring to the company's success in bringing needed water to the area from the windward side of the island through the construction of the Waiāhole Ditch in the early twentieth century). The area just inland from the shore held a small Honouliuli town with shops, residences, and small truck farms.

Demand for a free trade agreement between Hawai'i and the United States soon followed the Great Mahele, pushed by local businessmen in order to guarantee a secure market and therefore bank loans for sugar. The Hawaiian monarchy, under King David Kalākaua, also hoped to secure the islands' sovereignty by developing a firm economic base (Daws 2006; Kuykendall 1967). The United States, by then dependent on Hawai'i's sugar export and also interested in its strategic capacity, was particularly interested in its various harbors and waterways for both a commercial port and naval base. A Reciprocity Treaty of 1875 guaranteed that secure US market and, in exchange, in 1887 the United States gained exclusive entry into the large natural harbor of Puʻuloa, or Pearl Harbor (Daws 2006; Kuykendall 1967). Pearl Harbor also lies within ʻEwa district, just slightly to the east of the Honouliuli ahupuaʻa; in fact, Honouliuli borders the West Loch of Pearl Harbor (Sterling and Summers 1978). Initially, Pearl Harbor was for use in coaling and repairing of US ships; over time, it came to house its Pacific Fleet.

Following the overthrow of the reigning Hawaiian monarch, Queen Liliʻuokalani, by insurgents within the kingdom (most of whom were US citizens) in 1893 and a brief period as the Republic of Hawaiʻi, the islands were eventually annexed to the United States and became its Territory of Hawaiʻi in

The Honouliuli ahupuaʻa (shaded). Map of Oʻahu prepared by Hawaiʻi Territory Survey, 1929 (Sterling and Summers 1978).

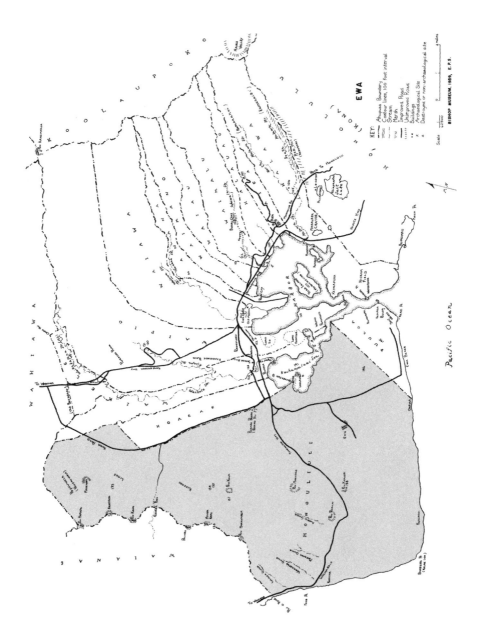

The Honouliuli ahupuaʻa (shaded). Map of ʻEwa prepared by Bishop Museum, 1959 (Sterling and Summers 1978).

1898 (Siler 2012; Kuykendall 1967). The US military presence in the islands would multiply over the next few decades, and in the early twentieth century Pearl Harbor became the preeminent American military facility in the Pacific.

Martial Law, Democracy, and Social Justice in Wartime Hawai'i

The Japanese attack on Hawai'i on a tranquil Sunday morning on December 7, 1941, was targeted on Pearl Harbor, which had recently come to house the US Pacific fleet, including its battleships lined up on "Battleship Row" and also its aircraft carriers (which fortunately were out to sea that day) (McKay 1946; Judd 1943). Bombs also fell on several other major US military installations in Hawai'i where aircraft were lined up wingtip to wingtip, making them easy targets for the Japanese and preventing US airmen from getting planes off the ground. In addition, bombs dropped on civilian residents and businesses in the surrounding area and in the city of Honolulu (some the result of "friendly fire" from misfired Navy anti-aircraft shells). The magnitude of destruction, both in the loss of lives of servicemen and civilians and of vital supplies, was devastating and took only minutes to be realized (McKay 1946; Judd 1943). In addition, the first prisoner of war was captured from a disabled Japanese midget submarine.

This attack was thought to be a preview of a dreaded land invasion by the Japanese, and by 11:30 a.m., Governor Joseph B. Poindexter after speaking with President Roosevelt, issued a proclamation invoking martial law and suspending the privilege of the writ of habeas corpus pursuant to Section 67 of the Hawaiian Organic Act (Anthony 1943; King 1942). Walter C. Short assumed the position of military governor shortly thereafter, replaced several weeks later by Delos Emmons. Later that day, President Roosevelt asked Congress to declare war on Japan in his "Day of Infamy" speech (Anthony 1943). On that one day, December 7, 1941, Hawai'i had become the center of the War in the Pacific.

The Territory of Hawai'i was the only locale within the United States to experience martial law. Invoking martial law has been used in situations of civil unrest, fear of imminent attack, or threat of war and insurrection; in such cases, the US government feared a society might become unstable or the traditional lines of authority could become eroded. Following the attack on Pearl Harbor, this situation certainly seemed a possibility in Hawai'i. Instituting martial law in Hawai'i allowed the US military to take control of the courts of law, law enforcement duties, and to designate policy and procedures that controlled civil liberties (Scheiber and Scheiber 1997). As a result, American ideals of democracy and social justice were quickly swept aside by military concerns for security and expediency (Scheiber and Scheiber 1997).

Under martial law lasting until October 27, 1944, a series of nearly 200 General Orders were issued by the Office of the Military Governor (OMG) outlining in detail who, what, when, and under what circumstances life was to be regulated (Anthony 1943). Martial law established curfews, blackouts, censorship, freezing of wages, restrictions on travel, mass fingerprinting, control of banks and businesses, and the temporary suspension, closing, or even military takeover of schools (King 1942; Anthony 1943; Margold 1942). Hawaiʻi's landscape was dramatically altered, especially on Oʻahu—important landmarks were camouflaged, beaches were strung with barbed wire, shelters were constructed, business doorways and windows were taped, machine-gun nests were set up at key locations, and access to military bases was restricted (King Kamehameha V Judiciary History Center 1991; Brown 1989). Gas masks were distributed, food and gas were rationed, and work restrictions and clothing identity badges were instituted for certain ethnic groups (Allen 1950; Dodge 1984). Military provost courts tried cases for the more minor crimes, with trials averaging five minutes and defendants not given copies of their charges; military commissions handled the more serious offenses (Anthony 1943; King 1942).

As a result of martial law, the lives of all of Hawaiʻi's peoples were changed—they were disrupted, disenfranchised, dismantled, and in some instances devastated (Office of the Military Governor 1945; Adler and Pinao 1995). This was particularly true of the more than 2,000 local residents who had been earlier identified on US Department of Justice and FBI lists (Scheiber and Scheiber 1997). Those lists consisted of individuals whose past or present personal ties or life circumstances linked them (at least in the minds of the American military, most of whom were unfamiliar with Hawaiʻi's peoples) to "enemy groups" and who were, therefore, suspected of questionable loyalty, as well as other individuals who were believed to act suspiciously (Roehner 2009).

Thus, those who were selectively targeted were rounded up beginning December 7, 1941, were very hastily tried, and thousands were interned, initially at Sand Island and other temporary camps located on Oʻahu and the neighbor islands. Opening in March 1943, Honouliuli was the last civilian internment camp to be constructed in Hawaiʻi, and most of the civilians still under custody were transferred there, or sent to internment camps or relocation centers on the mainland (Scheiber and Scheiber 1997). By that time, Hawai'i had also been designated as an important base camp to hold an increasingly very large and very diverse group of prisoners of war (Sato 1976), and several of the compounds at Honouliuli held POWs.

Internment and Imprisonment in Hawai'i

Honouliuli Internment and POW Camp's remote location, restrictions on access to and general secrecy surrounding military installations and activities, the lasting stigma and trauma associated with internment and imprisonment, as well as generational and cultural restrictions on speaking openly of such wartime hardships, have meant that Honouliuli's story is all but forgotten today.

On those occasions when Honouliuli's story has been told, it has frequently been subject to stereotypes and misunderstandings. Those members of the local community who know about this chapter of World War II history have believed that only individuals of Japanese ancestry were subject to internment, particularly elite Japanese males. Most believed that those who were retained were sent to camps on the US mainland; they have been surprised to learn about camps located in Hawai'i. Even less has been known about other individuals and groups who were interned within Hawai'i. Furthermore, very few have known about the wartime presence in Hawai'i of prisoners of war.

Circumstances and conditions of internment and imprisonment varied throughout the United States during World War II. Today, we know that the Hawai'i context, and especially that of the US Army's Honouliuli Internment and POW Camp, was like no other. It differed in terms of the number and types of peoples interned and imprisoned; the legal basis and process for internment under martial law; conditions within the Camp; relations among those within the Camp itself and outside the local community; as well as its profound and lasting impacts on those directly and indirectly involved and on subsequent generations in Hawai'i. These differences are significant for understanding the wider story of World War II internment and imprisonment, not only in Hawai'i but also in the wider context of the continental United States.

The first World War II internment activities actually began in Hawai'i. Even before the war began, some members of Hawai'i's Japanese community—those of the first generation who remained citizens of Japan, as well as others who were US citizens—had been specifically targeted for internment. However, they would be far fewer in number and percentage of that population than on the US mainland. They were, in fact, often males from among society's Japanese elite, but others were simply in the wrong place during the bombing of Pearl Harbor. Some, furthermore, actually identified themselves as Okinawans.

We have now learned that a few Japanese women were also interned. In addition, a few Japanese families, along with their young children, were sent from Micronesia to be interned in Hawai'i. And, while most of Hawai'i's more than 2,000 Japanese internees were in fact sent to various camps on the US mainland, they were often followed by their spouses and children who resided with them in the camps there.

In addition, the Federal Bureau of Investigation in Hawai'i also picked up nearly 140 residents of European descent for internment—of German, Italian, Austrian, Norwegian, Danish, Lithuanian, Swedish, Finnish, Irish, and Jewish heritage. Those classified as "German" or "Italian" alien enemies residing in Hawai'i were interned *en masse*, regardless of their actual ancestry or citizenship status. This included all able-bodied adults—husbands, wives, and their children over the age of 14. Internment in Hawai'i, then, cast a much wider net than just discrimination against resident Japanese.

Over the course of the war, Honouliuli Camp would hold approximately 300 internees who came from a wide variety of life circumstances and ethnic backgrounds. Significantly, most of those who were retained at or later returned to Honouliuli were American citizens held under the authority of martial law.

Those individuals who were singled out for internment were stigmatized, both during and after the war. The effect on loved ones left behind—spouses, the elderly or infirmed, and young children—was also devastating. They had been left to fend for themselves, treated with suspicion, and even avoided by others out of fear of perceived guilt by association. Indeed, internment continued to loom as a threat, with instances of pickups and interrogations continuing for several years. The lasting impacts of those experiences on family members are still felt today.

Adding to the complexity of internment at Honouliuli Camp, Hawai'i's largest prisoner of war camp was located immediately adjacent—this combination within one camp was rare for Hawai'i, as well as for the US mainland. POWs housed at Honouliuli included Japanese, Okinawans, Koreans, Filipinos, and others sent from various locations in the Pacific Theater—plus Italians picked up from the Atlantic Theater. They were guarded by an African American infantry unit.

The diverse backgrounds of the internees and the POWs held at Honouliuli significantly overlapped with the majority of peoples found in Hawai'i's local community and also many of the internees held at the Camp. This created highly varied and unusual conditions for imprisonment and internment. Honouliuli also served as a main transition point for internees and POWs sent to other destinations on the US mainland. While some categories of POWs were immediately evacuated to the US mainland, others remained and even mingled with or on very rare occasion actually lived within the local community.

Either directly or indirectly, World War II internment and imprisonment affected every person and most aspects of life in Hawai'i—while the war raged and even decades afterward. It profoundly changed family relationships, friendships, the practice of religious worship, dietary habits, the local economy, labor, etc. It also changed the entire political landscape. During the war, it served as an impetus for the distinguished records of the 100th Infantry Battalion and the 442nd Regimental Combat Team in the Atlantic campaign as well as local involvement in the Military Intelligence Service. Afterward, it helped to spark multiethnic labor movements, the "Democratic Revolution," and paved the way for some of the most progressive legislation in the nation. The Democratic Revolution's influences have continued to shape local debates on issues such as taxation, land reform, environmental protection, human, women's, and LGBT's rights, comprehensive health insurance, and collective bargaining—issues that are currently at the forefront of national and international debates, as well.

Breaking the Silence

In our research, we have found that there are volumes of information to learn about Honouliuli's story, but that information is scattered among various collections. While some oral histories have been collected and archived, what exists is largely anecdotal and simply descriptive. There has been little in-depth research or publication on the various aspects of the Honouliuli experience, on the full range of peoples housed there during World War II, or on the lasting impacts on families and the wider Hawai'i community. The challenge of more fully uncovering, critically analyzing and interpreting, and preserving in a scholarly publication what would otherwise be lost to history is taken up by our multidisciplinary University of Hawai'i-West O'ahu (UHWO) research team consisting of 10 faculty members from nine different academic disciplines.

The Honouliuli site is adjacent to the UHWO's mauka (inland) property, a visible link to our campus. As an archaeological site, the Honouliuli Internment Camp has been added to both the State of Hawai'i and the National Register of Historic Places and is under consideration to become a part of the National Park Service. With abundant features and artifacts, Honouliuli has the potential to provide important archaeological information about the administration of an internment and prisoner of war camp and how, in their everyday lives, people reacted to and coped with their confinement. Archaeologists have joined UHWO for three summer field schools at Honouliuli, providing a perspective on the physical remains. As a tangible link to the ways that fear and paranoia resulted in the suppression of civil rights during World War II, these remains can inform and add to discussion about the relationship of national security and the US Constitution.

In presenting the research of our community partners—especially Densho, the Japanese Cultural Center of Hawai'i, and Hawai'i's Judiciary History Center—along with our combined UHWO research in this volume, we share our findings that the Honouliuli site is not only locally very important to many different groups within our midst, but that it also holds national and international significance. The articles that follow aim to "break the silence" about internment and imprisonment in Hawai'i, particularly at the most significant site for such activities, Honouliuli Camp. In addition, we wish to tell a more complete, more complex story about Honouliuli, particularly about the lessons that site holds for challenges to democracy and social justice, especially during times of conflict. We also hope our readers will take away an understanding that Honouliuli's story and the lessons it holds are universal and timeless. In that sense, Honouliuli is *everybody's story.*

Articles in this Volume

Leilani Basham's "Ka I'a Hāmau Leo: Silences that Speak Volumes for Honouliuli" draws on Hawaiian language resources to describe and explain the landscape that housed the World War II Honouliuli Internment and Prisoner of War Camp. Her research examines 'ōlelo no'eau (proverbs), mele (songs, poetry), and mo'olelo (histories, stories) that relate to the ahupua'a (land division) of Honouliuli and the wahi pana (cultural sites) within its boundaries. The information contained in the oral and written traditions of the Hawaiian language highlights the historical and cultural richness of the ahupua'a of Honouliuli. The intrusion of an internment camp in its midst was largely unknown for many passing years.

To erase from memory and history the incarceration of internees and prisoners of war in the Honouliuli Camp is to lose the profound lessons learned only through exposing the injustices of war that threaten democratic principles. In their article "Finding Honouliuli: The Japanese Cultural Center of Hawai'i and Preserving the Hawai'i Internment Story," Jane Kurahara, Brian Niiya, and Betsy Young describe the efforts of the Japanese Cultural Center of Hawai'i (JCCH) and its Hawai'i Confinement Sites Committee to discover, collect, preserve, interpret, and educate the public, especially the schoolchildren, about Hawai'i's internment story, particularly for those of Japanese ancestry. These endeavors are accomplished through networks of community partnerships as well as state and federal support.

As our researchers discover facts and insights about the internment experience in Honouliuli Camp, the archaeologists, along with their UHWO students, uncover the physical evidence of its operations in wartime Hawai'i. Jeff Burton et al. dig into the past in "Hell Valley: Uncovering a Prison Camp in Paradise" and find two standing structures, building foundations, rock walls, artifacts, and other features of the 122.5 acre internment site that is now listed on the National Register of Historic Places. In addition to their fieldwork, Burton et al. use oral histories and archival research to document the day-to-day living conditions of the internees and prisoners of war. The significance of their research extends beyond its archaeological finds as the authors note the political, racial, ethnic, and social implications of the internment.

While the internees in Honouliuli Camp were mostly American civilians and resident aliens of Japanese ancestry, Alan Rosenfeld identifies people from a variety of ethnic backgrounds among the "German" and "Italian" internees, including individuals of Scandinavian and Irish backgrounds. These individuals were apprehended under the wide-ranging auspices of J. Edgar Hoover's Alien Enemy Control program. In "Neither Aliens nor Enemies: The Hearings of 'German' and 'Italian' Internees in Wartime Hawai'i," Rosenfeld details how justice is compromised by opting for security at all costs.

Suzanne Falgout points out that POW compounds were adjacent to the internee compound in Honouliuli Camp. As many as 4,000 POWs including Japanese, Okinawans, Koreans, and Filipinos from various locations in the Pacific Theater as well as Italians from the Atlantic Theater were incarcerated at Honouliuli. Falgout's research, "Honouliuli's POWs: Making Connections, Generating Changes," explains the varying conditions of imprisonment of the different POW groups that depended on their ethnicity, reputation, wartime political status, and connections made with members of their own group in the Camp, members of the local community, and the US military. These connections had local, national, and transnational significance, not only during the period of imprisonment but after the war as well.

In her article "Transnational Identities, Communities, and the Experiences of Okinawan Internees and Prisoners of War," Joyce Chinen focuses on local Kibei Nisei Okinawans (born in Hawai'i, taken back to Okinawa, and then returned to Hawai'i), POWs from the Pacific Theater, and POWs taken in the Battle of Okinawa. She notes that although the Okinawan internees and POWs were categorized as Japanese, they were culturally distinct from the Japanese population. Chinen investigates the reasons why the three Okinawan subgroups were imprisoned and describes how the local Okinawan community in Hawai'i responded to them.

Prior to the bombing of Pearl Harbor, various leaders in Hawai'i's Japanese community had already been identified by the FBI and US Justice Department as threats to national security in the event of war. Buddhist and Shinto priests were high on the US government's lists of potential enemy aliens and they were interned categorically. In "Reviving the Lotus: Japanese Buddhism and World War II Internment," Linda Nishigaya and Ernest Oshiro use rational choice theory to clarify some of the difficult individual and group decisions that were made by Buddhist priests and their leadership to protect the future of Buddhism and its followers in Hawai'i and the US mainland.

Amy Nishimura exposes civil rights violations based on religious identification that led to the incarceration of Shinto priestesses and disciples in Honouliuli Camp. The unjust treatment of two Japanese American priestesses imprisoned in Honouliuli Camp is revealed in "From Priestesses and Disciples to Witches and Traitors." From her examination of transcripts of the martial hearings of two priestesses, Nishimura uncovers their wrongful entrapment in a patriarchal, militaristic justice system that denied their true identities as lawful Japanese American Shinto priestesses.

The effects of internment extend far beyond the barbed-wire fences of confinement to family members left waiting in confusion and fear as was the case in Hawai'i, unlike the situation on the US mainland where whole families were interned. Susan Matoba Adler, whose Nisei parents were interned at Manzanar, explores "The Effect of Internment on Children and Families: Honouliuli and Manzanar." Through interviews and literature reviews, Adler finds that in Honouliuli and Manzanar the Japanese nuclear family unit weakened and the traditional roles of women changed during the period of displacement and political unrest.

How long and in what ways do the effects of wartime internment last? Focusing on the psychological effects of internment, Garyn Tsuru applies historical trauma theory in his examination of the intergenerational effects of trauma on three families of Honouliuli internees. Tsuru compares and contrasts the experiences of these families with what is known about families interned in camps on the US mainland in his article "Psychic Wounds from the Past: Investigating Intergenerational Trauma in the Families of Japanese Americans Interned in the Honouliuli Internment and POW Camp." Although the conditions of internment in Hawai'i under martial law differed from the US mainland, the wartime civil injustice suffered in both cases left interned families with lingering negative consequences for generations. ❖

References

Adler, Peter, and Noralynne Pinao. 1995. "American Democracy in Hawai'i: Finding a Place for Local Culture." *University of Hawai'i Law Review* 17:605–637.

Allen, Gwenfread. 1950. *Hawai'i's War Years: 1941–1945*. Honolulu: University of Hawai'i Press.

Anthony, Garner. 1943. "Martial Law, Military Government and the Writ of Habeas Corpus in Hawaii." *California Law Review* 31:477–514.

Brown, Desoto. 1989. *Hawaii Goes to War*. Honolulu: Editions Limited.

Daws, Gavan. 2006. *Honolulu: The First Century*. Honolulu: Mutual Publishing.

Dodge, Charlotte Peabody. 1984. *Punahou: The War Years, 1941–1945*. Honolulu: Punahou School.

Judd, Eva Marie. 1943. *Martial Law Journal*, December 7, 1941–March 10, 1943. Copy of typewritten typescript, King Kamehameha V Judiciary Center, Honolulu, Hawai'i.

King, Archibald. 1942. "The Legality of Martial Law in Hawaii." *California Law Review* 30(6):599–647.

King Kamehameha V Judiciary History Center. 1991. *Hawai'i under Martial Law: 1941–1944*. Honolulu: Friends of the Judiciary History Center.

Kuykendall, Ralph. 1967. *The Hawaiian Kingdom*. Vol. II, 1874–1893. Honolulu: University of Hawai'i Press.

Margold, (Sgd) Nathan R., Office of the Solicitor. 1942. Letter to the Secretary of the Interior. June 8.

McKay, Helen Willis. 1946. The Journal of Helen Willis McKay, December 7, 1941 to April 7, 1946. Manuscript M396. King Kamehameha V Judiciary History Center, Honolulu, Hawai'i.

Merry, Sally Engle. 2000. *Colonizing Hawai'i: The Cultural Power of Law.* Princeton: Princeton University Press.

Office of the Military Governor. 1945. General Orders, 1941–1945. Honolulu, Hawai'i.

Roehner, Bertrand M. 2009. "Relations between Military Forces and the Population of Hawaii, 1941–1945." Working Report. Paris: University of Paris 7.

Sato, Hank. 1976. "Honouliuli Camp: Footnote to a Dark Chapter." *Honolulu Star-Bulletin*, March 18.

Scheiber, Harry N., and Jane L. Scheiber. 1997. "Bayonets in Paradise: A Half Century of Retrospect on Martial Law in Hawai'i, 1941–1949." *University of Hawai'i Law Review* 19(2):477–648.

Siler, Julia Flynn. 2012. *Lost Kingdom: Hawai'i's Last Queen, the Sugar Kings, and America's First Imperial Adventure.* New York: Atlantic Monthly Press.

Sterling, Elspeth P., and Catherine C. Summers. 1978. *Sites of Oahu.* Honolulu: Bishop Museum Press.

Takaki, Ronald T. 1983. *Pau Hana: Plantation Life and Labor in Hawaii, 1835–1920.* Honolulu: University of Hawai'i Press.

Ka Iʻa Hāmau Leo: Silences that Speak Volumes for Honouliuli

Leilani Basham

ABSTRACT

This article will examine the silences that surround the iʻa hāmau leo (the silent-voiced fish) known as the pipi (oyster), which was a major food source for the ahupuaʻa (land division) of Honouliuli and the entire moku (district) of ʻEwa. I will do that by first describing the respect given to the pipi by Kānaka Maoli (the Native Hawaiian people) and the interdependence and interconnectedness between the pipi, the people, and their environment. This interdependence exemplifies the unique relationship that existed between the Native Hawaiian people and their environment, which was based on mutual respect and a seeking of pono—harmony and balance between the needs of people to extract resources from a place for life and livelihood and the needs of a place and its other inhabitants to their own life and livelihood. The article will then examine another form of silencing that resulted from various forms of colonial influences, which created a rift in the relationship that existed between Kānaka Maoli, the pipi, and the environment in which the people and the pipi once lived and thrived. Various Hawaiian resources form the foundation of this work. These resources will include ʻōlelo noʻeau (proverbial sayings), mele (song, poetry), and moʻolelo (histories, stories) that were written and published in Hawaiian language newspapers and books in the nineteenth and twentieth centuries. I will interpret these in terms of historical, political, and cultural content—in order to better understand and articulate the intimate relationship that Kānaka Maoli established and nurtured with their land base in order that we, of this and future generations, can give life to these places through the knowing of them, by giving voice to their names, and their stories, and thereby honoring their lives.

Leilani Basham, Associate Professor, Hawaiian-Pacific Studies, University of Hawaiʻi–West Oʻahu, 91-1001 Farrington Highway, Kapolei, HI 96707. The author can be reached at jbasham@hawaii.edu.

The main title of this article, "Ka i'a hāmau leo" comes from an 'ōlelo no'eau (proverbial saying)[1] that makes reference to the pipi (oyster) that was commonly found in the area known as ke awa lau o Pu'uloa (the many bays of Pu'uloa), that area that has since come to be known as Pearl Harbor. The 'ōlelo no'eau refers to the pipi as "ka i'a hāmau leo" or a "silent-voiced fish."[2] While in some cultural contexts, silence is seen as an oppressive action or one in which one is not allowed to voice its concerns, in the Hawaiian context, silence can be seen as a sign of disagreement or, in the case of the pipi, silence can be indicative of the reverence and respect that one must have and demonstrate when gathering the pipi.

These silences are especially relevant to this volume on the Honouliuli Internment and POW Camp as the camp is part and parcel of a larger silence surrounding the US military in Hawai'i. In terms of content, this article is not related to the internment camp itself, but is included here to provide insight into the history and social processes that preceded the camp and thereby ensure that this volume doesn't contribute to the further silencing of the voices of Honouliuli.

In this article, I will examine the silences that surround the i'a hāmau leo, first describing the respect given to the pipi by Kānaka Maoli (Native Hawaiian people) and the interdependence and interconnectedness between the pipi, the people, and their environment. I will then examine another form of silencing that resulted from various forms of colonial influences, which created a rift in the relationship that existed between the people, the pipi, and the environment in which the people and the pipi once lived and thrived. I will do this through the use and analysis of 'ōlelo no'eau, mele (song, poetry), and mo'olelo (histories, stories) that were written and published in Hawaiian language newspapers and books in the nineteenth and twentieth centuries. I will interpret them in terms of historical, political, and cultural content—in order to better understand and articulate the intimate relationship that Kānaka Maoli established and nurtured with their land base in order that we, of this and future generations, can give life to these places through the knowing of them, by giving voice to their names, and their stories, and thereby honoring their lives.

Ua lawa ka 'ikena i ke awa lau: A Culture of "Sufficiency"

The above heading "Ua lawa ka 'ikena i ke awa lau" is part of the third verse of a mele and it highlights an important cultural value of Kānaka Maoli and their perspective toward 'āina (land). This line describes the feeling of satisfaction that ke awa lau o Pu'uloa engendered in the people. This affection and connection are the focus of this section.

The mele, entitled "Makalapua," was composed in 1890 in honor of the future queen of the Hawaiian Kingdom, Lydia Lili'uokalani Kamaka'eha (de Silva 2003). The mele catalogs the then-princess and heir apparent's traveling on the O'ahu Railway & Land Co.'s (OR&L) railroad from its Kūwili station at Iwilei, near what is now downtown Honolulu, out to the Honouliuli station in 'Ewa. Lili'uokalani's journey on the train took place sometime in the six-month period between July 1890 when this segment of the railroad opened and her ascension to the throne as the queen of the Kingdom of Hawai'i following the death of her brother, David Kalākaua, in January 1891 (de Silva 2003). On the surface level, the mele is merely a travelogue, recounting the journey from Kūwili to Hālawa, past ke awa lau o Pu'uloa, and then on to Mānana, Waipi'o, and ending in Honouliuli.

A deeper interpretation of the mele, however, reveals a complex layering of expressions related to the social processes at play throughout Hawai'i at the end of the nineteenth century, and also specifically, within the moku (district) of 'Ewa. The mele asserts Hawaiian rights to lead the nation and the capabilities of the Kānaka Maoli leaders to do so, as seen in the first and last verses with the assertion that we follow the lead of Lili'uokalani ("Ho'ālo i ka ihu o ka Lanakila"). On the surface, these verses merely recount Lili'uokalani's traveling in the front of the train; however, with the train as a metaphor for the kingdom and an understanding that Lanakila is the name of the train but also translates as "success" and "victory," then this line is an assertion of Lili'uokalani's position as the leader of the nation and her ability to lead the kingdom to success and victory in the challenges it faces.

This mele also exemplifies the importance of Hawaiian perspectives toward 'āina through each verse's recounting of Hawaiian place-names and references to their various characteristics and attributes. The train itself, however, exemplifies the tensions between these Hawaiian ways of knowing and seeing 'āina—as an older sibling who cares for the people and is cared for in a reciprocal relationship of aloha (love, respect, affection)—and the perspectives of haole (Euro-American, Caucasian foreigners) toward land—as a commodity to be bought, sold, and "developed" for economic reasons as either real estate or as a part of a market agriculture, not grounded in the feeding of many, but with the growth of monetary wealth for a few (Kame'eleihiwa 1992).

Here is the mele in its entirety:

Makalapua

1. Eia mai au 'o Makalapua
   Hō'alo i ka ihu o ka Lanakila

2. 'O ke ku'e a ka hao a'i Kūwili
   Ka hiona 'olu a'o Hālawa

3. Ua lawa ka 'ikena i ke awalau

   Iā 'Ewa ka i'a hāmau leo

4. Ua pua ka uahi a'i Mānana
   Aweawe i ke kula o Waipi'o

5. I kai ho'i au o Honouliuli
   Ahuwale ke ko'a o Pōlea

6. Ha'ina 'ia mai ana ka puana
   Hō'alo i ka ihu o ka Lanakila

He inoa no Lili'uokalani
(Makalapua 1890)

1. Here I am, Makalapua
   Leading the prow of the *Lanakila*

2. The pistons move back and forth at Kūwili
   Down the pleasant descent of Hālawa

3. The seeing/knowing of the many lochs of
   Pu'uloa is satisfying
   The silent-voiced fish belongs to 'Ewa

4. The smoke rises at Mānana
   Streaming across the plain of Waipi'o

5. I am seaward of Honouliuli
   The coral flats of Pōlea are exposed

6. The refrain is told
   Leading the prow of the *Lanakila*[3]

Wahi pana (place-names, cultural sites) are a main focus of the mele. It mentions several ahupua'a (semi-independent land division) in the moku of 'Ewa (i.e., Hālawa, Mānana, Waipi'o, and Honouliuli) as well as ke awa lau o Pu'uloa. On the map below, notice the way that each and every single one of the 13 ahupua'a that comprise 'Ewa are directly connected to, curve around, and extend out into ke awa lau o Pu'uloa.

The third verse of the mele states, "Ua lawa ka 'ikena i ke awa lau," which translates as "The view of the many bays is satisfying." The word "lawa" in Hawaiian is translated as "satisfying" here, but can also translate to "enough" or "sufficient." It is important to note that these two words in English almost seem to indicate that something is barely enough, especially within a society in which "more is always better." In a Hawaiian context, however, "lawa" is more than just merely sufficient, it is ample and all that is needed in order to sustain life, not just in the here and now, but for future generations as well. The "ikena" referenced here speaks not only to the "view" of the many bays and lochs, but also the "knowing" of these places. This is an assertion that the value of this place is not for what we can *use* it for and for what resources may be extracted from it. Instead, it asserts that the awa lau of Pu'uloa are sufficient as they are, both in beauty and in use.

Sarah Nākoa, a kupa (native born) of 'Ewa describes her childhood in 'Ewa and of being raised gathering and eating pipi. She describes the appearance of the pipi as follows,

> He hākeakea a hinuhinu kona iwi. He nui a kaumaha ka pipi i like 'ole me kekahi mau pūpū a'u i 'ike maka ai i ko mākou 'āina (Nākoa and 'Ahahui 'Ōlelo Hawai'i 1979:22).

> Its shell is whitish and shiny. The oyster is large and heavy in a manner that is unlike any shelled-creature that I have seen in our land.

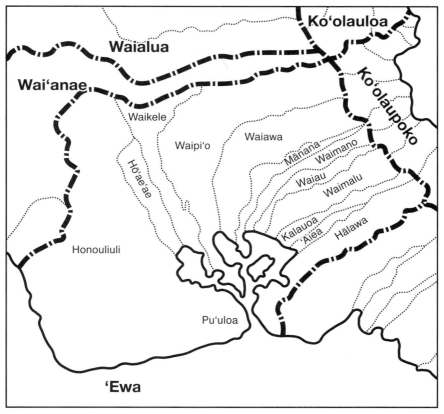

The moku of 'Ewa with ahupua'a indicated (Institute for Hawaiian Studies).

She also described the preparation and eating of the pipi as follows,

He 'ono 'oko'a nō ka 'aiwaha 'ana o ka i'a. 'O ka i'a i ho'omo'a 'ia ka'u i hānai 'ia mai ai. Ho'okomo 'ia ka pipi i loko o ka ipuhao me ka wai e paila ikaika ana. Hāmama wale a'e nō ka pipi ke mo'a iho ka i'a. He ke'oke'o ka 'i'o. He momona a he 'ono kona 'ai 'ana (Nākoa and 'Ahahui 'Ōlelo Hawai'i 1979:23).

This i'a has a different taste when it is eaten. I was raised eating this i'a in the cooked form. The oyster is placed inside of a pot with strongly boiling water. The oyster opens right up when it is cooked. The meat is white. Its eating is succulent and delicious.

Through these descriptions, the unique characteristics of pipi are highlighted. As further described by Nākoa and other authors, the relationship between the i'a hāmau leo and the wahi pana of 'Ewa is also unique.

Wahi pana are vitally important to Hawaiians and while we have experienced a great loss of knowledge of our language, our mo'olelo, and even our place-names, we continue to recognize the importance of 'āina and continue to have affection for it. This affection is evidenced in our naming of it, an act which honors its personality, individuality, and even its own inherent rights. Hawaiians named large areas of land—islands, districts, and ahupua'a–but they didn't stop there. As described by Pukui et al.,

Hawaiians named taro patches, rocks, and trees that represented deities and ancestors, sites of houses and heiau (places of worship), canoe landings, fishing stations in the sea, resting places in the forests, and the tiniest spots where miraculous or interesting events are believed to have taken place. (Pukui 1974:x)

Here are the names of the 13 ahupua'a that comprise the moku of 'Ewa, beginning at its border shared with the moku of Kona to the east and extending to its border with the moku of Wai'anae in the west.

1. Hālawa	8. Waiawa
2. 'Aiea	9. Waipi'o
3. Kalauao	10. Waikele
4. Waimalu	11. Hō'ae'ae
5. Waiau	12. Honouliuli
6. Waimano	13. Pu'uloa
7. Mānana	

While many of the ahupuaʻa names are still heard and known, most people are largely familiar with them only as names of elementary schools (i.e., Waiau, Waimalu) and shopping centers (i.e., Waikele, Waimalu). Usage of other ahupuaʻa names, however, have largely disappeared from daily usage (i.e., Kalauao), while others (i.e., ʻAiea), have grown in size due to their designation as a distinct zip code area by the US Postal Service. I would conjecture that most people (myself included prior to this research project) are not conscious of these wahi pana as ahupuaʻa extending from the mountain ranges on the inland side and curving around ke awa lau o Puʻuloa and extending down to the shoreline and out to sea.

Honouliuli is another traditional ahupuaʻa name that is not widely known or used. With the advent of this research into the Honouliuli Internment and POW Camp of which this article is a part, it's important that we don't make similar connections by which we begin to limit Honouliuli merely to the camp site. Honouliuli is the name of the entire ahupuaʻa in which the internment and POW camp sat. Honouliuli is by far the largest ahupuaʻa in ʻEwa. Perhaps due to its length and the difficulty of properly pronouncing the name Honouliuli, the ahupuaʻa has commonly come to be known by the names of either ʻEwa or ʻEwa Beach, or by the small (but growing!) residential areas found within it (i.e., Makakilo, Kapolei).

This process of erasure is part and parcel of the colonial history of Hawaiʻi that began at contact with Westerners in the late eighteenth century and escalated exponentially throughout the nineteenth century. The moku of ʻEwa is somewhat unique in the multifaceted nature of the colonialism it experienced. In the mid to late-1800s, following the privatization of land, ʻEwa was acquired and developed as both residential and commercial real estate and also as a part of an intensive agriculture-based economy. Both of these processes were instrumental in dispossessing Kānaka Maoli from not only their land, but also the very fabric of their society in terms of cultural and social practices. Land transformed into real estate and private property requires money not only at time of purchase but also on an ongoing basis for taxes. This need for money then became an impetus for Kānaka Maoli to become laborers for plantations, abandoning their land- and ocean-based subsistence lifestyle (Kameʻeleihiwa 1992; Kelly 1989). These two processes—an agriculture-based economy and privatization of land—were experienced throughout Hawaiʻi. In addition to these, however, ʻEwa experienced a military industrialization of "Pearl Harbor" that is largely unequaled in scope and intensity (Osorio 2010).

Mai wala'au o makani auane'i:
Interconnections of People and Elements

The above heading, "Mai wala'au o makani auane'i" is another 'ōlelo no'eau about the pipi. This proverb translates as "Don't speak lest the wind blows" and refers to the interconnection between the land and elements, the plants and animals, and the people. While the land and elements and the plants and animals are sources of life in terms of providing food and resources for humans, they are also understood and revered as both figurative and literal ancestors. In this section, I will explore the interconnections between the people, the pipi, and the wind—each with its own kuleana (rights, responsibilities).

As previously mentioned, the pipi are referred to as "ka i'a hāmau leo" or silent-voiced fish. This is not because the pipi themselves were silent, but because when fishing for them, it was the humans who needed to be silent. Some assert that the voices warn the pipi who would then dig down under the sand and soil, making it more difficult to find and gather them. Kānaka Maoli, however, were aware of a deeper connection that existed between the wind, the pipi, and the humans who gathered them. In actuality, there was another entity involved in the communication with the pipi—the wind. This is described in the 'ōlelo no'eau "Mai wala'au o makani auane'i" wherein the cause and effect are clearly delineated. If one spoke, the wind would blow and it was the wind that gave warning to the pipi.

Here is Nākoa's (1979) description of the effects of speaking while one is gathering the pipi. She wrote,

> A pēlā ihola ka mana'o nui o ka hāmau 'ana o ka leo i 'ole nō ho'i e 'ale'ale mai ke kai a 'ōlepolepo nō ho'i. Ke wala'au a pēia mai ke kai, 'a'ole hiki ke 'ike 'ia aku ua pipi waiwai nui lā me kona hale i hāmama, a 'a'ole ho'i hiki ke maopopo 'ia ka nui o nā pipi e loa'a me ka ma'alahi.

> And that is the main idea behind keeping the voice silent, so that the sea will not become choppy and murky as well. If you speak and the sea becomes like this [choppy and murky], then these highly-prized oysters with their open houses [shells] cannot be seen, and one cannot comprehend the size of the oyster meat with ease.

Here is another author's description of this phenomenon as he described it, and tested it, his first time out. The author was not a native of 'Ewa, but had married a woman from the area, and it was she who introduced him to the appropriate protocols when fishing for pipi. He described his first experience in the following manner:

Ao-a-o mai la kela iaʻu, ai hele kaua i kahakai mai walaau oe o makani auanei pilikia, oiai i ka makahiki 1870, e ikeia ana no keia ia o ka bipi, hele aku la maua a hiki i kahakai o Keamonaale ka inoa o keia wahi, he loʻi [*sic*] a malie loa keia la, aohe ani makani he laʻi malie ke kai a au aku la mau [*sic*]. ("Na Wahi Pana o Ewa" 1899a:2)

She advised me, when we go to the shoreline, don't speak or the wind will blow and we will have problems, since in 1870, this fish known as the oyster was still being seen. So we went until arriving at the shoreline, Keamonaale is the name of this place, and it was a calm and peaceful day, there was no wind and the ocean was calm and peaceful and so we waded out.

In the above section, the author's wife shares the practice of not speaking while fishing. The author, however, did not believe her and so tested it, as he described in the following manner,

Ia maua e au nei ike iho la i ka bipi he like me ka Papaua, a ke ohi ala me ka pane leo ole, a no ka pau ole o koʻu hoomaloka, ua kahea aku la au me ka leo nui. E mama? Nuiloa ka bipi ma keia wahi, a hoomau aku la no au i ke kahea ana. Aole i hala elima minute mahope iho oia manawa, ua uhipuia mai la maua e kamakani, akahi no a pau koʻu hoomaloka. ("Na Wahi Pana o Ewa" 1899b:2)

While we were wading, we saw oysters like the Papaua, and we were gathering them without speaking, but due to my continued disbelief, I called out with a loud voice. "Mama? There are a lot of oysters in this area," and I continued calling out. Not five minutes passed after that time, and we were enveloped by the wind, and only then did my disbelief end.

Through these descriptions, we are able to discern multiple pieces of information, foremost of which may be that in 1870, when military use of Pearl Harbor was minimal, pipi were still abundant and people were able to gather them. In addition, we have an eyewitness account of the cause and effect that speaking had—a clear indication of the intimate relationship between the wind and the pipi, and the people as well. The author's speaking was not just a sign of his disbelief but also a sign of his lack of respect for the pipi, the place, and the social and cultural practices of the people. This lack of respect had consequences, but in the case of the author, he learned his lesson and, from then on, treated the pipi, the place, and the people with the respect and care they demanded and deserved.

Iā ʻEwa ka Iʻa Hāmau Leo: ʻEwa's Responsibility to and for the Pipi

The title of this section also comes from the third verse of the mele "Makalapua" shown previously, and it asserts that the kuleana for ke awa lau o Pu'uloa rests with 'Ewa. In this section, I will highlight the conflicts and problems that arose when 'Ewa no longer was able to maintain that kuleana—when another entity, the US military, took it over and began its long legacy of disrespect and abuse of our lands and environment, plants and animals, and our people.

By the mid to late nineteenth century, ke awa lau o Pu'uloa had become embroiled in the colonial processes of the market-based agriculture, land privatization, and military industrialization. Not only were the people and land affected, but so were the pipi. Kānaka Maoli writing in the mid-1800s recognized the intersection between these colonial forces. One writer, Moses Manu (1885), makes a connection between the decrease of the Hawaiian population due to Western diseases and the decrease of pipi found in ke awa lau, writing,

> Mai ka wa i ike nui ai kela i-a ma Ewa, a i na makahiki mamua ae nei, oia paha ka makahiki 1850–53, oia hoi ka wa i luku nui ia ai keia lahui e ka mai hebera, ua hoomaka aku keia i-a e nalowale. (P. 1)

> From the time that this fish was seen frequently in 'Ewa until recently, perhaps in the years 1850–1853, which is the period of time when this nation of people (Hawaiians) were decimated by smallpox, this fish began to disappear.

Here, Manu highlights the vital connection between Kānaka Maoli and our environment, in which the life of our people is connected to the life of our environment. He then goes on to describe a possible correlation between this decrease of the pipi and other events in the following manner,

> I ka wa i nalo aku ai keia pipi, ua ulu ae la kekahi mea nihoniho keokeo ma na wahi a pau o ke kai o Ewa, a ua kapa iho na kanaka o Ewa i kona inoa he pahikaua, he mea oi keia. (Manu 1885)

> At the time that these oysters disappeared, a white jagged, serrated object arose in each and every place on the ocean side of 'Ewa, and the people of 'Ewa named this object a "pahikaua," which is a sharp, pointed thing.

I have chosen not to translate the word "pahikaua" above in order to provide an additional interpretation of it. Manu here is employing kaona (a hidden or multilayered meaning). On one level, the word "pahikaua" refers to another species of bivalve shellfish and so Manu's words could be interpreted to mean that the pipi was replaced by this other species. However, separated into two parts, the term "pahi" refers to a "knife" and "kaua" refers to "warfare." In this interpretation, Manu is more than likely referring to the guns and cannons of the US military's warships and is articulating his belief that the pipi were decreasing due to the impact of the military in the waters of ke awa lau o Puʻuloa.

Other authors also asserted this correlation between the US military's presence in ke awa lau o Puʻuloa and the decrease of pipi. By 1899–1900, when the author of the next piece was writing, even more had changed on political, economic, and militaristic levels. The Kingdom of Hawaiʻi had been overthrown in 1893, and in 1898, less than a year prior to its publication, the United States had illegally annexed Hawaiʻi through a joint resolution rather than a treaty as called for by its own constitution. Also in 1898, the United States had become an active combatant in the Spanish-American War and was using Hawaiʻi, and Pearl Harbor especially, as a place from which to deploy troops and warships. The industrialization of Pearl Harbor was continuing to increase as was its impact on the surrounding environment and community.

The unidentified author shows his concern over the irrevocable changes being experienced in the moku of ʻEwa in his title. He called his work, "Na Wahi Pana o Ewa i Hoonalowale Ia i Keia Wa a Hiki Ole ke Ike Ia." A quick look at the main title indicates that its focus is on the place-names and cultural sites of ʻEwa ("Nā Wahi Pana"), but a closer look at the title reveals a political message and motivation in that the author describes these place-names not simply as disappearing, which would be "nalowale," but as "hoʻonalowale ʻia," indicating that the place-names are intentionally being made to disappear. The title doesn't stop there but goes on to describe these places as things that had become "incapable of being seen" ("hiki ʻole ke ʻike ʻia").

Although this piece was published in the newspaper, it was not a single article, but rather appeared weekly in the newspaper *Ka Loea Kalaiaina* from June 1899 through January 1900. This newspaper was grounded in Kānaka Maoli political analysis, as indicated by its title, which refers to a "skilled" and "expert" ("loea") form of politics, known as "kālaiʻāina" in Hawaiian.

The article opens with the raising of a question that the author, and apparently the community, is asking, stating,

> Eia paha ka ninau a kahi mea, A pehea ihola hoi i nalowale ai na Bipi nei o Ewa? ("Na Wahi Pana o Ewa" 1899a:2)

> Here perhaps is a question of some, "And how did the Oysters of ʻEwa disappear?"

The author then goes on to answer the question through the sharing of a story about the abuse experienced by an elderly woman who resided in Honouliuli and who was fishing at ke awa lau o Pu'uloa. Although she had permission only to fish for crabs, she also gathered pipi at the same time. The author describes the event in this way.

> Aia no i Manana kekahi luahine kahi i noho ai, oiai keia e kaau Papai ana ma ke kai o Kaholona, me ke manao o ua luahine nei aohe mea na na oia e ike mai. Iaia nae e lalau ana i ka Papai, hemo pu mai la me ka bipi ua hele a makolukolu, ike ia mai la keia, a kii ia mai la a kahi huli—lau ana wawahi ia iho la—kiola ia aku la iloko o ke kai. A auhau ia mai la keia e uku i 25 keneta. ("Na Wahi Pana o Ewa" 1899a:2)

> It was at Mānana that an elderly woman lived, and while she was scooping crab at the shoreline of Kaholona, she thought that there was no one who could see her. Therefore, when she was grabbing the Crab, she also removed some oysters that had become plump, but she was seen and her basket was confiscated and destroyed—tossed into the ocean. And she was fined and made to pay 25 cents.

So, not only are her crabs and oysters discarded, but she is made to pay a fine for her actions. Although not specifically named, the "konohiki" ("caretaker," "overseer") of Pu'uloa is charged as the culprit in this abuse, and the konohiki of Pearl Harbor at the time was the US military (and the US government). Their presence and use and abuse of land had begun to impact Kānaka Maoli access to the land and food sources of Pu'uloa. In addition, taxes and other regulations imposed by the US government were impediments to the "seeing" and "knowing" of these places. Once again, we see the manner in which people's access to subsistence living is compounded by an additional need for cash funds.

As punishment for this abuse, Kānekua'ana, a spiritual guardian of the woman and of Pu'uloa intercedes, speaking through the woman and stating,

> E lawe hou ana wau i ka bipi i Tahiti i kahi a'u i lawe mai ai, aole e hoi hou keia bipi a pau na pua a keia kanaka i ka make, alaila; hoi hou ka bipi ia Hawaii nei. ("Na Wahi Pana o Ewa" 1899a)

> I am going to once again take the oysters to Tahiti to the place where I brought them from, this oyster will not return again until all of the "pua" of this person have died, then, the oyster will again return to Hawai'i.

Here then is described the true cause of the disappearance of the pipi as well as what it will take for them to return—the end of all of the "pua" of the current caretaker. Once again, I have chosen not to translate the word "pua" because of the kaona inherent in the word. On one level, it can refer to the "offspring" and "descendants" of an individual, however, it can also refer to all of that which "issues" or "emerges" from someone, in terms of speech and action even. As such, the essential lesson of this, the first moʻolelo to appear in this extended article about the place-names of ʻEwa is an assertion of the need for all remnants of the current caretaker and overseer, the United States and its military, to not just go away, but to be completely and simply "pau" (ended, finished).

Unfortunately, this goal has not yet been achieved. In the ensuing years of the twentieth and now into the twenty-first century, the legacy and impact of the US military in Hawaiʻi, and, especially in Pearl Harbor, continues. Part of that legacy is the Honouliuli (and other) internment and prisoner-of-war camps, which are the focus of the other articles in this publication. Another part of that legacy is the extreme degree of contamination of Pearl Harbor, which has been classified as a "Superfund contamination site" by the US Environmental Protection Agency since 1991. The EPA defines a "Superfund contamination site" as an "abandoned hazardous waste site," and provides Three-Mile Island as an example. While it is somewhat comforting to know that the EPA recognizes the need for cleanup, it is, however, still disturbing due to the fact that ke awa lau o Puʻuloa is hardly "abandoned," but still an active site that the US military continues to (ab)use. Even though the Pearl Harbor Naval Complex has been identified as a Superfund site, the media continues to report that the contamination is not dangerous. A *Honolulu Advertiser* article in 2006, described it as follows, "pollution at Pearl Harbor does not pose a public threat at current levels of use, *as long as residents don't eat fish or crabs caught in the basin*" [emphasis supplied] (TenBruggencate 2006). This caveat essentially means that Pearl Harbor is a threat, because the residents of Hawaiʻi, whether Kānaka Maoli or not, should be able to access our shorelines and their resources for food and recreation. The fact that we cannot—that the power of the US military means that they can incarcerate our citizens in internment camps (or other designated military installations) and destroy not just our environment, but the very foods we eat—is exemplary of an abuse of power which should not just be remembered, but questioned and critiqued. Only then will the "pua" of the US military's actions end.

Hopefully, the day will soon arrive when people will once again be able to gain both physical and spiritual sustenance from our lands and our seas—

when we can care for our ‘āina and its inhabitants with a respect exemplified in silence. Ironically, though, in the meantime, our voices are essential to bringing back the i‘a hāmau leo and the kānaka who love and respect it. We must act out and speak out on behalf of the i‘a hāmau leo—defending our ‘āina and asserting our rights to a reciprocal relationship with it. There is a time to be silent and a time to let the winds rise with our voices so our ‘āina are protected from further desecration and our pipi can once again respond to our silences—e ō mai, e ka i‘a hāmau leo. ❖

Glossary

ahupua‘a	semi-independent land division within a district
‘āina	land, earth
aloha	love, affection, respect, compassion
haole	Caucasian, white foreigner of American or European descent
ka i‘a hāmau leo	the silent-voiced fish (a metaphorical reference to the pipi)
kaona	hidden or multilayered meaning
ke awa lau o Pu‘uloa	the many bays of Pu‘uloa (a traditional reference to Pearl Harbor)
konohiki	caretaker, overseer, headman of an ahupua‘a land division under the chief
kuleana	rights, responsibilities
kupa	native born
mele	song, chant, poetry
moku	large district comprised of multiple ahupua‘a
mo‘olelo	history, story, fable, tale
‘ōlelo no‘eau	proverbial saying, wise saying
pipi	oysters
pua	progeny, descendants; to issue, appear, come forth, emerge, said especially of smoke, wind, speech
wahi pana	place-names, cultural sites

Notes

1. Throughout this text, the Hawaiian language will be used. Because of its status as an official language of the State of Hawai'i, these words will not appear in italics (except in quotes where italics appear in original). The first time a word is used, however, it will be defined in parentheses or within the text itself. Subsequent uses of the Hawaiian word will not be defined but will appear in the glossary. When warranted, additional information will be included within a footnote reference to help the reader better understand the meanings and uses of the word.

2. Note regarding use and translation of the word "i'a" in Hawaiian. The word "i'a" is translated as "fish," however, in Hawaiian, "i'a" is a term used for all foods that come from the ocean, whether they fall into the more narrow meaning of fish in English or not. Therefore, even though "pipi" ("oysters") are not considered to be fish in English, they are "i'a" in Hawaiian, as are "ula" ("lobsters") and even "limu" ("seaweeds").

3. All translations by author of this article unless otherwise noted.

References

de Silva, Kīhei. 2003. Hō'alo i ka Ihu o ka Lanakila, Three Train Chants for Lili'uokalani. *Kaleinamanu: Literary Archive.*

Kame'eleihiwa, Lilikala. 1992. *Native Land and Foreign Desires: How Shall We Live in Harmony? Ko Hawai'i 'āina a me nā koi pu'umake a ka po'e haole: pehea lā e pono ai?* A history of land tenure change in Hawai'i from traditional times until the 1848 Māhele. Honolulu: Bishop Museum Press.

Kelly, Marion. 1989. "Dynamics of Production Intensification in Precontact Hawaii." Pp. 82–105 in *What's New? A Closer Look at the Process of Innovation.* London: Unwin Hyman.

Makalapua. 1890. "Eia mai au 'o Makalapua / Hō'alo i ka ihu o ka Lanakila." Bishop Museum Mele Index. MS GRP 329.5.48. Honolulu, Hawai'i.

Manu, Moses. 1885. "He Moolelo Kaao no Keaomelemele." *Ka Nupepa Kuokoa.* April 25.

"Na Wahi Pana o Ewa." 1899a. *Ka Loea Kalaiaina.* June 3.

———. 1899b. *Ka Loea Kalaiaina.* June 10.

Nākoa, Sarah Keli'ilolena, and 'Ahahui 'Ōlelo Hawai'i. 1979. *Lei momi o Ewa.* Honolulu: Ahahui Olelo Hawaii.

Osorio, Jonathan Kamakawiwo'ole. 2010. "Memorializing Pu'uloa and Remembering Pearl Harbor." In *Militarized Currents: Toward a Decolonized Future in Asia and the Pacific.* Minneapolis: University of Minnesota Press.

Pukui, Mary Kawena. 1974. *Place Names of Hawaii.* Rev. and enl. ed. Honolulu: University of Hawai'i Press.

TenBruggencate, Jan. 2006. "Pollution Exposure Not High at Pearl Harbor." *Honolulu Advertiser.* January 5.

Finding Honouliuli:
The Japanese Cultural Center of Hawai'i and Preserving the Hawai'i Internment Story

JANE KURAHARA
BRIAN NIIYA
BETSY YOUNG

ABSTRACT

Since a chance phone call asking for the location of the Honouliuli Internment Camp site in 1998, the Japanese Cultural Center of Hawai'i has led efforts to preserve the Honouliuli site and to educate the community about the often neglected story of the internment of Hawai'i's Japanese Americans during World War II. This effort has come to involve many community partnerships as well as the involvement of the federal and state governments. This article outlines the efforts of the Japanese Cultural Center of Hawai'i and its Hawai'i Confinement Sites Committee to gain federal recognition and stewardship of the Honouliuli site, as well as its work to collect, preserve, and interpret the larger Hawai'i internee story to a broader audience, in particular Hawai'i's schoolchildren.

Jane Kurahara, staff associate, Japanese Cultural Center of Hawai'i, 2454 S. Beretania Street, Honolulu, HI 96826; Brian Niiya, content director, Densho, 1416 S. Jackson Street, Seattle, WA 98144; Betsy Young, staff associate, Japanese Cultural Center of Hawai'i, 2454 S. Beretania Street, Honolulu, HI 96826. Some of projects/programs described in this paper (a) are part of Education through Cultural & Historical Organizations (ECHO), a collaborative education partnership of museums and cultural institutions in Hawai'i, Alaska, Massachusetts, and Mississippi. Support is provided by the US Department of Education, Office of Innovation and Improvement; and (b) are based upon work assisted by a grant from the US Department of the Interior, National Park Service. Any opinions, findings and conclusions or recommendations expressed in this material are those of the author(s) and do not necessarily reflect the views of the US Department of the Interior.

In 1998, Honolulu television station KHNL was preparing to show the acclaimed film *Schindler's List*, set in the death camps of Nazi Germany. Wanting to make a local connection to the subject matter, a news reporter from the station called the Japanese Cultural Center of Hawai'i (JCCH), then a relatively new organization dedicated to sharing the history and culture of Japanese Americans in Hawai'i, to ask about internment camps built in Hawai'i to hold local Japanese Americans, specifically the camp called Honouliuli. Where, the reporter asked, had this camp been located? The volunteer staff of that organization's Resource Center was stumped by this request. Consulting knowledgeable people in the local community, the Resource Center staff received conflicting information on the location of Honouliuli. Though the staff recognized the historical significance of the internment of Japanese Americans from Hawai'i during World War II, the question from KHNL brought home how little most people knew about that experience. Over the next few years, the JCCH Resource Center dedicated itself to finding out more about that experience, and in the process, found itself involved in collecting material related to it, educating the public and Hawai'i's schoolchildren about it, and actively working to document and preserve the Hawai'i confinement sites such as Honouliuli. This essay provides a brief overview of those efforts.

The Japanese Cultural Center of Hawai'i was incorporated in 1987 as an offshoot of the Honolulu Japanese Chamber of Commerce. At the first fundraiser on March 1, 1988, campaign chair Joseph Pelletier and board president Walter Tagawa announced plans for the Center that would include a historical gallery, "a broad range of community programs and classes," and "accommodations for Japanese-related organizations" along with meeting rooms "for discussion and business events." (*Hawaii Herald* 1988) This basic vision of the JCCH has remained more or less unchanged. The Center was completed in two phases, with the first building, which included offices, a meeting room, and a teahouse, being completed in the fall of 1991. The second building, which included the exhibition gallery, gift shop, banquet facilities, martial arts *dōjō*, and parking, opened in 1994.

The JCCH Resource Center was not a part of the original plan. Staffed entirely by volunteers and situated in a small space adjacent to the historical gallery, it opened in May of 1997 with no budget and an unwieldy collection of donated books. The various strands of the JCCH's work on the Hawai'i internment story all emanated from the Resource Center, and the rise in the level of activity around the former paralleled the rise of importance of the latter.

The internment related activities of the JCCH can be divided into three broad categories: collection and preservation, interpretation and public education, and K–12 education. As the scope of these efforts increased over time, the Hawai'i Confinement Sites Committee (HCSC) was formed in 2005 to oversee these various efforts. Made up of core JCCH personnel as well as representatives from other interested organizations, the HCSC provided a broad base of expertise and labor to work on the many endeavors.

The story that JCCH and the HCSC focused on was that of Japanese Americans in Hawai'i who were sent to detention camps during World War II. It is much less well known, even in Hawai'i, than the story of the mass expulsion and incarceration of Japanese Americans living on the West Coast.[1] On the basis of years of surveillance of the Japanese American community in Hawai'i, the federal government had prepared custodial detention lists that it used as the basis for hundreds of arrests in the immediate aftermath of the Japanese attack on Pearl Harbor. Those arrested initially were almost entirely Japanese immigrant generation men, along with a smaller number of resident German, Italian, and other European Americans.[2] They were initially held in local detention facilities on the various islands for anywhere from a few days to several months, then were taken to the Sand Island camp in Honolulu Harbor. From there, the internees received hearings, and those who remained in detention were shipped to camps in the continental United States. In many cases, the families of these men "voluntarily" opted to join their husbands/fathers in the mainland camps. Additional arrests continued over the course of the war, with many of the later detainees being American citizen Kibei, Japanese Americans who had been born in the United States but raised and educated in part in Japan. When the Sand Island camp closed in March of 1943, the remaining population there was sent to Honouliuli, which was located in central O'ahu and opened at around the same time. Including the family members, a total of somewhere between 2,000 and 2,500 Japanese Americans living in Hawai'i were held in detention, a fraction of the wartime Japanese American population of around 160,000.[3]

A note on terminology: since the late 1970s, there has been much discussion as to what to call the forced removal and confinement of Japanese Americans during World War II and the camps they were held in. A pioneering article by Okamura (1982) argued that we should reject the euphemistic terminology imposed by the government such as "evacuation" (which implies that Japanese Americans were removed for their own protection) or "relocation centers" in favor of more accurate terminology such as "forced removal" or "concentration camps." Much debate on terminology ensued; see Murray (2008) and Daniels (2008) for overviews of this discussion. See also CLPEF (1996) and Noguchi (2012) for a discussion of the recent "The Power of Words" handbook. In line with what seems to be an emerging consensus on terminology in academia and within the Japanese American community, we avoid euphemistic terminology employed by the government. Japanese Americans from Hawai'i who were detained and incarcerated—as opposed to those on the West Coast who were forcibly removed under the authority of Executive Order 9066—are properly referred to as "internees," and the camps they were held in that were administered by the army or the Justice Department are referred to as "internment camps" or "detention camps." The euphemistically named "relocation centers" administered by the War Relocation Authority, will be referred to as "concentration camps" in line with most current usage. Although most Japanese immigrants were not allowed to become US citizens

Sand Island Internment Camp. Photograph courtesy of the US Army Museum.

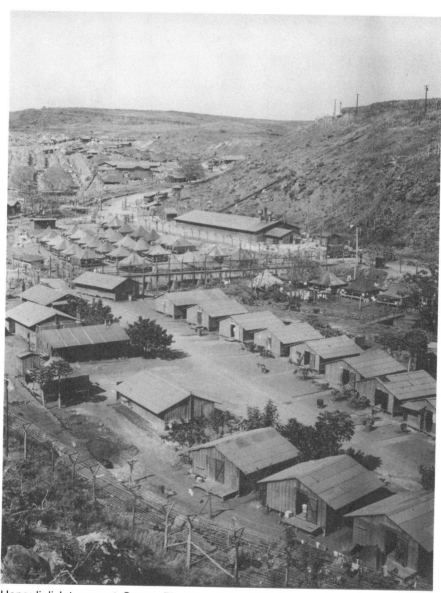

Honouliuli Internment Camp. Photograph by R.H. Lodge, Courtesy of JCCH /
Japanese American Relocation & Internment: The Hawaii Experience Collection.

prior to World War II, both the resident immigrants and their native-born American citizen children will be referred to as "Japanese Americans."

Collection and Preservation

Soon after the initial push to locate the site, the family of Otokichi Ozaki, a Hilo-based journalist and poet, approached the JCCH Resource Center about possibly archiving his papers. A significant portion of those papers centered on his internment during World War II and included letters written to him by family members and friends, poetry he composed about his wartime experiences, and radio scripts from his postwar radio show, several of which focus on his internment. The collection, which ended up filling over twenty standard archival boxes, was the first manuscript collection received by the Resource Center and was assigned the call number "AR1." The Resource Center staff learned about processing archival collections on the fly and successfully organized the Ozaki Collection and prepared finding aids. The Center prepared a small grant application to the Hawai'i Council for the Humanities to assist in the processing and to contract local historian Marie Strazar, who wrote an overview of the collection as part of the finding aid. Because much of the collection contained material written in Japanese, bilingual Resource Center volunteers set to work translating the material.

Otokichi Ozaki and son, Earl. Photograph courtesy of the Otokichi Ozaki Family Collection.

This first internment-based collection soon led to many others, including the Gladys S. Naitoh Collection, the Paul S. Osumi Collection, and the Ryuichi Ipponsugi Collection, all of which contain material documenting the internment experience of Hawai'i Japanese American families. The Patsy Saiki Collection includes material used in the writing of Saiki's landmark book *Ganbare! An Example of Japanese Spirit* (1982), while the Japanese American Relocation and Internment: The Hawai'i Experience/Dennis Ogawa Collection includes a wide range of material collected by Ogawa in the 1980s for a project on the internment of Japanese Americans in Hawai'i. Including material from the National Archives and interviews with internees and administrators of the Hawai'i camps, material from this collection became the basis for Ogawa and Fox (1986). For a list of internment-related collections held by the Resource Center, see Table 1.[4]

Table 1
JCCH Archival Collections Related to Internment

AR1	Otokichi Ozaki Collection
AR4	Gladys S. Naitoh Collection
AR5	Terumitsu Higashi Collection
AR14	Paul S. Osumi Collection
AR15	Bunka No Izumi Internment Sketches (copies of George Hoshida's sketches)
AR16	Dr. Victor Mori Family Papers
AR17	Toshio Saito Papers
AR18	Patsy Saiki Collection
AR19	Japanese American Relocation & Internment: The Hawaii Experience
AR27	Ryuichi Ipponsugi Collection
AR28	Usaburo Katamoto
Pending:	
	Rev. Toshiro Hirano Papers
	Doris Berg Nye Papers
	Soichi Obata Collection
Related:	
AR6	Catherine Embree Harris & Poston Relocation Camp
AR8	Mori Collection (Dr. Iga Mori's Diaries)

In addition to the archival collection, the Resource Center also added a small number of three-dimensional artifacts to its collection. Among them are craft objects made by internees while confined both in Hawai'i and in camps in the continental United States including shell necklaces made at Sand Island, miniature furniture made by Dan Nishikawa at Honouliuli, and a wood carving by Taichi Sato of his eleven-year-old daughter Harriet. Inmates created similar items at all of the various confinement sites for a variety of reasons, ranging from the pragmatic to the mental health related. But such items were often unique to particular camps or regions based on that camp's population or on materials unique to that area, as with the case of the shells found at Sand Island.[5]

Shell necklace. Courtesy of JCCH, Dan Toru Nishikawa Collection.

Fine art objects make up another category of camp related three-dimensional objects in the Center's collection. These include drawings and paintings of life in camp by artists such as Dan Nishikawa, Hiroshi Honda, and Bannosuke Yoshida. Honda's work has been the subject of two exhibitions at the Honolulu Academy of Arts, while Nishikawa's work provides rare glimpses of life at both Sand Island and Honouliuli. These works are again typical of the work done by Japanese American inmate artists at camps throughout the country.[6]

In 2003, the JCCH began to interview former Hawai'i internees and their family members as part of its oral history program. The Center adhered to academic oral history methodology that involves a pre-interview, the audio-only interview itself, transcription, review of the transcription by the interview subject, and the archiving of the final transcript. The interviews include a few former internees, along with many children of internees, some of whom joined their parents "voluntarily" in mainland camps. In addition, through

Honouliuli Women's Internment Barracks sketched by Dan Toru Nishikawa. Courtesy of the JCCH, Dan Toru Nishikawa Collection.

partnerships with the Go For Broke National Education Center and Densho beginning in 2009, the Center conducted additional interviews on video. See Table 2 for a list of oral histories in the JCCH collection.

Just as the Ozaki family materials led to the wide range of internment related materials the Resource Center has collected and is preserving, the initial inquiry about the location of the Honouliuli site has led to the identification of the site and many steps toward its ultimate preservation. In 2002, Resource Center staff identified the site of the Honouliuli Internment Camp with the assistance of Bert Hatton of Campbell Estate, the entity that owned the land the camp was built on at that time, along with local farmer Larry Jefts. In 2006, the JCCH worked with archaeologists Jeff Burton and Mary Farrell to conduct research on the five main confinement sites in Hawai'i: Sand Island and Honouliuli on O'ahu, Kīlauea Military Camp on the Big Island, Kalāheo Stockade on Kaua'i, and Ha'ikū Camp on Maui. The information gathered on this trip led to the publication of Burton and Farrell's *World War II Japanese American Internment Sites in Hawai'i* (2007) by the Center. One of their recommendations was for an archaeological study of the Honouliuli site.

In 2007, State Senator Will Espero introduced SB 1228, legislation calling for a memorial at the Honouliuli site that JCCH supported through testimony. Also in 2007, the parcel of land that includes the Honouliuli site was sold to Monsanto, a large multinational agricultural company. The company was aware of the Honouliuli site at the time of the purchase and made it clear to JCCH at the initial meetings that it wanted to preserve Honouliuli as a historic site. Over the past six years, the Center has worked with Monsanto in charting the best possible course to accomplish this.

A significant element of any future plans was a better sense of the archaeology of the site. With the assistance of funding from the Conservation Fund, National Trust for Historic Preservation, and National Park Service, Burton and Farrell returned to Honouliuli in February 2008 to conduct a five-day survey of the site with the assistance of 25 volunteers from JCCH. Among other developments, this survey revealed the presence of two standing buildings from the administration area of the camp, in addition to scores of foundations and other remains from the camp. Burton and Farrell returned to Honouliuli the following year to do more work at the site, and, since 2010, the pair has been conducting summer field schools at the site through the University of Hawai'i–West O'ahu. The pair also authored a nomination for

Table 2
Oral Histories in JCCH Collection

Hisashi Fukuhara

Kaetsu Furuya

Minosuke Hanabusa

Grace Sugita Hawley

Edward K. Honda [son of Hawai'i internee artist Hiroshi Honda]

George Hoshida

Jukichi Inouye

Carolyn Shizuko Izumo

Sidney I. Kashiwabara

Mabel I. Kawamura

Masamizu Kitajima

Iwao Kosaki

Tamotsu Masui

Morris Matsumoto

Gyokuei Matsuura

Stanley M. Miyahara

Carol Tatsuko Murakawa

Shigeo Muroda

Yuuichi Nakamura

James A. Nakano

Doris H. Nye

Kenjiro Ohara

Muriel Chiyo Onishi

Toshio Saito

Rodney A. Santiago

Sarah Yomogi Okada Sato

Mitsuko Sumida

Rev. Seikaku Takesono

Janet Chieko Uehara

Robert Yamamoto

Shizuo Yoshikane

Honouliuli for the National Register of Historic Places. It was added to the state historic register in 2009 and to the national register in 2012.[7]

Another important element of the site preservation planning was political. While the landowner had made it clear that it was willing to give up the land to an entity that would insure its preservation, it was unclear what the entity would be. The HCSC and the landowner looked at three possibilities: federal management of the site through the National Park Service (NPS), state management through the Department of Land and Natural Resources (DLNR), or a nongovernmental organization, presumably a nonprofit. For various reasons, both the HCSC and the landowner felt that the first option was clearly the best choice given the resources and ultimate access the NPS could provide as well as discussions with local NPS staff indicating their willingness to take on the Honouliuli site.

Once this decision had been reached, the HCSC reached out to the Hawaiʻi congressional delegation to seek legislation that would form a special resource study for Honouliuli, a necessary first step in the process. (While there are other avenues for a site to come under NPS jurisdiction—most notably by presidential decree—such avenues required that the land already be owned by the federal government. While the landowner was by this time willing to donate the land to the federal government, there was no federal agency that was able to accept it.) A special resource study would be a directive from Congress to the NPS to conduct a study of the site for "national significance, suitability, and feasibility" in determining its fitness for becoming an NPS unit. The congressional delegation—Senators Daniel Inouye and Daniel Akaka and Representatives Neil Abercrombie and Mazie Hirono—were extraordinarily receptive to the idea and worked together to put the necessary legislation together. Ultimately, it was included in Section 125 of the Defense Appropriations Bill of October 2009 where it was passed into law. Ultimately, the legislation called for a special resource study of all 13 confinement sites in Hawaiʻi. (In addition to Honouliuli and the other four sites noted above, the study also included other short-term holding centers—mostly local jails—where detainees were held right after their arrests.)

In late 2010, the NPS assigned a staff person to its Honolulu office to lead the special resource study. While the NPS has been directed to investigate all thirteen sites, it decided to focus on Honouliuli first given the favorable conditions at that site. Thanks to the archaeological work and historic register nominations for Honouliuli that had already been completed, the "national significance" and a good portion of the "suitability and feasibility" had already been established. The main remaining piece was to conduct a series of hearings that would allow public comment. These sessions took place on O'ahu, Hawai'i island, Maui, and Kaua'i in 2011. Based on our attendance at these sessions, public response was uniformly positive.[8] As of this writing, we are awaiting a draft set of recommendations, after which another set of public scoping sessions will take place before a final recommendation is made to Congress.[9]

Interpretation and Public Education

As collection and preservation efforts progressed, interpretation and public education followed. The purpose of these efforts was twofold: (a) in order to build support for Honouliuli preservation efforts—both political support that would be needed in the special resource study process and financial support—we wanted as many people as possible to know about the Hawai'i internment story; and (b) as an end in itself: we study history to gain insight into the present and future; this story is an important one in the ongoing debate on civil liberties in times of war and more broadly, on stigmatizing people based on their race, religion, or other external criteria. As such, the Center tried to use as many platforms as possible to get the story out.

As part of its regular programming, JCCH has a small (about 1,000 square feet) exhibition gallery for temporary exhibitions on the aspects of the Japanese American experience in Hawai'i. In 2004, the Center featured an exhibition titled "Dark Clouds Over Paradise: The Hawai'i Internees Story" featuring objects from the collection and archive at the time. The exhibition was inspired by an interview with former internee Jack Tasaka, then 90 years old, who offered his help with the exhibition if it was completed within a year given his advanced age. The exhibition opened at JCCH in June of 2004 and was augmented by a series of public programs that summer. With funding provided by a grant from the Hawai'i Council for the Humanities, a traveling version of the exhibition was produced in the fall of 2006. Consisting of twelve self-standing photo and text panels, this version of "Dark Clouds" like the original provided a broad overview of Japanese Americans living in Hawai'i who had been detained both in Hawai'i and in the continental United States. It also included a list of internee names. The traveling exhibition debuted at the Pacific Tsunami Museum in Hilo and traveled extensively over the next few years to venues that included the Kailua-Kona Public Library, the Kaua'i

Dark Clouds Over Paradise
The Hawai`i Internees Story

Sand Island Detention Center, O`ahu

What day will I see
My children again?
I am overcome
As I hug each child
One at a time.

On the night of December 7, 1941, various leaders of the immigrant Japanese community in Hawai`i were greeted by local and federal authorities. Some had their bags packed already in anticipation of what was to come; others hurriedly readied their belongings and said goodbye to their families. Their wartime odyssey had begun.

By the following evening, 345 Japanese in Hawai`i had been detained. Over the course of the coming weeks and months, some 10,000 people living in Hawai`i would be investigated, resulting in the detention of 1,569 individuals, of whom 1,250 were Japanese.

Harriet (Saito) Masunaga had her first permanent, when she was 11 years old. Her mother sent a photo showing her new hairdo to her father, Taichi Sato, who was sent from Hawai`i to be interned on the Mainland (Santa Fe). Out of a single piece of wood, Mr. Sato carved her likeness and sent it back to her.

Fingerprinting of internee for FBI records, February 17, 1942.

Traveling Exhibit, Dark Clouds Over Paradise: The Hawaii Internees Story. Courtesy of the JCCH.

Community College Library, the Kaua'i Museum, three high schools in Kaua'i, and many venues on O'ahu including the Kapolei Public Library, and at Days of Remembrance and other events. In addition to the thousands of people who have seen the exhibition in its travels, more people were exposed to the story through the newspaper articles and TV/radio spots that accompanied the various openings of the exhibit. This publicity is a valuable by-product of a traveling exhibition.

Publications reach a different, geographically dispersed audience and provide a more in-depth treatment of the story. In the early 2000s, two Resource Center volunteers began projects to translate important Japanese language memoirs by Hawai'i Issei about their internment experiences. In 1948, esteemed journalist Yasutaro Soga, one of the leaders of Honolulu's prewar Japanese community, published a detailed account of his internment titled *Tessaku seikatsu* (*Life behind Barbed Wire*). Written by an experienced journalist—Soga was 68 years old when he was interned and had been a journalist in Hawai'i for over forty years—Soga's book contains detailed descriptions of every aspect of his four-year internment odyssey that took him from Sand Island to a succession of camps on the mainland. Although the vivid accounts in his book have often been quoted by those writing about Hawai'i during World War II—see Okihiro (1991) and Kashima (2003) for but two examples—there had never been a full translation. Inspired in part by Soga's example, Suikei Furuya, a Honolulu businessman, wrote his internment memoir titled *Haisho tenten*, which was published in Honolulu in 1964. Additionally, a committee was formed to consider the possibility of commissioning a publication based on the Otokichi Ozaki papers held by the Resource Center. As committee member Dennis Ogawa saw it, the three books could form a trilogy of stories about the Hawai'i internees.

The first to see publication was Soga's book (2008) translated by Kihei Hirai. A banker by profession who first came to Hawai'i on business and who settled there after his retirement, Hirai volunteered at the Resource Center as a translator and took on Soga's book as his project. Assisted by other Resource Center translators Shige Yoshitake and Florence Sugimoto—both of whom were Nisei familiar with many of the local names and idioms—Hirai finished up the manuscript and submitted it to the University of Hawai'i Press for consideration. With the additions of introductory pieces by scholars Dennis Ogawa and Tetsuden Kashima, the book was published in 2008 under the title *Life behind Barbed Wire: The World War II Internment Memoirs of a Hawai'i Issei*.

In the meantime, the Ozaki committee raised money and commissioned local writer and editor Gail Honda to craft a manuscript out of the documents. Working with the Ozaki family, translators from the Resource Center, and volunteer managing editor Sheila Chun, Honda produced a manuscript that was reviewed by the committee and JCCH staff. JCCH published the book (with a distribution agreement by the University of Hawai'i Press) in 2012 under the title *Family Torn Apart: The Internment Story of the Otokichi [Muin] Ozaki Family*. Arrested shortly after the attack on Pearl Harbor, Ozaki was interned at Sand Island and sent to various internment camps on the mainland. His young family opted to join him in the mainland camps, but they remained separated for over a year in different mainland camps due to government bureaucracy before finally being reunited. The story is told through letters and Ozaki's poems and scripts from his postwar radio show in which he recalled his wartime experience.

The third book in the trilogy, Furuya's *Haisho tenten*, was originally published in Japanese in 1964, and has been translated by Tatsumi Hayashi, another retired Japanese businessman (and airline executive) turned Resource Center volunteer. Though structurally similar to Soga's book, on which it was modeled, Furuya's story is that of a man a generation younger than Soga, who as the title—which roughly translates to "Internment Here and There"—indicates, was sent to a bewildering number of mainland camps. The translation of that book is scheduled to be published by JCCH in 2014.

In 2009, Congress passed PL 109-441 that authorized up to $38 million in federal matching grants to preserve the Japanese American World War II confinement sites and to share the lessons and stories of that experience. The following year, the Japanese American Confinement Sites (JACS) Grant Program came into being, with an initial federal appropriation of $1 million. With the success of the "Dark Clouds" exhibition, the HCSC decided to submit an application for a new wayside exhibition on Honouliuli that could be displayed outdoors at pilgrimages and even at the site itself. The application was among those selected for funding, with a total budget of $61,000. A grant from the Island Insurance Foundation provided the matching funds for the project. The HCSC contracted Mo'ili'ili Blind Fish Tank, Inc. (MBFT) Media to produce the exhibition. It was completed in 2011 under the title "Right from Wrong: Learning the Lessons of Honouliuli." While outlining the history of internment of Japanese Americans from Hawai'i and Honouliuli, this exhibition also includes information about the recent preservation efforts and meaning of Honouliuli in the present and future. It debuted at the Hawai'i Okinawan Festival, held over Labor Day weekend in Kapiolani Park and attended by some 50,000 people. It has since been displayed at Days of Remembrance and other events and can be viewed daily in the JCCH courtyard.

Wanting to reach a broader—and younger—audience than those drawn to publications and exhibitions, the JCCH applied for a grant in the second year of the JACS program in 2010 for a documentary film on the Hawai'i internment story. The Center had previously produced a short film on Honouliuli for the 2010 Day of Remembrance, which had been widely screened to a highly positive response. The JCCH received a grant for $117,626 for the film; matching funds were provided by grants from the Gerbode Foundation, the Island Insurance Foundation, and the Japanese American Citizens League (JACL) Honolulu Chapter. Filmmaker Ryan Kawamoto was contracted to produce the film for JCCH. Under the title *The Untold Story: Internment of Japanese Americans in Hawai'i*, the hour-long documentary debuted at the Hawai'i International Film Festival in October 2012 and has been screened for appreciative audiences on O'ahu, Hawai'i, Kaua'i, and Maui. It was shown on Hawai'i PBS stations and released on home video in 2013.

Beyond such interpretive vehicles as the exhibitions, books, and the documentary film, special events have also been a part of the public education strategy. Days of Remembrance (DoRs) have become important commemorations in the Japanese American community nationwide since the first event in Seattle in 1978. Today, they are held annually in some twenty cities nationwide, on or around the February 19 anniversary of Executive Order 9066, the presidential directive that authorized the mass forced removal and incarceration of Japanese Americans on the West Coast.[10] Since 2008, JCCH has been partnering with the Honolulu Chapter of the Japanese American Citizens League (JACL) in putting on the Honolulu event. (JACL had been organizing the Honolulu events since the 1980s.) The 2008 event included the first ever pilgrimage to the Honouliuli site and was held to coincide with the first archaeological survey of the site. Because the pilgrimage was limited to fewer than 100 participants due to logistical difficulties at the site, a separate event was held at the JCCH ballroom that was attended by some 600 people. Subsequent annual events have drawn large and enthusiastic crowds and substantial media coverage, which has increased local support and interest in the Hawai'i internment topic. In 2011, the Center organized a second pilgrimage to the Honouliuli site.

Honouliuli

JAPANESE CULTURAL CENTER OF HAWAI'I
Honoring our heritage. Embracing our diversity. Sharing our future.

Right from Wrong: Learning the Lessons of Honouliuli

Why Bother?

IIIA. The Human Toll

The total number of internees was small, less than 1 percent of the more than 157,000 people of Japanese descent living in Hawai'i in 1940. It has been pointed out, however, that the impact of the internment was greater than is reflected by sheer numbers because those arrested were often leaders of the community. Amongst the internees, for example, the government had targeted Japanese language school principals and teachers, Buddhist priests, martial arts instructors, business leaders, Japanese consulate staff, and others who might have had direct dealings with Japan. Key community institutions such as Japanese language schools, Buddhist temples, and even a few Japanese Christian churches were closed.

THERE IS NOTHING...

ikusa hodo
kanashiki wa nashi
sekaijyu no
kanashiki koto no
koko ni atsumaru

There is nothing
More sorrowful than war.
Here alone,
All of life's sadness
Is brought together.

—Yasutaro "Keiho" Soga, Poets
Behind Barbed Wire, Bamboo
Ridge Press (1983)

Drawing of Honouliuli mess hall by Dan T. Nishikawa depicts detainees dressed down to their skivvies as a means of enduring the oppressive heat.
(JCCH Collection)

"Hell Valley"

Honouliuli represented isolation and injustice to all who were interned there. Mosquitoes and the intense heat trapped in the gulch added to their misery. They called Honouliuli "Jigoku Dani," or Hell Valley.

Photo: Hawai'i
Plantation Village
Collection

Wayside Exhibit, Right from Wrong. Courtesy of the JCCH.

Beyond the DoRs and pilgrimages, the JCCH has sponsored other special programs including book events and public lectures, featuring such acclaimed authors as Jeanne Wakatsuki Houston (2007), Lane Hirabayashi (2010), Gary Okihiro (2011), and Greg Robinson (2011). JCCH staff and volunteers also make regular presentations on the Hawai'i internment story to local community groups upon request.

K–12 Education

Hawaii's schoolchildren represent one of the most important audiences for the lessons of the Hawai'i internment story. The core lessons of what can happen if we stereotype and stigmatize can have very practical implications for students in their everyday life and can also be a platform for sharpening research and writing skills. While the Center has worked with teachers and students going back to a 1999 internment workshop attended by seventy teachers as well as many individual students seeking assistance on school projects, the core educational efforts came about after 2005 when the Hawai'i State Department of Education (DOE) issued new benchmarks for their teachers. Among these benchmarks were specific references to the removal and incarceration of Japanese Americans in the Modern History of Hawai'i course (then taught in grade 9) and the US History course (then taught in grade 10). For the first time, Hawai'i's schoolchildren would be required to learn about

Pilgrimage to Honouliuli. Photograph courtesy of the JCCH.

this important topic. But resources on the Hawai'i internment story were few and far between. Given the material collected in the Resource Center, JCCH was in a position to provide resources that would allow teachers to meet these new benchmarks.

The first step came in 2006 in the form of a Hawai'i Internment Discovery Box, the latest in a series of such boxes containing primary and secondary sources (both books and audiovisual material) and suggested lesson plans on a given topic. These boxes can be borrowed by schools for one-week periods for a nominal charge. The internment box included copies of many of JCCH's primary sources on Hawai'i internment as well as secondary sources and videos. Five internment discovery boxes were created, including two on O'ahu.

While appreciated by some teachers, there were two main problems with the Hawai'i internment boxes. The sheer volume of material in them proved daunting to all but the most interested teachers. Given the number of topics the benchmarks required them to teach, they did not have the time to wade through all this material to create relevant lessons for their classes. Second, the uniformity of the benchmarks meant that schools typically taught particular topics at more or less the same time, and thus generally needed the boxes at more or less the same time. With only a few boxes to lend, the Center could reach only a handful of schools.

The next iteration aimed to solve these problems. Resource Center education volunteers—all of whom were former schoolteachers or school librarians—carefully went through the primary sources in the internment discovery boxes and selected highlights in several topical areas, with input from a focus group of teachers. These documents were copied and compiled into an approximately 250-page binder titled "World War II Hawaii Internees' Experiences Resource Folders." With the assistance of a grant from the Honolulu Chapter of the JACL, two hard copies of the folders were produced and distributed in 2007 to every public high school in the state, one to the school library and one to the social studies department.

A final refinement came with the assistance of a grant from the federal Education through Cultural and Historical Organizations (ECHO) program. This funding allowed the JCCH to contract a former DOE assistant superintendent and four highly respected social studies teachers to create instructional units using our primary sources to specifically address the benchmarks in the Modern History of Hawai'i, US History, and Participation in Democracy classes. The Center also was able to contract nine other teachers to review these units and six others to test them in the classroom. These carefully authored, reviewed, and tested units were then made available to all teachers—as well as to the general public—electronically, through a website, http://www. hawaiiinternment.org/. In cooperation with the DOE, the Center publicized the units through DOE channels and also conducted workshops for social studies teachers on Hawai'i, Kaua'i, Maui, and O'ahu where the units were unveiled. Through these increasingly specific iterations—internment discovery boxes available for borrowing, resource folders distributed to every school, and instructional units designed for specific classes—Hawai'i's social studies teachers have a variety of tools available to address the benchmarks regarding the internment of Japanese Americans from Hawai'i during World War II.

Though specifically designed as a vehicle for distributing the internment instructional units, the "Hawaii internment" website contains much additional information and resources: descriptions, finding aids, and samples of internment related collections at JCCH; a short version of the Honouliuli video developed for the 2010 DoR; an internment timeline; electronic versions of the "World War II Hawai'i Internees' Experiences Resource Folders"; and an overview essay on the topic. The JCCH is in the process of updating the site and more fully integrating it with the new JCCH website.

The most recent development in our educational efforts has been to use the power of the Honouliuli site as a living resource. Thanks to the 2011 and 2012 JACS grants and aided by collaborations with the Honolulu Japanese Junior Chamber of Commerce, Monsanto, the NPS, and community volunteers, the Center has been able to facilitate gulch tours for hundreds of visitors.

The 2011 grant funded the gulch tours pilot program that included high school classes, college classes, and members of the general public. Although the site looks very different from the World War II period, upon being engulfed in the isolation, heat, humidity, and mosquitoes, the sense of place of what the internees called "Jigoku Dani" (Hell Valley) became very real to them, not just something out of a textbook. In a similar inquiry process used by the site archaeologists, the facilitators involved the visitors in the exploration and investigation of the site remains and artifacts. To extend upon their findings, the facilitators engaged the visitors with primary source material such as historic photographs and maps. The most powerful resources for engendering empathy for the internees and their families were the poignant stories, poems, and songs of their unjust imprisonment. Students have commented on the significant impact from the numerous candid imprisonment stories from internee Jack Tasaka, who was a prolific writer and historian. The art of internee Dan Nishikawa documented the 1943 camp scenes and camp life. The humility, inner strength, and forgiving spirit of internee Sanji Abe—who astonishingly had been a territorial senator before he was interned—are evident in his letters.[11]

The 2012 grant was extended to include twelve public and private high schools. These students applied the lessons from World War II history and the tours of Pearl Harbor and Honouliuli Internment Camp to create projects related to current social justice issues. The outstanding student projects were shared and celebrated at a culminating event: "Inspired by History, Hawai'i's Youth Take Action," held at the JCCH on April 13, 2013.

In an article in the *Honolulu Star-Advertiser*, Sacred Hearts Academy student Keala Parker-Lee wrote, upon reflecting on her Honouliuli site experiences:

> Seeing the remnants of buildings and hearing true stories of families who went through this traumatic experience taught me that we must stand up to social injustices.

A student group on tour to Honouliuli. Photograph courtesy of the JCCH.

As American citizens, we are promised many things through the Constitution, but the most important thing we are promised is our freedom.

Let my generation never force its citizens into situations where their rights to freedom are completely forgotten. May my generation never make these same mistakes. (Parker-Lee 2013)

Since the fateful call from KHNL some fifteen years ago, much has happened that has added to our knowledge about the story of Japanese Americans from Hawai'i who were interned during World War II. But there is still much to be done. Though substantial progress has been made toward the preservation of the Honouliuli site, we are still several steps from it becoming an NPS unit and many more from it being open and accessible to the general public.[12] There is also much to be done with the other sites, whether a historical marker at the Sand Island site, signage or other commemoration of the Kīlauea site, or

Clockwise from top: Internees Sanji Abe, Dan Toru Nishikawa, and Yoshitami Jack Tasaka. Photographs courtesy of the JCCH, Abe, Nishikawa, and Tasaka Collections.

archaeological exploration of the Haʻikū and Kalāheo sites.[13] There are many other important collections still out there in the community that need to be preserved, more Days of Remembrance to organize, and more schoolchildren to educate. With growing support from the local community as well as an active volunteer base that has supplied much of the labor for all this activity, we are confident that we will never again be puzzled when someone asks us where the Honouliuli site is. ❖

Notes

1. The story of the mass removal and incarceration of Japanese Americans from the West Coast has been written about extensively, even exhaustively. For a small sample of the most significant works, see Densho (2012).

2. For more on European American internees from Hawaiʻi, see Alan Rosenfeld (2014). There were also a handful of women who were arrested and detained; see Amy Nishimura (2014) for accounts of two of those women.

3. On the detention of Japanese Americans from Hawaiʻi, see Saiki (1982), Nakano and Nakano (1983), Ogawa and Fox (1986), Knaefler (1991), Okihiro (1991), Kashima (2003), and Robinson (2009). See also Susan Matoba Adler (2014) for a list of several children sent from Micronesia.

4. Finding aids for some of these collections can also be downloaded at http://www. hawaiiinternment.org/collections.

5. There have been several studies of craft objects made by Japanese Americans confined in the various types of camps during World War II. The first was Eaton (1952) by a pioneering folk art chronicler. Dusselier (2008) explores the meanings of these objects, while Hirasuna (2005) is a lavishly illustrated companion book to a recent exhibition.

6. The two Honda exhibitions are "Reflections of Internment: The Art of Hawaii's Hiroshi Honda" (Honolulu Academy of Arts 1994) and "Hiroshi Honda: Detained" (Honolulu Academy of Arts 2012); the first was accompanied by a companion booklet featuring essays by Franklin Odo and Marcia Morse along with color images of many of the displayed paintings. Among the overview studies of fine arts in the camps are Gesensway and Roseman (1987) and *The View from Within* (Japanese 1992), the latter a companion book to an exhibition of the same name. There are several studies of the work of individual Japanese American artists from the concentration camps, including Kim (2000) and Johns (2011).

7. See the article by Burton et al. (2014) for detailed information on the progression of the archaeological work and the findings from each trip to the site.

8. This has not been the case in similar efforts to commemorate mainland confinement sites. See, for instance, Murray (2008) and Bahr (2007) for accounts of the opposition to site commemoration of California's Manzanar camp.

9. For the background and current status of the efforts, see "Honouliuli Special Resource Study" (National Park Service 2010).

10. For more on the history and evolution of Days of Remembrance, see Iwamura (2007), Murray (2008), Nakagawa (2012), and Takezawa (1995).

11. For more on Abe, see Nakamura (2012).

12. The NPS currently manages three Japanese American confinement sites: Manzanar National Historic Site, Minidoka National Historic Site, and Tule Lake Unit of the Valor in the Pacific National Monument.

13. In November of 2012, JCCH staff did additional interviews in Kaua'i with local residents who remembered the Japanese American internment camp in Kalāheo in an attempt to verify its location.

References

Adler, Susan Matoba. 2014. "The Effect of Internment on Children and Families: Honouliuli and Manzanar." In this issue.

Bahr, Diana Meyers. 2007. *The Unquiet Nisei: An Oral History of the Life of Sue Kunitomi Embrey*. New York: Palgrave Macmillan.

Burton, Jeffrey F., and Mary M. Farrell. 2007. *World War II Japanese American Internment Sites in Hawai'i*. Tucson, AZ: Trans-Sierran Archaeological Research; Honolulu: Japanese Cultural Center of Hawai'i Resource Center.

Burton, Jeff, Mary Farrell, Linda Kaneko, Linda Maldonato, and Kelly Altenhofen. 2014. "Hell Valley: Uncovering a Prison Camp in Paradise." In this issue.

CLPEF Network. 1996. "CLPEF Resolution Regarding Terminology." Retrieved December 21, 2012 (http://www.momomedia.com/CLPEF/backgrnd.html#Link%20 to%20terminology).

Daniels, Roger. 2008. "Words Do Matter: A Note on the Inappropriate Terminology and the Incarceration of the Japanese Americans." Los Angeles: Discover Nikkei. Retrieved December 21, 2012 (http://www.discovernikkei.org/en/journal/2008/2/1/ words-do-matter/).

Densho. 2012. "Web Resources, Printed Resources and Videos." Seattle: Retrieved December 25, 2012 (http://www.densho.org/resources/default.asp?path=directory.asp).

Dusselier, Jane. 2008. *Artifacts of Loss: Crafting Survival in Japanese American Concentration Camps*. New Brunswick, NJ: Rutgers University Press.

Eaton, Allen H. 1952. *Beauty Behind Barbed Wire: The Arts of the Japanese in Our War Relocation Camps*. New York: Harper.

Furuya, Suikei. 1964. *Haisho tenten [Internment from Camp to Camp]*. Honolulu: *Hawaii taimususha*.

————. Forthcoming. *Haisho Tenten: A Hawai'i Issei's Odyssey from Internment Camp to Camp*, translated and annotated by Tatsumi Hayashi. Honolulu: Japanese Cultural Center of Hawai'i.

Gesensway, Deborah, and Mindy Roseman. 1987. *Beyond Words: Images from America's Concentration Camps*. Ithaca, NY: Cornell University Press.

Hawaii Herald. 1988. "Japanese Cultural Center of Hawaii." March 18:5.

Hirabayashi, Lane Ryo. 2010. Book Talk: Japanese American Resettlement through the Lens: Hikaru Carl Iwasaki and the WRA's Photographic Section, 1943–1945. Japanese Cultural Center of Hawai'i, August 14.

Hirasuna, Delphine. 2005. *The Art of Gaman: Arts and Crafts from the Japanese American Internment Camps, 1942–1946*. Berkeley, CA: Ten Speed Press.

Honda, Gail, ed. 2012. *Family Torn Apart: The Internment Story of the Otokichi [Muin] Ozaki Family*. Honolulu: Japanese Cultural Center of Hawai'i.

Honolulu Academy of Arts. 1994. "Reflections of Internment: The Art of Hawaii's Hiroshi Honda." Exhibit with companion booklet with essays by Franklin Odo and Marcia Morse. Honolulu, Hawai'i.

————. 2012. Hiroshi Honda: Detained. Exhibit. Honolulu, Hawai'i.

Houston, Jeanne Wakatsuki. 2007. Untitled talk, Japanese Cultural Center of Hawai'i, November 4.

Iwamura, Jane Naomi. 2007. "Critical Faith: Japanese Americans and the Birth of a New Civil Religion." *American Quarterly* 59(3):937–968.

Japanese American National Museum. 1992. *The View from Within: Japanese American Art from the Internment Camps, 1942–1945*. Los Angeles: UCLA Wight Art Gallery and UCLA Asian American Studies Center.

Johns, Barbara. 2011. *Signs of Home: The Paintings and Wartime Diaries of Kamekichi Tokita*. Foreword by Stephen H. Sumida. Seattle: University of Washington Press.

Kashima, Tetsuden. 2003. *Judgment Without Trial: Japanese American Imprisonment during World War II*. Seattle: University of Washington Press.

Kim, Kristine. 2000. *Henry Sugimoto: Painting an American Experience*. Berkeley, CA: Heyday Books.

Knaefler, Tomi Kaizawa. 1991. *Our House Divided: Seven Japanese American Families in World War II*. Honolulu: University of Hawai'i Press.

Murray, Alice Yang. 2008. *Historical Memories of the Japanese American Internment and the Struggle for Redress*. Stanford: Stanford University Press.

Nakagawa, Martha. 2012. "Days of Remembrance," Densho Encyclopedia. Seattle: Densho. Retrieved December 25, 2012 (http://encyclopedia.densho.org/Days%20of%20Remembrance/).

Nakamura, Kelli. 2012. "Sanji Abe," Densho Encyclopedia. Seattle: Densho. Retrieved April 7, 2013 (http://encyclopedia.densho.org/Sanji%20Abe/).

Nakano, Jiro, and Kay Nakano, ed. and trans. 1983. *Poets Behind Barbed Wire.* Honolulu: Bamboo Ridge Press.

National Park Service. 2010. "Honouliuli Special Resource Study." Washington, DC: US Department of the Interior. Retrieved December 23, 2012 (http://www.nps.gov/pwro/honouliuli/index.htm).

Nishimura, Amy. 2014. "From Priestesses and Disciples to Witches and Traitors: Internment of Japanese Women at Honouliuli and Narratives of 'Madwomen.'" In this issue.

Noguchi, Andy. 2012. "JACL Ratifies Power of Words Handbook: What Are the Next Steps?" Los Angeles: Manzanar Committee. Accessed on December 21, 2012 (http://blog.manzanarcommittee.org/2012/07/15/jacl-ratifies-power-of-words-handbook-what-are-the-next-steps/).

Ogawa, Dennis M., and Evarts C. Fox. 1986. "Japanese Internment and Relocation: The Hawaii Experience." Pp. 135–138 in *Japanese American: From Relocation to Redress,* edited by Roger Daniels, Sandra C. Taylor, and Harry H. L. Kitano. Salt Lake City: University of Utah Press.

Okamura, Jonathan Y. 1982. "The American Concentration Camps: A Cover-Up through Euphemistic Terminology." *Journal of Ethnic Studies* 10(3):95–108.

Okihiro, Gary Y. 1991.*Cane Fires: The Anti-Japanese Movement in Hawaii, 1865–1945.* Philadelphia: Temple University Press.

———. 2011. Keynote Address. 2011 Day of Remembrance. Monsanto, Kunia, Hawai'i. February 27.

Parker-Lee, Keala. 2013. "Letters to the Editor." *Honolulu Star-Advertiser.* March 14. Retrieved June 29, 2013 (http://search.proquest.com/docview/1316870459?accountid=136522).

Robinson, Greg. 2009. *A Tragedy of Democracy: Japanese Confinement in North America.* New York: Columbia University Press.

———. 2011. Martial Law in Hawai'i. Japanese Cultural Center of Hawai'i, August 17.

Rosenfeld, Alan. 2014. "Neither Aliens nor Enemies: The Hearings of 'German' and 'Italian' Internees in Wartime Hawai'i." In this issue.

Saiki, Patsy Sumie. 1982. *Ganbarre! An Example of Japanese Spirit.* Honolulu: Kisaku. Honolulu: Mutual Publishing.

Soga, Yasutaro (Keiho). 1948. *Tessaku seikatsu.* Honolulu: The Hawaii Times, Ltd.

———. 2008. *Life behind Barbed Wire: The World War II Internment Memoirs of a Hawai'i Issei,* translated by Kihei Hirai. Honolulu: University of Hawai'i Press.

Takezawa, Yasuko. 1995. *Breaking the Silence: Redress and Japanese American Ethnicity.* Ithaca: Cornell University Press.

Hell Valley:
Uncovering a Prison Camp in Paradise

JEFF BURTON
MARY FARRELL
LISA KANEKO
LINDA MALDONATO
KELLY ALTENHOFEN

ABSTRACT

Even as scholars of the University of Hawai'i–West O'ahu (UHWO) research team begin to uncover the history of Honouliuli Internment and Prisoner of War Camp (State Site No. 50-80-08-9068), archaeologists have been uncovering its physical remains. For decades, Honouliuli lay lost and forgotten, hidden in a densely vegetated gulch and surrounded by agricultural fields, 14 miles northwest of Honolulu. With the assistance of the Japanese Cultural Center of Hawai'i volunteers and UHWO archaeology students, over 130 archaeological features have been discovered and documented, and the site is now listed on the National Register of Historic Places. Contributing resources in the 122.5-acre archaeological site include two standing buildings, numerous building foundations, rock walls, fence remnants, artifact scatters, and other features. As an internment site, Honouliuli represents the fragility of constitutional rights and the effects of martial law; as a POW camp, Honouliuli exemplifies the management of enemy troops as the military balanced the need for national security and the need to comply with

Jeff Burton, Manzanar National Historic Site, P.O. Box 426, Independence, CA 93526, jeffburton@nps.gov; Mary Farrell, Trans-Sierran Archaeological Research, P.O. Box 840, Lone Pine, CA 93545, mollyofarrell@gmail.com; Lisa Kaneko, University of Hawai'i–West O'ahu, 91-1001 Farrington Highway, Kapolei, HI 96707; Linda Maldonato, University of Hawai'i–West O'ahu; Kelly Altenhofen, Jean LaFitte National Historic Park and Preserve, National Park Service, 419 Decatur Street, New Orleans, LA 70130-1035.

the Geneva Convention. This article describes how oral histories, archaeo-logical fieldwork, and archival research have been integrated to document the physical remains of the Honouliuli Internment and POW Camp. This interdisciplinary approach has contributed small but important details about the site on the one hand, and broader and more universal implications about how ethnicity and status play out on the other.

Honouliuli Internment and Prisoner of War Camp is a mid-twentieth-century archaeological site in a lush valley on the beautiful island of O'ahu. The Hawaiian name, "Honouliuli," means "blue harbor" or "dark bay." But the site had another name that was not so idyllic: Japanese Americans who were interned there during World War II called it "Jigoku Dani," or "Hell Valley." The camp held US citizens, resident aliens, and thousands of prisoners of war (POWs). As the other articles in this volume attest, researchers in diverse fields are uncovering the hidden history of Honouliuli. The research is revealing new information about the reach of martial law, its effects on individuals and groups, and the treatment of Hawaiian civilian internees as well as prisoners of war. In this article we discuss how Honouliuli as a *physical* place can contribute to the research and interpretations.

Most fundamental, it was the search for the physical location of the Honouliuli Internment and Prisoner of War Camp that focused attention on the history. As discussed in Kurahara, Niiya, and Young's article (this issue), a local TV station called the Japanese Cultural Center of Hawai'i (JCCH) to ask where the Honouliuli Internment and Prisoner of War Camp was located. JCCH Resource Center volunteers set about to learn more about civilian internment during World War II and to make it better known to the people of Hawai'i and beyond (Niiya 2008). Led by Jane Kurahara and Betsy Young, the all-volunteer JCCH team found unpublished manuscripts and contemporary reports, photographs, and descriptions; with these in hand, they searched for the physical location of Honouliuli. Useful clues came from R. H. Lodge's *Waipahu at War* (1949) and Patsy Saiki's *Ganbare!* (1982). Lodge was a for-mer division overseer of the Oahu Sugar Company who became an official army photographer. His book documents wartime activities that occurred on the Oahu Sugar Company land, and includes a map of military zones near Waipahu and five photographs of the Honouliuli Camp in operation. *Ganbare!* is a collection of internee stories, one of which described the Honouliuli Camp and its location in a hidden gulch.

Lodge depicted one military area within the ahupua'a (a traditional Hawaiian land division, usually extending from the uplands to the sea) of Honouliuli, which is one of 13 traditional land divisions in the moku (district) of 'Ewa; the Honouliuli ahupua'a includes the entire watershed from Honou-liuli Gulch into Kaihuopala'ai, the West Loch of Pearl Harbor. The military area depicted on Lodge's map was roughly six miles mauka (inland) from the coast, and fit Saiki's description of being "well-hidden": the gulch is only 500 to 700 feet wide at the area depicted, with steep slopes enclosing it some 100 feet below the surrounding agricultural fields.

However, the site, which at the time of JCCH's search was owned by the Campbell Estate, was not immediately recognizable. Instead of the sunbaked valley visible in historic photographs, thick vegetation blanketed the slopes and floodplain. Koa haole (*Leucaena leucocephala*) trees and Guinea grass (*Panicum maximum*) made it difficult to see even the contours of the land, and the most salient features were the modern road and Board of Water Supply developments. It appeared impossible to walk off the paved road without a machete. However, the JCCH researchers were able to confirm they had found the

The 1920 aqueduct visible in R. H. Lodge's World War II photographs is still present today.

right spot when they verified that a concrete aqueduct and a large metal pipe visible in one of Lodge's historic photographs of the camp were still present.

Internment in Hawai'i vs. Mainland "Relocation"

Honouliuli and the other internment sites in Hawai'i had been only briefly mentioned in an archaeological overview of Japanese American confinement sites because so little was known of them (Burton et al. 2002). On the mainland, Japanese American imprisonment during World War II has been the focus of legal action, political movements, and historical research for decades. There were far greater numbers of people involved, and historic blueprints, plans, and War Relocation Authority documents provide precise information about the original locations of the "Relocation Centers."

On the mainland, four sites have been set aside by the federal government to provide opportunities for public education and interpretation of the incarceration of Japanese Americans during World War II: Manzanar National Historic Site, California; Minidoka Internment National Monument, Idaho; Nidoto Nai Yoni ("Let it not happen again") Memorial, Bainbridge Island, Washington; and the Tule Lake Segregation Center, California.

It could be argued that those four National Park Service historic sites, along with the Heart Mountain Interpretive Center and other internment-related sites and exhibits on the mainland, tell the story of World War II internment sufficiently already, and indeed, the history of internment in Hawai'i has much in common with that on the mainland. As on the mainland, the internment in Hawai'i was justified at the time as a military necessity, but was later found to be an unjust abrogation of civil rights. On both the mainland and in Hawai'i, official government investigations conducted before the war indicated that the resident Japanese aliens and the Japanese American citizens were not likely to pose a threat to US security, and that only a small number of persons should be detained (Kashima 2003). On both the mainland and in Hawai'i, internment resulted in economic hardships and long-lasting psychological and social repercussions, and epitomizes how civil rights can be brushed aside in a time of crisis. The mainland commemorative sites illustrate some of the challenges the United States faces, even today, balancing constitutional rights with homeland security.

But despite the similarities, internment in Hawai'i differed in several key ways from the internment on the mainland during World War II. These differences increase the importance of telling this story, and preserving the

Honouliuli Internment and Prisoner of War Camp. The first key distinction between the mainland and Hawaiʻi is that the internment in Hawaiʻi was authorized by martial law, rather than Executive Order 9066. Martial law left little imprint on the landscape, so Honouliuli is a rare physical manifestation of those numerous wartime restrictions, which had a profound effect on all the citizens of Hawaiʻi. Internment camps loomed as a threat even to those not held for long periods of time; for example, Saiki (1982) relates the story of a terrified man dragged into an internment camp in Hawaiʻi because a neighborhood warden accused him of violating blackout regulations.

Second, internment in Hawaiʻi directly affected a smaller, but more diverse, segment of the population. On the mainland, the vast majority of internees were of Japanese ancestry: 100 percent of the Japanese Americans living on the mainland's West Coast were interned, the majority of them American citizens. Similarly, the Japanese Americans interned in Hawaiʻi included US citizens, who in fact outnumbered the resident aliens who were interned. However, in contrast, less than two percent of the Hawaiian residents of Japanese ancestry or birth were interned. As discussed by Rosenfeld (2014), the heritage of Hawaiian civilian internees included Japanese, Okinawan, German, Italian, Austrian, Norwegian, Danish, Russian, Lithuanian, Swedish, Finnish, Irish, and British. As Rosenfeld documented, the military government in Hawaiʻi can be credited with preventing the large-scale internment of civilians of Japanese ancestry, but it took a stern and broad approach to interning residents of German or Italian ancestry or birth and others.

Third, although the more-limited internment in Hawaiʻi was less damaging to the morale of the general population, it may have had even more insidious effects on those individuals interned. Internment on the mainland was psychologically and financially devastating for the internees, but the entire Japanese American population on the West Coast was directly affected. Therefore, it would have been difficult to argue that this entire population, including US military veterans, the elderly, and babies, was potentially guilty of treason. In Hawaiʻi, the individuals were singled out, and therefore stigmatized and treated as though there could have been a valid reason for their internment. The effect on the individuals and their families would have been even more devastating (see, for example, Kashima 2003), and in some cases, children were left to fend for themselves when parents and older siblings were interned (Adler 2014; Nye 2005; Rosenfeld 2014).

Finally, Kashima (2003) points out another aspect distinguishing internment in Hawai'i from that on the mainland—the secrecy imposed and maintained by the military: "Many Japanese Americans in Hawai'i [and other residents] are still unaware of the full story of forced detention and removal of island persons to the mainland and the existence of the [internment] camps. Martial law and use of the military-security classification restricted information about the entire wartime episode" (Kashima 2003:85).

The secrecy surrounding internment in Hawai'i has come to an end, thanks largely to the research efforts of the Japanese Cultural Center of Hawai'i and faculty and students at the University of Hawai'i–West O'ahu (UHWO). Jane Kurahara of JCCH discussed the finding of the Honouliuli site at a conference about internment in Little Rock, Arkansas (Kurahara 2004). After hearing her presentation and meeting Kurahara, Jeff Burton, the principle author of the mainland overview (Burton et al. 2002), worked with the JCCH and obtained a grant from the National Park Foundation to complete an archaeological overview of Japanese American internment sites in Hawai'i (Burton and Farrell 2007). That overview documented 13 former

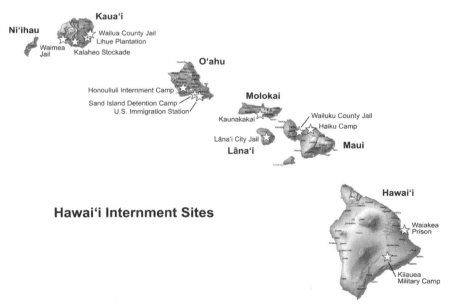

The 13 World War II internment sites discussed in Burton and Farrell (2007).

internment sites, located on the islands of Hawai'i, Kaua'i, Moloka'i and Lāna'i, as well as O'ahu, and a few additional temporary internment sites have since been identified. Because of the immediacy of the roundup and arrests, existing jails, schools, immigration stations, and military installations were initially used to confine internees. Some of the sites had been used to hold fewer than a dozen internees, others held hundreds. Honouliuli was the last to be constructed, opening in March 1943, and the largest, built to house both civilian internees and prisoners of war.

Honouliuli as an Archaeological Site

Because access to the site was limited, the archaeological overview of Hawai'i Japanese American internment sites included only a cursory assessment of the Honouliuli Internment and Prisoner of War Camp, based on a reconnaissance visit of just a few hours in 2006 (Burton and Farrell 2007). It was quickly determined that the aqueduct and the pipe visible in Lodge's historic photographs were not constructed as part of the internment camp: a "1920" date is inscribed in the cement of one of the aqueduct's post supports, and the pipe is part of an inverted siphon that conducted water across, rather than to, the gulch. Both the aqueduct and the siphon were part of the Waiāhole ditch system, constructed in the early twentieth century to bring water from the windward side of O'ahu to the drier leeward side for sugarcane irrigation (Wilcox 1998). However, even during the hurried reconnaissance, Burton noted several features likely dating to World War II, including two concrete slabs approximately 50 by 100 feet in size, one located where a large building is visible in a historic photograph. Also potentially associated with the internment camp were cesspools, a manhole, a steel tank, rock walls, and concrete debris.

Other features, such as corrals and abandoned vehicles, appeared to be more recent. The City and County of Honolulu's Board of Water Supply had developed and fenced three areas for wells and a treatment plant. The treatment plant was located where a large building is shown in one of the Lodge photographs of the Honouliuli Internment and Prisoner of War Camp. The original camp entrance road had been replaced with a paved road entering the gulch from the ridge to the east. Also within the boundary of the camp were two structures reportedly part of an abandoned chicken farm, but time did not allow inspection of that area. Large satellite dishes and a small building for KITV-News4 have been installed on the slope adjacent to the access road. Dense Guinea grass and koa haole trees limited visibility and access, so it was impossible to do even a preliminary assessment of the entire area. It was not clear if the junglelike vegetation hid more World War II features and artifacts, or if most of the area had been cleared or disturbed during later use. Nevertheless, even in that cursory visit, Honouliuli appeared to have potential as an archaeological site. Compared to the other Hawai'i internment sites included in the overview, Honouliuli retains a remarkable degree of integrity, and has the greatest potential to evoke the isolation and remoteness of the internment camp experience. Most of the known sites used to intern civilians in Hawai'i during World War II have been significantly modified. For example, at Sand Island only the road pattern and a remnant of the Italian prisoner of war camp have escaped obliteration by modern developments; World War II–era buildings at both the Wailuku and Wailua county jails have been replaced; and internment facilities at Ha'ikū are gone (Burton and Farrell 2007).

Integrated Research

A reporter who accompanied Burton and the JCCH team during the 2006 inspection of Honouliuli wrote an article about the site and included a description of a small slab of concrete with names inscribed (Gordon 2006). Rodney Santiago contacted JCCH to report that those names were his relatives; he had grazed cattle and horses in Honouliuli Gulch for over 40 years, beginning in 1958. Santiago noted that when he grazed cattle in the gulch, sidewalks, rock alignments, and other features could be easily seen; the vegetation that made travel off the road treacherous had grown up only recently. This oral history confirmed that Honouliuli held promise as an archaeological site. In February 2008, Burton and Farrell conducted further archaeological investigations assisted by two dozen volunteers recruited by the JCCH and Ron Beckwith of the National Park Service (Burton and Farrell 2008). By this time, the Monsanto Hawaii company had purchased the part of the Campbell Estate that included the Honouliuli site, and facilitated the research.

Generally, archaeologists conduct a survey by systematically walking transects back and forth across a given study area, at regular intervals. Because of the vegetation at Honouliuli, regular transects were not possible. Instead, we focused on areas that seemed most likely to have World War II–era features, based on the Lodge photographs. The photographs provided overviews of the Honouliuli Internment and Prisoner of War Camp, showing a sea of tents, closely spaced barracks, fences, guard towers, and other structures. With the aqueduct and siphon visible in the Lodge photographs of the camp as landmarks, we searched for and matched other features visible in the photographs. Archival information discovered by the JCCH provided more details, which allowed interpretation of the Lodge photographs. Particularly useful was a 1943 report of the Office of Military Governor (Springer 1943:2) that described the camp:

> The kitchen and mess hall for Japanese internees is equipped to feed up to one thousand internees. The internees live in prefabricated sixteen-man de-mountable barracks. All latrines have modern plumbing with hot and cold showers. A post exchange is available for the purchase of cigarettes, tobacco, and miscellaneous items for sale. There is also a tailor shop, an equipped dental office, and a dispensary for necessary medical treatment. A recreation field has been cleared and fenced in for the use of the internees....

> The prisoner of war section of the Camp has been divided into separate enclosures to take care of Japanese officers, enlisted men, and noncombatant Japanese prisoners of war. As a result of the Gilbert Island operation and the capture of Korean noncombatant prisoners of war, it has been found

R. H. Lodge photograph of Honouliuli, courtesy of Hawai'i's Plantation Village.

necessary to construct an additional enclosure to separate the Japanese from the Koreans. There are two large prisoner of war kitchens and mess halls, each with facilities to feed one thousand or more prisoners. In the prisoner of war section there are cold water showers and pit latrines. Prisoners of war live in pyramidal tents, usually six to eight men in a tent.

Even with the photographs and descriptions providing clues, dense stands of six- to eight-foot-tall Guinea grass obscured the ground surface so thoroughly that remnants of buildings or foundations were difficult to find. Survey was more intuitive and opportunistic than systematic: crew members made their way through the vegetation, often feeling features with their feet before they could see them. Occasional clearings in the vegetation allowed more thorough inspection; some clearings with relatively sparse vegetation indicated where foundation slabs lay buried under a few inches of sediment.

Field recording included descriptive notes, plan maps drawn to scale using compass and tape or pacing, field sketches, and digital photography. Recent sediments and plants were removed from some of the partially buried features to facilitate measuring and mapping. Following Monsanto's stipulation for this and subsequent work, no artifacts were collected. The locations

Volunteers searching for a foundation slab.

of features, isolated artifacts, and recent cultural features were recorded using aerial photographs and Global Positioning System (GPS) technology.

During the survey, over 100 features and numerous artifacts were recorded. Features include concrete slabs from latrines, showers, and other buildings, septic tanks, cesspools, manholes, small concrete slabs, footings, rock walls, piled concrete debris, bridge abutments, and inscriptions in concrete and rock. Two of the features were particularly surprising. One was a small concrete-lined pond constructed in the internee area. Such landscape features are fairly common at the mainland camps, where incarcerees constructed and nourished gardens and ponds to ameliorate the harsh surroundings. The second was the standing wood-frame building at the chicken farm. Closer inspection showed that it had several World War II–era characteristics and that in spite of some modifications it probably did date to the camp. The second structure at the chicken farm was constructed atop a World War II–era foundation, and appears to incorporate lumber and roofing recycled from the camp.

JCCH had arranged some publicity for the archaeological work, and Burton was invited to give a talk about the results at ʻIolani Palace. After

The "chicken farm," originally constructed during World War II.

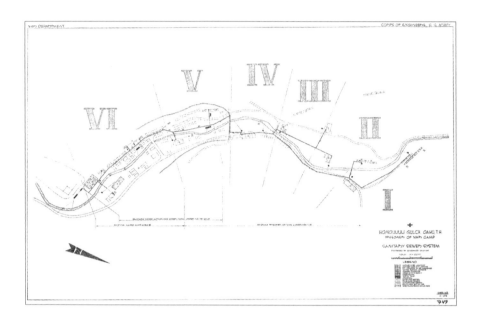

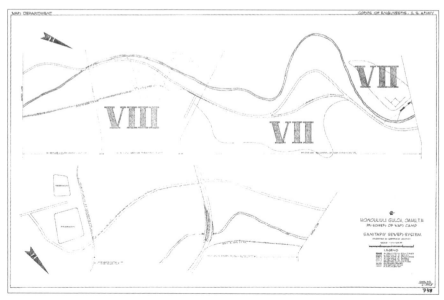

Blueprints of the Honouliuli "Sanitary Sewer System." Courtesy of US Army, Schofield Barracks, Cultural Resources.

that talk, David Cox, the Cultural Resource Specialist at Schofield Barracks, provided two historic plan maps, or blueprints, of Honouliuli that he had found (US Army n.d). Labeled "Honouliuli Gulch, Oahu, T. H. / Prisoner of War Camp / Sanitary Sewer System," the blueprints consist of two sheets that depict the location of the stream, buildings, and roads. Only features of interest to the sewer system are labeled, and the blueprints are not complete: no fences or guard towers are depicted, and some buildings visible in historic photographs are not shown.

The blueprints are undated, but the legends differentiate between "existing" facilities, "authorized" facilities, and "proposed" facilities. The blueprints thus appeared to date to sometime in the middle of the camp occupation, after the original wastewater disposal system was determined no longer adequate, but well before the end of the war when new facilities would have been unnecessary. This inference is supported by a manhole cover discovered during archaeological survey. Depicted as part of the "authorized" system on the blueprint, the manhole cover has "Nov. 4, 1944" inscribed in it. It seems likely, then, that the blueprints date to shortly before November 1944, when this part of the sewer system was "authorized" but not yet "existing."

Manhole cover with "Nov. 4, 1944" date.

The blueprints show over 150 buildings at the camp, which is subdivided into areas or compounds designated by Roman numerals I–VIII. Five of the areas are labeled as prisoner-of-war compounds (I–V), one as "Guard Camp Area" (VI), and one as "proposed POW compound" (VII). Through oral histories, historic photographs, and internee art, we know that Compound V was where civilian internees were held. West of the stream were the Japanese American men. East of the stream, Japanese American women were to the north, and European Americans were housed to the south.

Because the blueprints provided clues about where additional features might be found, we decided to do a second session of fieldwork in 2009 to provide more data to nominate the site for listing on the National Register of Historic Places. Listing on the National Register does not guarantee preservation or protection, but it does confer recognition of a historic place's significance, and can help qualify a property for certain historic preservation funds or grants. Again JCCH recruited volunteers, and obtained additional R. H. Lodge photographs from the files of Hawai'i's Plantation Village, in

KITV-News4 filming the clearing of a foundation during the 2008 volunteer survey.

Waipahu. During every season of the archaeological work, photographs and other documents collected by the JCCH played a crucial role in the research. We compared the blueprints and historical photographs with known features, such as the aqueduct or stream, to determine likely locations for additional features. The presence of archaeological features like foundations or walls could be used to reconstruct exactly where, and to what direction, historic photographs had been taken. Pinning down photo points often resulted in the discovery of additional features visible in the photograph but obscured by vegetation. JCCH arranged media coverage of the archaeological projects, which generated publicity that in turn generated the donation of more historic photographs and documents.

Field methods were similar to previous work: in some cases irregularities in the ground surface, such as depressions or mounds, or a change in the density or type of vegetation, provided clues about feature locations. Twenty-five new features were discovered and recorded; the blueprints led us to depressions where latrines had been located, shower buildings, cesspools, and septic tanks, but rock walls and road and ditch segments were found as well (Burton and Farrell 2009).

Cleared shower building in Compound III.

Water and sewer systems are not usually considered the stuff of archaeological dreams. But at the mainland prison camps, it is precisely these types of structures that leave the most substantial remains. On the mainland, the Japanese American "Relocation Centers" were purposefully established in remote and undeveloped areas of the country. In many cases these hastily constructed prison cities became the largest settlements in their respective regions. While those incarcerated lived in flimsy barracks without indoor plumbing or cooking facilities, the sewer systems had to be designed for dense concentrations of people. The POW and internee mess halls at Honouliuli have more substantial foundations than the mess halls at many of the mainland camps, perhaps, as the Office of the Military Governor reported in the passage quoted above, each was designed to feed 1,000 people, while the mainland camp mess halls usually served only 300 to 400 people.

UHWO Field School

In 2010 we conducted the third field season of archaeological investigations at Honouliuli (Burton and Farrell 2011a), which was the first session led by UHWO. The UHWO faculty includes scholars interested in diverse

Cesspool in Compound III.

aspects of Honouliuli history, as illustrated by the other articles in this issue. A grant from the National Park Service through the Japanese American Confinement Sites (JACS) Grant Program facilitated the purchase of needed archaeological equipment and supplies. The JACS Grant Program was established by Congress (Public Law 109-441, 16 USC 461) for the preservation and interpretation of US confinement sites where Japanese Americans were detained during World War II.

In addition to the interdisciplinary focus, the UHWO connection also brought students with their own interests and expertise to the project. For example, Kelly Altenhofen, a National Park Service wildlife biologist, took the field class because of his interest in history and in Hawai'i. Altenhofen is also a veteran familiar with military archives and records. One of the Lodge photographs archived at Hawai'i's Plantation Village shows a soldier striding out of a wood-frame building; a four-part sign identifies the building as "Headquarters Prisoner of War Processing Station / Compounds 6, 8, and

R. H. Lodge photograph, courtesy of Hawai'i's Plantation Village.

9, Civilian Internee Stockade / 162 Prisoner of War Processing Company / Anti-Tank Company, 372nd Infantry." By contacting military historians, museum technicians, and archivists in Hawai'i, Maryland, the District of Columbia, and Ohio, Altenhofen was able to track down the record of the 372nd Infantry, an African American unit in the segregated US military. They were assigned to Hawai'i in May of 1945, thus providing a *terminus post quem* ("no earlier than") date for at least that one Lodge photograph, and perhaps others. During World War II, African American units in the military were often relegated to support roles, such as truck driving, convoy operations, and food preparation. It is ironic that at Honouliuli, US soldiers segregated because of their race guarded civilian internees who were incarcerated because of their race or ethnic background.

Drawing of the Japanese American compound, showing the location of a guard tower by Dan Nishikawa dated "1943 / 5-10"; courtesy of JCCH.

The photographs and blueprints also inspired a search for the foundations of a guard tower visible in historic photographs and depicted in one of the drawings Dan T. Nishikawa created while he was interned at Honouliuli. Nishikawa's drawing shows the guard tower as just east of a fork in the perimeter road; the view would have been from the Japanese American compound, on the west side of the gulch. The same tower is visible in one of Lodge's photographs, confirming that Nishikawa was drawing the actual landscape, rather than an imagined composite. In the presumed guard tower vicinity, there was no evidence of the footings visible on the ground surface, but a leveled area was noted just east of the fork in the perimeter road. A tall, deteriorated fence post looked like it might have been part of the original security fence, but debris from a recent small rockfall had been pushed onto the leveled area to clear the adjacent road. Archaeology students removed the rockfall debris, and found the four guard tower footings a few inches below the ground surface.

Archaeology students were also determined to find another guard tower partially visible in historic photographs on the west edge of the internment camp. Only the upper portion of the guard tower is visible in the historic photographs, but it appeared to be near the boundary between Compound VI

R. H. Lodge photograph, showing the guard tower that Nishikawa drew center left. Courtesy of Hawai'i's Plantation Village.

(the guard area) and Compound V (the civilian internee area). Not only was the guard tower foundation found, a rock stairway that led to it was discovered during the search. The stairway represented a substantial investment of labor, but it had been completely obscured by grasses and other vegetation, and was not visible in any of the historic photographs.

In some cases the historic photographs provided clues as to the types of features that might be present, even when they do not appear directly. Two features, with tall metal chimneys suggesting incinerators, are visible in historic photographs outside the mess hall in Compound IV. Although those incinerators were removed sometime before the current Board of Water Supply building was constructed where the mess hall once stood, we assumed there would have been similar incinerators near mess halls in the other compounds. We knew the general location of the mess hall in Compound I based on photographs and blueprints, and found the incinerator, almost completely obscured by vegetation, just makai (toward the ocean) of where the mess hall would have been.

Uncovered concrete footings for the guard tower depicted in Nishikawa's drawing and the Lodge photograph.

Mapping the stairway during the 2010 UHWO field school.

Portion of R. H. Lodge photograph enlarged to show the incinerators at the Compound III mess hall.

Remains of a similar incinerator in Compound I.

During the 2010 field school, we were visited in the field by 100-year-old Hanako Hashimoto, the wife of Koji Hashimoto, and her daughter and son, Elsie Hyde and Francis Hashimoto. The family had visited Koji Hashimoto when he was interned at Honouliuli, and Hashimoto and his family returned to Honouliuli in 1948. Their five photographs from the 1948 visit show that by then most of the buildings had been removed but many concrete slab foundations remained. Elsie Hyde provided copies of the photographs to the UHWO and JCCH. All of the Hashimoto photographs provide enough visual information to determine where they were taken.

New archival resources were also discovered after the 2010 fieldwork, when JCCH obtained 38 photographs from Kendall Olsen, whose grandfather Glenn Heern was a Military Police (MP) at Honouliuli. Twenty-one of the photographs could be identified as taken at Honouliuli; together these provide a candid view of some of the ways the military police passed their leisure time at the camp. The Heern photographs helped guide the next season's fieldwork, in the summer of 2011 (Farrell and Burton 2012). Students in the UHWO archaeological field methods class, with assistance from volunteers recruited

1948 photograph by Koji Hashimoto, courtesy of JCCH, Elsie Hyde collection.

Photograph by Glenn Heern, member of the Military Police at Honouliuli, depicting two of his fellow soldiers on the sidewalk in front of the Compound VI latrine and shower building. Courtesy of JCCH.

UHWO field school students in same location as soldiers in Glenn Heern photograph.

through the UHWO Anthropology Club and by JCCH, uncovered and mapped many of the features visible in the Heern photographs, including a sidewalk, retaining walls, and the foundation of a latrine and shower building that forms the backdrop for some of the pictures. Scraps of wire mesh were identified as likely from the trellis visible in the photographs. Students recreated some of the shots, standing and sitting in the same places that the MPs had stood and sat 70 years before. There is an interesting distinction in the Heern collection. Many of the photographs are informal but posed portraits of individuals and groups; almost all the settings are casual, and all the subjects are Caucasian. But there are also photographs of African American soldiers, taken from afar, as the soldiers are standing in formation. The photographs suggest little interaction between Heern's unit and members of the African American segregated 372nd Infantry.

African American soldiers of the 372nd Infantry in formation at Honouliuli. Glenn Heern photograph, courtesy of JCCH.

The 2011 fieldwork also focused on discovering what might remain at the area labeled "proposed prisoner of war compound VII" in the Army blueprints. By the time R. H. Lodge took photographs of the camp, there were over 80 tents in a rectangular fence enclosure in this area, guard towers at each of the three corners visible in the photograph, nine small buildings (probably latrines) along the fence, a long building (possibly a mess hall) at the back of the compound opposite the entrance gate, and another building outside the fence near the entrance. Yong-ho Ch'oe (2009) notes that Korean POWs were at Honouliuli beginning in late 1943 or early 1944, and Springer's 1943 report (excerpted above) notes that an additional enclosure was needed at Honouliuli to house Korean noncombatants captured during the Gilbert Island (now called Kiribati) operations. The area designated Compound VII on the blueprints is likely the area that housed Korean noncombatants. Its location, makai from the guards' area, suggests less security than the other POW compounds, and in fact, in the Lodge photograph, a few dozen people, presumably prisoners, are seated *outside* the fenced area. Less-stringent security would be expected for the Korean POWs, given their antagonism toward the Japanese. As Ch'oe documents, many Korean captives strongly opposed Japan, which had forcibly annexed Korea and instituted colonial rule in 1910. Ch'oe recounts the story

R. H. Lodge photograph of Compound VII. Courtesy of Hawai'i's Plantation Village.

of three captured Koreans who had actively and heroically assisted the US military until the end of the war once again reduced them to POW status.

Survey in Compound VII in 2011 discovered sections of the original entrance road, a large enameled metal light shade, and what appear to be remnants of the security fence. The remains of a wooden building were found bulldozed over the edge of a steep slope that leads down to Honouliuli Stream. Most of the surrounding trash that could be observed during a cursory inspection appears to date to the 1960s and 1970s, but the structure itself may date to World War II, and more careful recording would help determine whether its construction methods and materials are similar to other military structures of that era.

In 2012, students again expanded the investigations at Honouliuli to bring their own expertise and passion to the research. The results of all the students' research will be incorporated into the final report, but two examples

Name inscribed in guard tower foundation.

are included here, to illustrate the range of information that might be garnered from the archaeological remains at Honouliuli. Linda Maldonato took an interest in the inscription written in the concrete of the guard tower foundation that had been uncovered the previous year:

R. N. Hotchkis
8/13/43

Close examination of the inscription showed that there could have been a missing letter at the end of the name, since the concrete was crumbled. In the 1930 Federal census, a Rollin N. Hotchkiss was living in Euclid Village, Cuyahoga, Iowa. This Hotchkiss was estimated to have been born in 1879, and was listed as 51 years old at the time of the census, which would have made him about 64 at the time that name was inscribed in the concrete at Honouliuli. But in Rollin N.'s household is also listed a Rollin M. Hotchkiss, who was 18 in 1930. Although many older men served in the military during World War II, it seemed more likely the younger Rollin would have been the one inscribing his name in the concrete. Maldonato checked the 1940 census and found young Rollin listed as "Hotchkiss, Rollin Jr" indicating that the 1930 transcription with the different middle initial was in error.

Through enlistment records digitized in the National Archives and available online (US Army 2002), Maldonato found Rollin's serial number. He had enlisted at Camp Blanding, Florida, on April 29, 1942; his civilian occupation category was listed as "semiskilled chauffeurs and drivers, bus, taxi, truck, and tractor," and he was single with no dependents. Hotchkiss's records were among the millions of service records catastrophically destroyed by fire in 1973, so Maldonato searched for other sources of information. The March 23, 1951, edition of the *Daytona Beach Morning Journal* noted that Hotchkiss had entered Halifax Hospital. In the Florida death index, Rollin Neale Hotchkiss is listed as having died in 1955, at Volusia, Florida. His tombstone at Arlington National Cemetery is, of course, much more formal and poignant than the inscription in the concrete at Honouliuli:

Rollin Neale Hotchkiss

OHIO

CPL CMP

WORLD WAR II

FEBRUARY 15 1911

AUGUST 9 1955

Maldonato has not yet been able to locate descendants or other relatives of Hotchkiss, but notes that the fact that he is buried at Arlington means he either retired from the military, or was medically disabled. The latter seems more likely, because he died before he could have served the minimal 20 years required for retirement. Derived from a name scratched in wet cement, these preliminary findings have opened up other avenues that might help flesh out this picture of one of the guards at Honouliuli.

Lisa Kaneko was another student in the 2012 field school who has contributed original research and questions to the study, focusing on the laundry building in the Guard Camp area, in Compound VI. Compound VI housed not only staff barracks but also administrative and utility buildings, and to date, more features have been found in that compound than in any of the other sections of the camp. Buildings identified on the blueprints include a laundry, a dispensary, and three water-borne latrines. As Falgout notes (2014, citing the Territory of Hawai'i, Office of the Military Governor), laundry was done three times per week, and bedsheets were changed every 15 days. Given the regular schedule for laundry and the fact that the laundry building was one of the largest structures at the site, it seems likely that the laundry was intended to serve the entire camp.

Kaneko, however, challenged the assumption that the prisoners had access to the large laundry building, and conducted her own analysis. First,

Prisoners of war at work, with the laundry building in the background. Photograph by Glenn Heern, courtesy of JCCH.

the laundry facility was at the far southern end of Compound VI, which in the original camp design was as far from the nearest prisoner compound as it could get. If the laundry facility was intended for use by all members of the camp—guards and internees and POWs alike—the facility likely would have been located in a more centralized location, such as the northern end of Compound VI, which bordered Compound V, the Internee area, or even within one of the POW or internee compounds. Located as it was, prisoners would have had to traverse the entire length of the Guard area in order to reach the laundry facility. Kaneko notes that it would be unlikely for the military to consciously plan to share a space—much less a living area—with POWs or mistrusted civilian internees. The second geographic consideration is the location of the laundry facility adjacent to the original outermost border of the camp. Although Compound VII was eventually built south of Compound VI to house additional POWs, the Army blueprints show that the laundry facility existed when Compound VII was still only a proposal. It seems unlikely that a facility intended to be utilized by incarcerated individuals would have been

Laundry building foundation partially exposed during UHWO field school.

located next to the outermost border of a prison encampment, where there might be a greater potential for successful escape.

Kaneko contacted Doris Berg Nye, who was a young teenager when she visited her interned parents, first at Sand Island and then at Honouliuli (Nye 2005). As described by Nye (2012), the internees "had their own laundry…" and would "… boil their clothes, swirling them with paddles. All was done by hand." Nye further described how internees at the Sand Island and Honouliuli internment camps would wash "[l]arge items [by] boiling them in a little open-sided hut with a tin roof…" while "small personal items were washed by hand then draped (on the German side) in their tents or little houses on [the] Japanese side" (Nye 2012). Internees would either volunteer or be assigned the all-day task. Nonpersonal items were hung on lines that were located near the outdoor laundry facility. As described by Nye, "there was no collection of laundry to be shipped outside for cleaning. No laundry machines at Honouliuli, no electricity for the detainees…" (Nye 2012). According to Nye, not even linens were washed at the large Compound VI laundry: sheets and blankets were also washed by boiling and the use of washboards (Nye 2012). This ethnographic account supports the contention that the internees were not able to use the laundry facility. In fact, although washing machines might seem a necessity for a large prison nowadays, Kaneko noted that washboards were far more common in the 1940s. Washing-machine companies manufactured aircraft parts and other military-related goods during the war (Whirlpool n.d.), and for at least one company, washboard production peaked in 1941 (Columbus 2011).

The oral history also indicates that the little open-sided hut with a tin roof laundry facility that Nye described might have been constructed in each compound. Kaneko found examples of what such a laundry facility might look like at Hawai'i's Plantation Village, where a contemporary reconstructed outdoor laundry facility consists of a flat concrete foundation, drain trough, and metal roof. This model will inform future surveys at Honouliuli, and will lead to more accurate identification of potential laundry facilities in the prison compounds.

Reviewing other oral histories for laundry clues, Kaneko also found evidence that may indicate POWs had fewer security restrictions than the internees. In his ethnographic account, Richard H. Y. Chun describes Italian prisoners of war who worked at the Schofield Barracks laundry facility alongside the civilian workers starting in 1943 or 1944 (Center for Oral History 1994:1118). Chun further pointed out that the Italian laundry workers were prisoners of war and were not Italians from Hawai'i. These POWs were likely from the Schofield Barracks POW compound (see Falgout 2014), but their ability to work alongside civilians in the laundry suggests that the enemy military enjoyed more freedom than the civilian internees who had been living peacefully in Hawai'i. Did POWs eventually have access to the large laundry facility at Honouliuli, even as the civilian internees continued to use small huts and washboards? Differential access to resources, as well as to relative freedom, may be visible in the archaeological record, which in turn would have implications for the social and cultural context of the site.

Conclusion

The Honouliuli Internment and Prisoner of War Camp illustrates the power of place in remembering, discovering, and commemorating an important aspect of World War II history. As described by Kurahara and others (2014), JCCH-sponsored pilgrimages to the site have increased local awareness of internment in Hawai'i. Likewise, the archaeological investigations have brought the history to the community's attention: media coverage brought each field season's results to a wider audience, which in turn generated donations of historic photographs, oral histories, and more volunteers. Exposing and analyzing building foundations and other features have anchored the historic photographs to real, discernible places on the ground, which have become integral parts of current JCCH tours of the site. Students and volunteers have contributed countless hours of both physical labor and archival research; working in the harsh physical conditions at Honouliuli, students and volunteers experienced the heat, lack of breezes, and insects that plagued the World War II prisoners. For visitors, volunteers, and students, the physical remains at the Honouliuli Internment and Prisoner of War Camp provide tangible connections to the lives of the civilian internees, POWs, and guards who once lived there.

The archaeological documentation has also expanded opportunities for preservation and interpretation at the site: with data obtained from the archaeological investigations, the Honouliuli Internment and Prisoner of War Camp was listed on the National Register of Historic Places in March 2012 (Burton and Farrell 2011b). Further, the archaeological work has provided the basis for the site's inclusion in a National Park Service Special Resource Study, in which Honouliuli will be considered for National Historic Landmark status and National Park Service management.

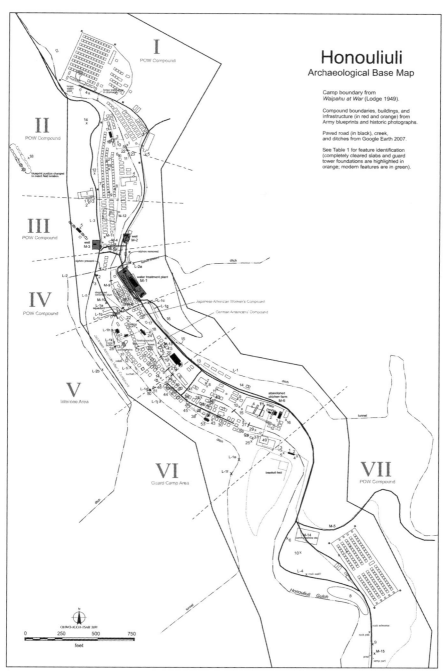

Honouliuli Archaeological Base Map.

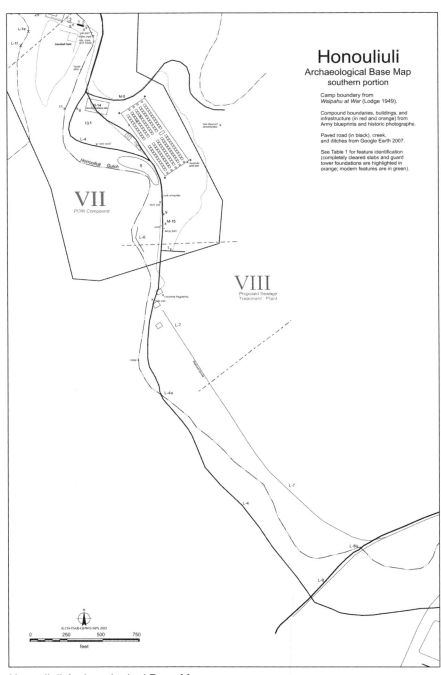

Honouliuli Archaeological Base Map.

There are undoubtedly more features and artifacts hidden under vegetation at Honouliuli, and more questions and research topics that could be addressed (see Farrell [2013] for a summary of ongoing archaeological work at Amache, Kooskia, Manzanar, and other Japanese American internment sites, and Listman, Baker, and Goodfellow [2007] for a summary of history and archaeological potential at mainland POW camps). As a tangible link to an event in which fears and prejudices led to the suppression of civil rights during World War II, Honouliuli can inform today's discussions about the treatment of immigrants and minorities, the history of racial relationships, and the interplay of national security and the US Constitution. With UHWO's involvement in continued research, and the National Park Service's involvement in management, the Honouliuli site will become even more effective in raising awareness of this aspect of Hawaiian history. ❖

References

Adler, Susan Matoba. 2014. "The Effect of Internment in Hawai'i on Children and Families." In this issue.

Burton, Jeffery F., and Mary M. Farrell. 2007. World War II Japanese American Internment Sites in Hawai'i. Trans-Sierran Archaeological Research and Japanese Cultural Center of Hawai'i Research Center.

———. 2008. Jigoku-Dani: An Archaeological Reconnaissance of the Honouliuli Internment Camp, O'ahu, Hawai'i. Honolulu: Trans-Sierran Archaeological Research and Japanese Cultural Center of Hawai'i Research Center.

———. 2009. Addendum 1: 2009 Field Work. Jigoku-Dani: An Archaeological Reconnaissance of the Honouliuli Internment Camp, O'ahu, Hawai'i. Trans-Sierran Archaeological Research and Japanese Cultural Center of Hawai'i Research Center.

———. 2011a. Addendum 2: 2010 Field Work. Jigoku-Dani: An Archaeological Reconnaissance of the Honouliuli Internment Camp, O'ahu, Hawai'i. Trans-Sierran Archaeological Research and Japanese Cultural Center of Hawai'i Research Center.

———. 2011b. National Register Nomination, Honouliuli Internment and POW Camp. Nomination accepted by Keeper and listed on the National Register March 2012.

Burton, Jeffery F., Mary M. Farrell, Florence Lord, and Richard Lord. 2002. Confinement and Ethnicity: An Overview of World War II Japanese American Relocation Sites. Seattle: University of Washington Press.

Center for Oral History, Social Science Research Institute, University of Hawai'i-Mānoa and National Park Service United States Department of the Interior. 1994. "Oral History Interview with Richard H. Y. Chun (RC)." Pp. 1110-1154 in An Era of Change: Oral Histories of Civilians in World War II Hawai'i, transcribed by J. Sato. Volume IV. Honolulu: University of Hawai'i.

Ch'oe, Yong-ho. 2009. Korean Prisoners-of-War in Hawai'i during World War II and the Case of US Navy Abduction of Three Korean Fishermen. *The Asia-Pacific Journal*, 34–1-09, August 24, 2009. Retrieved March 14, 2010 (http://japanfocus. org/-Yong_ho-Ch_oe/3266).

Columbus Washboard Company. 2011. "Columbus Washboard History." Retrieved August 2, 2012 (www.columbuswashboard.com/).

Daytona Beach Morning Journal. 1951. Local News. "At The Hospitals Halifax Admission." March 23: 8.

Falgout, Suzanne. 2014. "Honouliuli's POWs: Making Connections, Generating Changes." In this issue.

Farrell, Mary M. 2013. "Archaeology of Japanese American Incarceration." Retrieved June 1, 2013 (http://encyclopedia.densho.org/).

Farrell, Mary, and Jeff Burton. 2012. Addendum 3: 2011 Field work. Jigoku-Dani: An Archaeological Reconnaissance of the Honouliuli Internment Camp, O'ahu, Hawai'i. Trans-Sierran Archaeological Research and Japanese Cultural Center of Hawai'i Research Center.

Gordon, Mike. 2006. "Under Honouliuli Brush, Dark History." *Honolulu Advertiser*. February 5.

Kashima, Tetsuden. 2003. *Judgment Without Trial: Japanese American Imprisonment during World War II*. Seattle: University of Washington Press.

Kurahara, Jane. 2004. "Putting a Face to a Place" workshop in the conference "Life Interrupted: the Japanese American World War II Experience in Arkansas," Japanese American National Museum & University of Arkansas, Little Rock, funded by the Winthrop Rockefeller Foundation. Little Rock, Arkansas. September 25.

Kurahara, Jane, Brian Niiya, and Betsy Young. 2014. "Finding Honouliuli: The Japanese Cultural Center of Hawai'i and Preserving the Hawai'i Internment Story." In this issue.

Listman, John, Christopher Baker, and Susan Goodfellow. 2007. "Historic Context: World War II Prisoner-of-War Camps on Department of Defense Installations." Department of Defense, Legacy Resource Management Program.

Lodge, R. H. 1949. *Waipahu at War: The War Record of a Hawaiian Sugar Plantation Community*. Waipahu: Oahu Sugar Company.

Niiya, Brian. 2008. "Journey to Honouliuli," in *Discover Nikkei*, April 17, 2008. Retrieved December 30, 2012 (www.discovernikkei.org/en/journal/2008/4/17/journey-to-honouliuli/).

Nye, Doris. 2005. "Internment and Abandonment." Retrieved December 31, 2012 (www.foitimes.com/internment/Berg2.htm).

———. 2012. Personal communication / email correspondence with Lisa Kaneko. August 1–2, 2012.

Rosenfeld, Alan. 2014. "Neither Aliens nor Enemies: The Hearings of 'German' and 'Italian' Internees in Wartime Hawai'i." In this issue.

Saiki, Patsy Sumie. 1982. *Ganbare! An Example of Japanese Spirit.* Honolulu: University of Hawai'i Press.

Springer, Louis F. (Lt.). 1943. "Control of Civilian Internees and Prisoners of War in the Central Pacific Area." Territory of Hawai'i, Office of the Military Governor, 'Iolani Palace, Honolulu.

US Army. N.d. Honouliuli Gulch, Oahu, T.H., Prisoner of War Camp Sanitary Sewer System, prepared by Sewerage Section, Corps of Engineers. Drawing No. C-204, sheets 1 and 2.

———. 2002. World War II Army Enlistment Records, created 2002, documenting the period ca. 1938–1946 - Record Group 64. National Archives and Records Administration. Retrieved December 31, 2012 (http://aad.archives.gov/).

Wilcox, Carol. 1998. *Sugar Water: Hawai'i's Plantation Ditches.* Honolulu: University of Hawai'i Press.

Whirlpool (USA) N.d. "Whirlpool Corporation History." Retrieved August 2, 2012 (www.whirlpoolcorp.com/about/history.aspx).

Neither Aliens nor Enemies: The Hearings of "German" and "Italian" Internees in Wartime Hawai'i

ALAN ROSENFELD

ABSTRACT

Although officially billed by J. Edgar Hoover as an "Alien Enemy Control" program, an examination of the Federal Bureau of Investigation's wartime internment of civilians in Hawai'i reveals that the bureau grossly overstepped the authority provided under the Alien Enemies Act. Specifically, the hearing board transcripts of those detained as German and Italian alien enemies demonstrate that wartime authorities in martial law Hawai'i proceeded emphatically on the side of caution and security, even at the expense of justice. In fact, those apprehended for the purposes of "Alien Enemy Control" and subsequently interned at the Sand Island and Honouliuli detention camps included numerous US citizens—both by naturalization and by birth—and several men who had served in the US Armed Forces. One could also find people from a variety of ethnic backgrounds among the ranks of Hawai'i's "German" and "Italian" internees, ranging from civilians of Scandinavian descent to an Irish American woman and a family of Jewish refugees from Nazi-occupied Austria. The stories of this diverse array of internees underscore the importance of defending democratic principles, particularly in moments of crisis.

Alan Rosenfeld, University of Hawai'i–West O'ahu, 91-1001 Farrington Highway, Kapolei, HI 96707. This material is based upon work assisted by a grant from the Department of the Interior, National Park Service. Any opinions, findings, and conclusions or recommendations expressed in this material are those of the author and do not necessarily reflect the views of the Department of the Interior. The author can be reached at alan3@hawaii.edu.

In the spring of 1942, with her country embroiled in the Second World War, private citizen Clara Ludders stood before a four-person alien enemy hearing board in Honolulu awaiting one of three possible fates: outright release, release on parole, or continued internment. The fact that she had already been interned for more than a month before her hearing began—despite never being charged with a crime—was not at all unusual. The fact that Ludders was physically removed from the makeshift courtroom while an FBI agent presented evidence that she would never even hear, describing Ludders as "anti-English" and as an alleged supporter of Adolf Hitler (Ludders 1942:1), was also standard procedure. Furthermore, Ludders's lack of legal counsel and her inability to confront the anonymous informants whose "tips" prompted her arrest were also defining features of internee hearing board procedures in wartime Hawai'i (Ludders 1942; Internee 1942).

What *is* noteworthy about Ludders's case, however, is that she was a United States citizen of *Irish* ancestry, a rather unsettling point when one considers that the legal basis for Ludders's incarceration—the Alien Enemies Act of 1798—was predicated on the notion that she was a German alien enemy. In truth, Ludders was neither an alien nor an enemy. Born and raised in San Francisco, Ludders had lived for nearly 30 years in Hawai'i, where she raised two children with her husband Hugo, a naturalized US citizen of German birth. The couple's oldest child, William, graduated from Stanford University in 1939, before surrendering a lucrative position as an aviation engineer with a Lockheed Corporation subsidiary following the attack on Pearl Harbor in order to serve in the United States Navy (Ludders 1943). At no time during her hearing was Ludders's US citizenship called into doubt, and the only question raised concerning her ethnic heritage stemmed from the board members' desire to learn whether her parents had resided in the "Northern or Southern counties" of Ireland before emigrating to the United States. Nevertheless, the hearing board, citing the subject's alleged "strong pro-Nazi sympathies" and disloyalty toward the United States, sentenced Clara Ludders to continued internment for the duration of the war. The Irish American mother of two thus became one of the dozens of US citizens confined as "Germans" at the Sand Island and Honouliuli detention centers (Ludders 1942). Ludders's case is one of many that calls our attention to the degree to which an obsessive drive for security often trumped racial prejudice as the underlying impetus for the trampling of citizens' civil liberties during a time of war.

This article offers the first comprehensive study of civilian internee hearing board cases in wartime Hawai'i. Although several previous studies have mentioned Hawai'i's hearing boards in passing (Commission 1997; Okihiro 1992; Scheiber and Scheiber 1997; Kashima 2003; Scheiber, Scheiber, and Jones 2009; Rosenfeld 2011b), these accounts ultimately rely on internal memoranda from Hawai'i's wartime military government and a cursory description of the territory's hearings boards provided by journalist Gwenfread Allen in *Hawaii's War Years* (Allen 1950).[1] Unfortunately, while Allen's text—which was commissioned by the territorial legislature following the conclusion of the war— generally offers a comprehensive archival-based account of wartime Hawai'i, the author did not have access to the hundreds of hearing board transcripts that are currently housed in the National Archives in College Park, Maryland. As we shall see, the stories of Hawai'i residents interned as Germans or Italians under J. Edgar Hoover's "Alien Enemy Control" program—brought to life in their hearing board transcripts—force a revision of several previous assumptions concerning the wartime confinement of civilians in martial law Hawai'i.

Martial Law And Internment

Narratives of internment have understandably focused on the larger scale developments on the West Coast of the US continent, where President Franklin D. Roosevelt's Executive Order 9066 in February 1942 prompted the forced removal and mass incarceration of 120,000 ethnic Japanese civilians—mostly US citizens—into an archipelago of inland camps managed by the War Relocation Authority (Weglyn 1976; Daniels 1993; Robinson 2001; Kashima 2003; Hayashi 2004; Muller 2007). In sharp contrast, Hawai'i has been presented as an idyllic counterpoint where comparatively progressive attitudes toward race and the "spirit of aloha" (Commission 1997:261) combined to ensure a moderate approach to internment. After all, only about 1 percent of Hawai'i's 159,000 ethnic Japanese civilians were subjected to any form of confinement or "evacuation" during the war, despite Secretary of the Navy Frank Knox's recommendation of "taking all the Japs out of Oahu and putting them in a concentration camp on some other island" (Commission 1997:272). However, a consideration of martial law conditions and a close examination of internment hearings reveal a marked absence of aloha within Hawai'i's wartime government. As Hawai'i's Military Governor General Delos C. Emmons later testified under oath, his administration "leaned over backward in interning people in order to achieve as much security as [it] possibly could" (Allen 1950:144). A closer look at the confinement of non-Japanese civilians will illuminate the apparent contradiction between the general's comments and Hawai'i's comparatively modest internment figures.

The sudden and dramatic Japanese attack on Pearl Harbor (and other military installations on the island of O'ahu) on the morning of December 7,

General Delos Emmons (seated) and Lt. Colonel Thomas Green (standing) over-saw the implementation of martial law and civilian internment from their offices in 'Iolani Palace. Photo courtesy of Hawai'i War Records Depository, Hamilton Library, University of Hawai'i at Mānoa.

1941, coupled by the perceived threat of a Japanese land invasion, fueled the declaration of martial law and a rapid implementation of preexisting plans for the arrest of local civilians whose loyalty might be called into question. In fact, army officers in Hawai'i had been planning for the enactment of military rule over the island territory long before the actual opening of hostilities with Japan (Scheiber and Scheiber 1997). Territorial Governor Joseph Poindexter, himself a federal appointee, would later testify that his hurried proclamation of martial law within hours of the Pearl Harbor attacks occurred reluctantly and only "at the request of the Army" (Anthony 1975:9). The actual typed declaration that Poindexter issued on the afternoon of December 7 had mysteriously appeared on the desk of his attorney general earlier that afternoon, apparently drafted by someone in the War Department (Anthony 1975)—most likely Lt. Colonel Thomas H. Green (Scheiber and Scheiber 1997). As such, Poindexter was abruptly replaced by Lt. General Walter C. Short, as Hawai'i's civilian government gave way to a newly established Office of the Military Governor that took up residence in 'Iolani Palace and effectively ruled over the mid-Pacific territory until October 1944.

The rule of martial law in Hawai'i fostered a drastically different environment for the internment of alleged alien enemies than existed on the American continent. Most significant, military rule ensured a substantial degree of control over the *entire* civilian population, even without wide-ranging internment (Anthony 1975; Scheiber and Scheiber 1997). Martial law provided the armed forces with an abundance of methods to monitor and restrict local residents, including curfews and blackouts; censorship of newspapers, radio broadcasts, and private mail; and the surveillance of telephone conversations. Governing the civilian populace through a series of directives and general orders, the territory's wartime leaders abolished trial by jury, suspended the privilege of habeas corpus, and enforced the closure of civil courts that were fully capable of functioning (Anthony 1943, 1975; Scheiber and Scheiber 1990, 1997). With the rights of due process suppressed indefinitely, civilians were tried in provost courts, with either a single military officer or a local plantation manager serving as a judge. There were no warrants, no written charges, no juries, no trial transcripts, and no rights to appeal; parties were advised not to obtain legal counsel. These wartime provost courts, which heard at least 37,000 civilian cases, were bastions of hard-nosed efficiency, handing down guilty verdicts in at least 90 percent—and perhaps even 99 percent—of the cases, while reducing the average trial time to just five minutes (Scheiber and

Scheiber 1990, 1997). However, in addition to the unchecked power Hawai'i's martial law government wielded over the islands' general population, military leaders conspired with the Federal Bureau of Investigation's Honolulu field office to arrest and detain any individual citizens whose loyalty to the US government could even remotely be called into question.

The rule of martial law and the unusual level of collaboration between the US Army and the FBI in Hawai'i helped achieve the apprehension of 430 local civilians—including 85 individuals classified as German or Italian—by the night of December 8, 1941, that is, within 32 hours of the enactment of martial law and more than 48 hours *before* declarations of war upon Germany and Italy (Hoover 1943–1944; Kashima 2008; Rosenfeld 2011b). J. Edgar Hoover would later boast that the massive dragnet operation in Hawai'i, which was undertaken with the cooperation of military authorities and local police (Kashima 2003), occurred "with the greatest dispatch in accordance with pre-arranged plans" (Hoover 1943–1944:408). Indeed, the sudden stream of arrests marked the culmination of several years of careful preparations. Already in the mid-1930s, then Lt. Colonel George S. Patton—the army's senior-ranking intelligence officer in Hawai'i—developed a report calling for martial law and the taking of civilian hostages in the territory in the event of an outbreak of war with Japan (Okihiro 1992; Kashima 2003; Coffman 2003). Meanwhile, the FBI reopened its Honolulu office in August 1939 for the express purpose of monitoring ethnic Japanese, German, and Italian civilians for possible acts of espionage or sabotage, with its staff expanding rapidly from a single agent before its 1934 closure to 16 full-time agents at the time of the Pearl Harbor attack (Okihiro 1992). The primary responsibility of Special Agent in Charge Robert L. Shivers was to compile a custodial detention list of potentially dangerous individuals to be used as a resource for civilian internment (Kashima 2003). Indeed, the army's Military Intelligence Division (MID) and the Office of Naval Intelligence (ONI) had been assiduously compiling their own versions of this list in Hawai'i for years (Okihiro 1992; Robinson 2001; Kashima 2003; Scheiber et al. 2009).

Wartime tensions fueled the expansion of intelligence agency activities on a national level, and in that sense the prominent role the FBI played in the internment of civilians in Hawai'i was hardly unique. By the end of the war, Hoover's "Alien Enemy Control" program would achieve the arrest and internment of more than 30,000 people, including 11,507 ethnic Germans, 2,730 ethnic Italians, and 16,853 ethnic Japanese civilians—oftentimes

United States citizens (Kashima 2003).[2] In the late 1930s, as political tensions mounted steadily across the globe, Hoover attempted to maneuver himself into a preeminent position within the US intelligence matrix, with a vision of becoming what Rhodri Jeffreys-Jones has described as "the overall tsar of a super-intelligence agency" (Jeffreys-Jones 2007:109). He received a crucial show of support when President Roosevelt placed the FBI in charge of coordinating domestic sabotage and espionage investigations in September 1939 (Theoharis and Cox 1988; Jeffreys-Jones 2007). Hoover's position was further augmented through the public announcement of an agreement brokered by Roosevelt that granted the FBI ultimate authority—vis-à-vis the MID and ONI—in areas involving the investigation of civilians (Theoharis and Cox 1988). Politicians were also quite willing to provide the resources Hoover demanded to meet security threats, as congress and the president's cabinet vastly expanded the FBI's budget allocations for counterespionage, fingerprinting technology, and personnel in 1939 and again in 1940 (Jeffreys-Jones 2007).

At the same time, improved support for the FBI came with rising expectations and pressure. Although the FBI successfully dismantled two Nazi spy rings operating in New York (Jeffreys-Jones 2007), the bombing of Pearl Harbor exposed embarrassing rifts among the US intelligence organizations that had provoked Hoover's bureau into withholding critical information regarding the possibility of an impending Japanese attack (Jeffreys-Jones 2007). In the months that followed, navy Secretary Frank Knox (Weglyn 1976; Commission 1997; Robinson 2001; Kashima 2003) and members of the congressional Tolan Committee (Commission 1997) were among those who voiced stinging critiques of intelligence-gathering efforts in wake of the Pearl Harbor attack. These officials publicly proclaimed that Japanese fifth column activity had enabled the December 7 attack, despite the existence of at least one previous government report chronicling the "extraordinary degree of loyalty" (Weglyn 1976:34) that existed among Hawai'i's Nikkei residents (Commission 1997; Scheiber and Scheiber 1997; Robinson 2001).

The Klaus Mehnert affair constituted yet another—if less prominent—black eye for intelligence operatives in Hawai'i, bolstering subsequent calls for expanded surveillance efforts and the internment of civilian suspects in the islands. A German national, Mehnert held a faculty position at the University of Hawai'i in the years leading up to the war. In a sensationalist 1940 book entitled *The Fifth Column Is Here*, George Britt caused a stir by asserting that the respected scholar was a Nazi spy, based on an essay Mehnert had published in a German academic journal the previous year in which he discussed fleet maneuvers at Pearl Harbor. Although Mehnert's text had been prescreened by US military authorities in Hawai'i, the story was amplified by coverage Britt's book received in *Time* magazine in August 1940 (Mehnert 1983). University officials stood behind Mehnert, only to see him exit Hawai'i to accept a lucrative position as editor of an English-language magazine—*XX Century*—published by the Nazi regime in Shanghai (Wasserstein 1999). By the fall of 1941, local newspapers lamented that authorities had allowed a purported spy to operate so freely in Hawai'i (Mehnert 1983). Thus, even before December 7, Hoover was forced to grapple with criticism that his bureau was not doing enough to combat espionage (Theoharis and Cox 1988). Furthermore, President Roosevelt seemed to favor William J. Donovan as his proverbial "Mister X," naming the Hoover nemesis as the head of a newly created Office of Strategic Services (OSS)— forerunner to the CIA—in 1942 (Theoharis and Cox 1988; Jeffreys-Jones 2007).

Despite the aforementioned fractures in the federal intelligence community, the Territory of Hawai'i effectively served as a laboratory for an extraordinary level of cooperation between the FBI, MID, ONI, and the islands' predominantly white oligarchy. Just months after its 1939 reopening, the Honolulu FBI office began exchanging files and custodial detention lists with the MID and ONI (Okihiro 1992; Scheiber et al. 2009). The relationship intensified in October 1941 as the army relocated its MID contact office to the Dillingham Building on Bishop and Merchant Streets in downtown Honolulu, sharing a floor with the FBI's Honolulu office (Okihiro 1992; Coffman 2003). Following the Pearl Harbor attack, the two agencies deepened their collaborative efforts yet again by physically merging their offices (Okihiro 1992). Although the ONI preserved a degree of independence in Hawai'i (Coffman 2003), it maintained a live telegraph connection with the FBI-MID joint headquarters, while local ONI boss Captain I. H. Mayfield attended weekly meetings with his FBI and MID counterparts (Okihiro 1992). Finally, the military's intelligence gathering efforts in Hawai'i relied heavily upon cooperation with members of the local oligarchy—such as high-ranking employees of the "Big Five" corporations (Okihiro 1992)—the very same talent pool that would be tapped to staff the hearing boards.

Although internee hearing boards were a nationwide undertaking, the rule of martial law in Hawai'i ensured that board procedures differed substantially from those in place on the continent. While internees in the 48 states had their cases heard by all-civilian boards, the hearing boards in martial law Hawai'i always contained an active officer of the US Army, who served as the board's executive and recorder. Although one civilian member received the title of board president, it was the army officer who unquestionably dominated the proceedings. As executive and recorder, it was his prerogative to proclaim the hearing open, summon and excuse witnesses, direct the questioning of the internee, and officially pronounce the hearings closed.[3] The uniformed army officer also apprised each internee that these were *military* hearings" accorded as a "matter of justice" rather than as a matter of right, echoing the official position of the FBI (Hoover 1943–1944). As such, the standard rules of jurisprudence need not apply. Under the ominous shadow of martial law, these hearings functioned much like the provost courts. In absence of written charges and cross-examinations, individual suspects were routinely sentenced to unspecified periods of confinement based on "flimsy or non-existent evidence" (Scheiber and Scheiber 1997:495).

The Wahiāwa District Court served as a provost court during the period of martial law. Photo courtesy of Hawai'i War Records Depository, Hamilton Library, University of Hawai'i at Mānoa.

The composition of the civilian portion of the hearing boards, stacked with Caucasian male elites, clearly worked to the detriment of Hawai'i's internees, the vast majority of whom were of Japanese ancestry. On the island of O'ahu—where most of the cases were heard—the wartime authorities formed three separate hearing boards. Civilian members included retired army Judge Advocate Lt. Colonel Edward Massee, Hawaiian Trust Company President P. K. McLean, future territorial Attorney General Edward N. Sylva, University of Hawai'i President Dr. Arthur L. Dean, estate director Mark A. Robinson, and Frank Thompson Jr., son of the prominent island attorney who represented the Hawai'i Sugar Planters' Association. This was hardly a trial by one's peers. On the "Garden Isle" of Kaua'i, the sole hearing board was comprised of Major George Tivy plus three civilians—C. E. S. Burns, Hector Moir, and Lindsay Faye—who managed the Līhu'e, Kōloa, and Kekaha sugar plantations and

Former University of Hawai'i President Dr. Arthur Dean (dark suit and tie), shown here with Admiral Chester Nimitz, served on one of the three hearing boards established on the island of O'ahu. Photo courtesy of Hawai'i War Records Depository, Hamilton Library, University of Hawai'i at Mānoa.

thus presided over the hearings of many of their own employees (Harada 1942; Furuya 1982; Inouye 1982).

Additional post-hearing practices in martial law Hawai'i worked to the detriment of internees in ways that differed from continental cases. According to the procedures outlined by J. Edgar Hoover, hearing boards in the 48 states made recommendations to the local US Attorney, who possessed final authority on internment decisions (Hoover 1943–1944). This was obviously not possible in martial law Hawai'i, where the power of the attorney general had been usurped by the Office of the Military Governor. Instead, the recommendations of each hearing board were reviewed by a committee consisting of the local chiefs of the FBI, MID, and ONI. Since these were the very same individuals who had overseen the creation of the custodial detention lists that determined who would be apprehended, the odds of release tilted significantly against Hawai'i's internees. Tellingly, in cases in which the single army officer dissented from the three civilian board members' decision for release or parole, the intelligence agencies enforced the *minority* opinion and recommended internment. There are further cases in which the intelligence officers ignored unanimous recommendations of the hearing boards for release or parole in order to enforce the extended internment of individuals whose loyalty they questioned.[4] In essence, this meant that federal prosecutors retained the right to overrule their own handpicked judges. Each case culminated when it reached the desk of Lt. Colonel Thomas H. Green at the Office of the Military Governor in 'Iolani Palace, with Green consistently upholding decisions for prolonged detention. Finally, internees in Hawai'i were forced to sign a waiver in order to gain their parole or release, promising to "forever discharge" the federal government and the military "from any and all manner of action or actions, cause and causes of action, suit, controversies, trespasses, damages judgments, executions, claims, claims for damages, and demands whatsoever, in law or equity" (Orenstein 1942). Failure to consent to this comprehensive waiver of rights resulted in continued confinement (Commission 1997; Kashima 2003).

The fact that internees in Hawai'i—but not those on the mainland—were theoretically entitled to attorneys did not result in any amelioration of civil rights abuses. First of all, internees were informed that legal counsel would only be available at their own expense (Kashima, 2003; Rosenfeld 2011b). Furthermore, since they only learned of the possibility of legal counsel during their actual hearings, any request for a lawyer would only have extended their periods of pre-hearing confinement. It is thus exceedingly rare to find cases of internees who retained attorneys, with many of them either explicitly expressing financial constraints or likely fearing that taking such a measure would have been interpreted as a sign of guilt.[5] Owing to the climate of fear in wartime Hawai'i and the reign of martial law, there are also reports of internees undergoing a preliminary set of interrogation sessions at the joint FBI-MID offices in the Dillingham Building in which they were threatened by military personnel with brandished weapons and forced to sign false declarations (Allen 1950; Commission 1997; Nye, 2009b; Scheiber et al. 2009). However, owing to the military governor's decision to forcibly close the civil courts, little recourse was available to contest unfair treatment by wartime authorities.

Loyalty under Trial

The case of Carl Magnus Torsten Armfelt provides a striking example of how the additional power granted to federal intelligence agencies in Hawai'i undermined any notions of due process. Just 23 years old at the time of his arrest, Armfelt was a United States citizen—by birth—who had served two-and-a-half years in the US Army before receiving an honorable discharge with a classification of "excellent character." Much like Clara Ludders, Armfelt became engulfed in an FBI probe even though he was neither of German nor Italian descent. A member of a blue-blood Scandinavian family, Armfelt was of Swedish heritage on his mother's side while his estranged father was a Finnish count. In many ways, Carl fell victim to political machinations on the European continent. By the time the United States had entered World War II, Sweden had been occupied by Nazi Germany and Finland was at war with the Soviet Union—at that time a US ally. Although Armfelt admitted to activities on behalf of a Finnish relief fund during his December 19 hearing, the civilian board members concluded that his "sympathy towards Finland in her struggle against Russia is perfectly understandable" (Armfelt 1941:23) and therefore recommended his release on parole. However, Captain Dixon Avery, in his role as executive and recorder, issued a dissenting opinion and reconvened the board on Christmas Eve for a closed session in which FBI agent George E. Allen testified that Armfelt was a "fanatical follower of Hitler" and a "member of an informal discussion group maintained by permanent individuals of Nazi and pro-Fascist sympathies" (Armfelt 1941:25). This hearsay evidence was enough to trump Armfelt's US citizenship and military service, resulting in a revised movement for continued internment. Needless to say, the intelligence agency heads upheld this decision. Carl Armfelt's case— quite possibly the first internee hearing in Hawai'i—demonstrated wartime authorities' ability to manipulate cases to arrive at a predetermined outcome. Armfelt thus joined Clara Ludders as one of the many US citizens confined at the Sand Island and Honouliuli detention centers, ostensibly as German alien enemies (Armfelt 1943).

The examination of hearing board transcripts thus shatters the previous assumption that the "FBI used the same criteria in Hawai'i as on the mainland" (Kashima 2003:74) for assembling lists of civilians who would be apprehended as alien enemies in the event of war. In fact, the threshold for classification as a Nazi or fascist sympathizer in Hawai'i appears to have been set significantly lower. To be sure, internment on the US continent was not limited to people of Japanese, German, and Italian descent. Austria had been annexed to the Nazi Reich in the Anschluss of 1938, meaning that people of Austrian descent in the US were also classified as Germans for purposes of internment. Additionally, the American declaration of war against Axis allies in June 1942 resulted in the internment of foreign nationals from Bulgaria, Hungary, and Romania (Kashima 2003).

However, people who would not have raised any suspicion on the mainland quickly found themselves confined behind barbed wire in martial law Hawai'i, including local high school students, veterans of the US Armed Forces, Jewish refugees, and—as we have seen—American citizens who did not possess any ancestral ties to countries at war with the United States. Gertrude Schroeder was a teenage student at the Catholic all-girls Sacred Hearts Academy in Kaimukī. Mario Valdastri had fought for the US Army in France during the First World War. Norwegian composer and Honolulu Symphony Orchestra co-founder Alf Hurum, with his native country under Nazi occupation, also found himself interned as an alien enemy. So did the Austrian-born architect Alfred Preis, who would later design the USS *Arizona* Memorial in Pearl Harbor. Jewish refugees Ernst and Zdenka Orenstein and their teenage son, Otto, had fled their home city of Vienna to escape Nazi persecution, traveling to the other side of the world only to be locked up at the Sand Island detention center in Honolulu Harbor as alien enemies. Even though the hearing board recommended their "unconditional release," the couple spent nearly five months in confinement (Orenstein 1942; Orenstein 1942a, 1942b).

In the continental United States, the sheer enormity of the German and Italian communities—combined with their extensive integration into the social fabric of American life—ruled out any program of mass internment. At the beginning of the Second World War, Germans and Italians constituted the two largest foreign-born populations in the country, and if one included those with at least one German- or Italian-born parent, these two ethnic communities numbered more than 10 million people (Fox 2000a, 2000b). Federal authorities therefore pursued a policy of selective internment that bore some resemblance to the targeted arrests of ethnic Japanese civilians in Hawai'i. In addition to statements collected from informants, FBI agents on the mainland relied on newspaper and magazine subscription lists, overseas assets and remissions, visits to Axis countries, and the activities of close relatives in those countries when evaluating an individual's loyalty and potential for engaging in subversive behavior (Fox 2000a, 2007). The most powerful indicator was a person's membership in the pro-Nazi Amerikadeutscher Volksbund (German American Federation) or "Bund," which had organized a sold-out spectacle at New York City's Madison Square Garden in 1939 (Krammer 1997; Fox 2000a; Commission 1997).

In the Territory of Hawai'i, however, far removed from any Bund activities, neither membership in proscribed organizations nor subscriptions to suspicious publications played a prominent role in internment cases. Formal pro-Nazi or pro-fascist organizations did not exist, and foreign publications mentioned in hearing board transcripts were limited to medical journals and the innocuous German magazine *Hausfrau* (*Housewife*). Instead, under the leadership of Robert L. Shivers, Honolulu's FBI office monitored the territory's relatively small German and Italian communities in their entireties and interned people *en masse* in the days and weeks after the United States entered the war. In fact, in a letter addressed to J. Edgar Hoover on December 4, 1941, Robert Shivers stated that the accompanying custodial detention lists contained "*all* of the known Germans residing in the Territory of Hawaii" (Shivers 1941). He even assured Hoover that "there [could] be no improvement" to the plan, since "arrangements" had been made for the "specific handling of *each and every individual* alien German and Italian in the Hawaiian Islands" (Shivers 1941). It is thus not surprising that the postwar study commissioned by Hawai'i's territorial legislature found that FBI agents had arrested "practically every German and Italian alien in Hawai'i with the exception of the aged and infirmed" (Allen 1950:42; Holian 1998).

The correspondence between Shivers and Hoover also reveals the FBI chief's undeniable awareness of the internment of US citizens under his "Alien Enemy Control" program. In the aforementioned letter from Shivers to Hoover just days before the Pearl Harbor attack, the Honolulu office head informed his superior that, "in addition to the names of the aliens who are considered dangerous and for whom custodial memoranda have been prepared, there were also listed American citizens of German descent of similar classification" (Shivers 1941). Unambiguous as this December 4 statement might be, it is still only recognition of the intent to intern citizens, since the United States had yet to enter the war. However, the arrest reports sent by Shivers to Hoover in the weeks after the declaration of war separated ethnic German and Italian internees neatly into categories of US "citizens" and "aliens" (Shivers 1942). This distinction was also maintained in internal communication drafted by Hoover himself. Specifically, in a memorandum to L. M. C. Smith of the Special Defense Unit on December 18, 1941, Hoover provided separate lists of "alien enemies" and those "apprehended as United States Citizens of German Ancestry in the Territory of Hawaii" (Hoover 1941). Of course, even this internal message is not entirely truthful, as the early arrests of civilians in Hawai'i included US citizens of Danish, Swedish, Finnish, and Norwegian descent.

In fact, the internment of US citizens in Hawai'i had become public knowledge long before Hoover published a defense of his "Alien Enemy Control" program in the 1943–1944 volume of the *Iowa Law Review*. Hans Zimmerman was the first of three German American internees from Hawai'i to file for a writ of habeas corpus after he had been transported to Camp McCoy in Wisconsin. Although the American Civil Liberties Union eventually intervened on behalf of more than a dozen US citizens in the same predicament, Zimmerman—with assistance from his wife, Clara—was the first to push forward with his case. A naturalized citizen who had served in the US Army before building a lucrative medical practice in Honolulu, Zimmerman found himself condemned to internment for the duration of the war, despite having summoned some of the territory's leading figures to his defense during his hearing. Clara Zimmerman eventually took her husband's petition all the way to the US Supreme Court, only to have the War Department shrewdly avoid the possibility of a decision that would undermine military rule in Hawai'i by releasing Hans before the case could be heard (Anthony 1975; Rossiter 1976; Scheiber and Scheiber 1990, 1997). The plight of Zimmerman and the other citizens shipped from Hawai'i to Camp McCoy and their habeas corpus challenges received coverage in both of Honolulu's leading newspapers, while territorial Attorney General J. Garner Anthony used the Zimmerman case to challenge the legality of martial law in Hawai'i in a scathing critique published in the *California Law Review* (Anthony 1943). The issue even reached the desk of the president, as Secretary of War Henry

Stimson wrote Roosevelt in April 1942 to recommend returning the internees to Hawai'i (Stimson 1942).

Hoover's "Cloak Of Citizenship"

Taking their cue from bureau head J. Edgar Hoover, the agents of Honolulu's FBI office viewed dual and naturalized citizens in Hawai'i as potential spies and saboteurs. Hoover, in his essay for the *Iowa Law Review*, expressed distrust for what he called "the naturalized citizen whose cloak of citizenship is a sham and who is dangerous to the nation's security" (Hoover 1943–1944:407). He even discussed the FBI's ongoing efforts to have certificates of naturalization revoked in federal courts in cases of presumed disloyalty or lack of allegiance, although this information gave his readers the false impression that citizenship protected suspects from FBI internment measures. The cases of Hawai'i's wartime internees demonstrate the intense suspicion with which the FBI viewed them. Not only did Honolulu agents apprehend naturalized citizens of German and Italian descent, they even arrested Hawaiian-born wives of naturalized citizens, including Bertha Berg and Clara Ludders—both of whom were confined at Sand Island and Honouliuli.

The peculiar case of Mario Valdastri supports General Emmons's assertion that military authorities "leaned over backward in interning people" in wartime Hawai'i (Allen 1950). While other Hawai'i residents—including Carl Armfelt, Arthur Baltrusch, Alexander Varis, and Hans Zimmerman—had served in the US Armed Forces before their periods of internment, Valdastri had actually seen combat as an American soldier in France during the First World War, before receiving an honorable discharge in 1919. At the time of the Second World War, Valdastri owned a house sitting on nine acres of property in Kailua, having built up a successful contracting business in Honolulu (DiStasi 2001). In the end, Valdastri's citizenship, military valor, and fine standing in the community mattered little in comparison to the closed testimony of FBI agent George E. Allen. Although Valdastri's citizenship and service were never questioned, Allen claimed that the subject was "regarded as pro-fascist and pro-Nazi," referencing "meetings of local Italians at his Kailua home" and a close friendship Valdastri had formed with consulate official Giovanni Muratori, at least until the Italian consulate in Honolulu was closed down. While it probably didn't help his cause to admit harboring "fascist leanings" until 1935, Valdastri's associations with Italian nationals and former consulate employees were deemed sufficient evidence of "subversive activities." In a December 22 hearing that lasted less than an hour—including the closed testimony of the

FBI agent and the deliberations of the board—US citizen and army veteran Mario Valdastri was ordered to remain in confinement (Valdastri 1942). Not even a spirited letter-writing campaign, in which Valdastri contacted President Roosevelt and asked to be shipped to the "most exposed and dangerous spot" in order to "sacrifice [his] life for [his] country" (DiStasi 2001:147) was enough to overturn the board's decision. Other Hawai'i cases suggest that military service and civilian employment on military bases, far from being regarded as irrefutable proof of one's loyalty, could actually provoke concerns that an individual was engaging in acts of espionage or sabotage.

The hearing of Anna "Nikky" Walther shows how in the absence of more concrete indicators such as membership in proscribed organizations or subscriptions to pro-Nazi literature, Hawai'i's FBI agents became dependent upon the most problematic form of evidence—the allegations of anonymous informants. Nikky and her husband, Herb Walther, were both naturalized US citizens of German birth, who were widely regarded as responsible community members and patriotic Americans. She volunteered time making bandages for the Red Cross and the couple had organized a fundraiser for the "Committee to Defend America." During Nikky's hearing, local civil servant August Hasselgreen testified that, "the Walthers [were] better Americans than a lot of local born" (Walther, Anna 1942:23). Similarly, John Cass Stevens of the Hawaiian Electric Company stated under oath that, "in every respect, everything [he] ever heard from Mrs. Walther [had] always been ... pro-American" (Walther, Anna 1942:18). Indeed, it seems that the FBI trusted Nikky Walther enough to recruit her as an informant. Nikky named a local FBI agent who had arranged an "interview" in which she was asked to "contact German people to find out what things were" (Walther, Anna 1942:10). Nikky even testified having joined a church at the behest of the FBI agent and acknowledged having provided him with "statements" in support of the bureau's counterespionage efforts (Walther, Anna 1942:10).

During the course of her hearing, however, Nikky Walther was quickly transformed from a patriotic informant to a tragic victim of hearsay and supposition. Following standard procedures, Nikky was barred from the courtroom for the presentation of FBI testimony, in which agent George E. Allen reported that the German-born Walther had expressed support for Hitler and had claimed to have conducted spy work for Austria in 1927, when she was still a teenager. In her defense, Walther assured the board that she had no sympathy for Hitler and had "never been connected with any government agency" (Walther, Anna 1942:13), either in Austria or Germany. She recounted a humble adolescence, in which she shuffled from one German-speaking city to another—Bonn, Cologne, Hamburg, Munich, and Vienna—finding employment as a domestic servant before getting married and emigrating to the United States in 1927. Her only political activity seems to have been involvement in a "group of about 50 young people" (Walther, Anna 1942:7) in Vienna that supported a new—but democratic—social order in the wake of the devastation of the First World War. Furthermore, the timeline she provided indicated that her period of residence in Vienna (and her accompanying political activity) ended when she was just 15 years old—in 1923. While this testimony should have removed any suspicions of espionage work on behalf of Austria or support for Hitler, the board's follow-up questions reveal a complete ignorance of contemporary European politics. Incredibly, Walther was next

Before her arrest as an alien enemy, naturalized US citizen Nikky Walther participated in Red Cross events like this one, preparing surgical dressings for wounded soldiers. Photo courtesy of Hawai'i War Records Depository, Hamilton Library, University of Hawai'i at Mānoa.

asked if "the *Anschluss* had taken place" (Walther, Anna 1942:8), an event that did not occur until 1938—a full 11 years after her arrival in the United States.

Despite the board's confusion and the anonymous allegations provided to the FBI, Nikky Walther's case probably would have ended in a decision of release on parole, if not for a peculiar turn of events. John Cass Stevens, called as a witness in support of the internee just an hour earlier, was asked to return as a government witness, resulting in the removal of the internee from the room. Once again, Stevens confirmed that Nikky Walther had "never once" indicated any admiration for Hitler, and had consistently expressed herself "very badly at the German attitude" (Walther, Anna 1942:26). However, this time the witness claimed that he had been "over-entertained" at the Walthers' home, adding that "there was a little too *much* Americanism" (Walther, Anna 1942:26) voiced in his presence. One can only wonder whether George E. Allen or another FBI agent convinced Stevens to suddenly resurface at the hearing with a radically revised version of his testimony. The hearing board immediately arrived at a new verdict: "as in the case of her husband ... there was abundant evidence of expressions of loyalty to the United States which to the board seemed excessive, raising questions as to their sincerity" (Walther, Anna 1942:27). Although one of the board's civilian members officially dissented, the local chiefs of the three federal intelligence agencies upheld the majority decision for continued internment (Walther, Anna 1942). Hence, a new precedent was set: not only could US citizens be interned for acts of disloyalty, they could also be punished for an apparent *excess* of patriotic loyalty.

The Pains of Internment

The internment experience tore apart Hawai'i's families, even in cases in which a husband and wife were both subject to detainment. One poignant example can be found in a letter sent to the International Red Cross by a group of 13 male US citizens interned at Camp McCoy. The internees—all Hawai'i residents—expressed hope at "establishing communication with [their] wives and sister" who had "all been detained in Honolulu" prior to the men's forced departure to Wisconsin. After informing the Red Cross that mail communication had been "hopelessly interrupted," the petition closes with a simple yet heartfelt entreaty: "please tell us where our wives are" (Walther, Gunther 1942).

Just as married couples were divided, so too were parents separated from their children. When a hearing board recommended the internment of Kurt and Margaret Moderow for the war's duration, its members noted that the couple had "no known relatives [in Hawai'i] to properly take care of their child." The board therefore pleaded with wartime authorities to devise "some arrangement" that would allow the three-and-a-half-year-old Kurt Jr. to "stay with [his] mother during the period of internment" (Moderow 1942). However, other young children—their parents having been whisked away at a moment's notice—were left to fend for themselves amidst the chaos and confusion that followed the attack on Pearl Harbor. When the FBI arrested Joe and Dora Pacific on December 8, the couple's nine-year-old daughter remained alone at home (Morrison and Knerr 1990; Pacific 1994). Similarly, when agents picked up Fred and Bertha Berg later that evening, they left seven-year-old Anita in the care of her 11-year-old sister, Doris, with both children assuming for weeks that their parents had been killed (Nye 2009a, 2009b). Interned US war veteran Mario Valdastri was not permitted to attend the wedding of his only daughter, Frances, whose life was tragically cut short in an automobile accident before her father's release. Mario's son later wrote that his mother, Josephine, "never forgave them for what they did to [their family]" (Valdastri 2001:151).

Material losses were also severe. Previously prosperous families fell into poverty, as their incomes were halted and their assets frozen. Herb and Nikky Walther lost their car, home, and furniture for failing to meet payments while interned (Morrison and Knerr 1990; Fox 2007). Faced with the same predicament, Joe Pacific lost his shoe and luggage repair shop (Morrison and Knerr 1990). Before the war, Bertha Berg had run a successful nursing home in Nu'uanu, but she was unable to prevent her enterprise from collapsing while she wasted time away on Sand Island (Nye 2009a). Just like their Japanese counterparts, German and Italian internees continued to experience the social stigma of internment after the war, repeatedly encountering obstacles to gainful employment. Otto Orenstein was rejected for a job with the Bank of Hawaii due to his internment history, while his father, Ernst, missed out on several business opportunities before eventually finding work on a neighbor island sugar plantation (Fox 2007). Fred Berg—who had earned a Master's degree at the University of Cologne—was dismissed from a position at a Coca Cola bottling factory after the war out of fear that he might poison the beverages (Fox 2007; Nye 2009a).

Conclusion

The hearing board records of US citizens interned as German and Italian enemies demonstrate how the rule of martial law impinged upon civil liberties in ways that distinguish the Hawai'i case from narratives of wartime confinement on the continent. In martial law Hawai'i, where Japanese nationals and Japanese Americans accounted for over 37 percent of the civilian population, wartime leaders implemented a policy of selective internment thoroughly unlike what unfolded in the 48 states, where the proportionately smaller Japanese American population was forcibly "relocated" *en masse*. While authorities on the US mainland carried out a more limited incarceration of individuals in the country's enormous German and Italian communities, members of these comparatively tiny ethnic groupings in the Hawaiian Islands faced a much higher probability of confinement. Although it is clear that on the US West Coast "Japanese Americans were initially interned on far slimmer evidence than German Americans" (Hayashi 2004:77), what transpired in Hawai'i was closer to the reverse.

The point here is not to engage in a discourse of competitive victimization. When one considers the cultural suppression faced by Hawai'i's much larger Nikkei population, including the censorship of newspapers and closure of language schools, shrines, and temples (Nishigaya and Oshiro 2014)—one can only conclude that the Japanese American community of Hawai'i faced the most severe and "manifest deprivation of constitutional liberties" (Scheiber and Scheiber 1997) in wartime Hawai'i. Indeed, while the maltreatment of naturalized US citizens of European descent warrants our attention, it is worth noting that Japanese Issei were not even eligible for American citizenship, due to anti-Asian prejudice and discriminatory immigration laws. J. Edgar Hoover's attempt to find legal justification for his "Alien Enemy Control" program in Section 21, Title 50 of the US Code—otherwise known as the Alien Enemies Act of 1798—was an outright sham. This law only empowered the federal government to detain foreign nationals whose country was at war with the United States, and not to incarcerate lawful US citizens—whether they were of German, Japanese, or any other heritage—on the mere assumption that they could not be trusted.

The evidence presented here challenges the notion that wartime internment in Hawai'i occurred merely as a manifestation of a protracted "race war" (Okihiro 1992:272) against people of Japanese ancestry. Instead, it seems that outside pressure to respond to a security threat in the island territory—combined with bureaucratic inertia—resulted in the arrest, incarceration, or removal of more than 2,500 innocent local residents under the authority of martial law (Rosenfeld 2011a). At least 135 civilians of European heritage were arrested in the Territory of Hawai'i and subsequently detained at the Honolulu

Immigration Office and in army-run internment camps on Sand Island and at Honouliuli,[6] but this was hardly the result of a deeper level of prejudice against Germans and Italians in Hawai'i than existed on the continent. In fact, although these local residents were portrayed publicly as German and Italian "alien enemies," Hawai'i's wartime confinement sites held internees from a wide range of national and cultural heritages. In addition to ethnic Germans, Italians, and—of course—Japanese, one could find people of Austrian, Danish, Finnish, Irish, Korean, Lithuanian, Norwegian, Okinawan, and Swedish descent in Hawai'i's camps, in addition to European Jews escaping Nazi persecution. In line with the findings of more recent studies of internment (Hayashi 2004; Scheiber et al. 2009), the diversity of this pool of internees suggests that racial bigotry—while it existed—played a less decisive role than the first wave of scholars tackling this topic surmised.

One cannot underestimate the degree of pressure officials in Washington, DC exerted on Hawai'i's military government in an effort to implement a much more comprehensive internment program. Navy Secretary Frank Knox was far from alone in his repeated demands for a mass incarceration or evacuation of the islands' Nikkei civilians (Weglyn 1976; Fox 1988; Kashima 2003; Scheiber and Scheiber 1997; Robinson 2001; Scheiber et al. 2009). Those joining him in calling for harsher measures in the territory included US Army Chief of Staff General George C. Marshall (Weglyn 1976; Robinson 2001; Scheiber et al. 2009) and President Franklin D. Roosevelt (Weglyn 1976; Robinson 2001; Kashima 2003; Coffman 2003; Kashima 2008). Yet Military Governor Delos Emmons continually dragged his heels on the issue, citing labor needs, logistical problems, the danger of transport, war priorities, and any other excuse he could muster (Commission 1997; Scheiber and Scheiber 1997; Robinson 2001; Kashima 2003; Coffman 2003; Scheiber et al. 2009). In this sense, Emmons has rightly been described as the "shield of Hawai'i's Nisei" (Coffman 2003:79), even if he was motivated more by pragmatism than a love of liberty. Similarly, Robert L. Shivers and his staff at the Honolulu FBI—while serving as willing cogs in Hoover's disingenuous "Alien Enemy Control" program—simultaneously supported Emmons's more moderate approach to Nikkei internment, assuring federal investigators that Hawai'i's Japanese American population was "98% loyal" to the United States (Weglyn 1976; Robinson 2001).

When it came to the islands' German and Italian residents, however, the bureaucratic brush was far too broad and the arms of the American intelligence agencies far too clumsy to accurately delineate the lines between friend and foe within these small communities. "Mass" internment in this case was entirely possible and the custodial detention lists were already drafted. When war hostilities ensued with the attack on Pearl Harbor and paranoia reigned in the days and weeks that followed, the FBI and MID moved to apprehend and detain the entire lot. The arrest of Bernard Julius Otto Kuehn—a German citizen who was eventually tried and convicted of spying on behalf of the Japanese (Fox 2007)—coupled with the embarrassment of the Klaus Mehnert affair doubtlessly convinced intelligence officers that Germans in Hawai'i posed a genuine security risk. At the very least, the pressure to show results was real, and Honolulu FBI agents' wave of arrests in early December 1941 earned them the public praise of bureau chief J. Edgar Hoover (Hoover 1943–1944).

Operating in the midst of a war zone where the threat of an impending Japanese land invasion was taken seriously—at least, in the immediate aftermath of the Pearl Harbor attack—the authorities' unwavering emphasis on security was not entirely irrational or unfounded. But evidence suggests that law-abiding citizens, patriotic Americans, and productive community members greatly outnumbered the actual "alien enemies" inside of Hawai'i's camps. In fact, 33 of the 36 "German" and "Italian" internees whose names appear on camp rosters and reports from Honouliuli were US citizens.[7] More important, for all of the innocent civilians confined behind barbed wire in Hawai'i—including the more numerous Japanese and Japanese American detainees—wartime arrest and incarceration constituted a grave injustice, with consequences that lasted far longer than the duration of their internment. It is incumbent upon the rest of us to learn from their experiences so that their suffering did not occur in vain.

Above all, their stories teach us that we are all potentially at risk. When faced with war, martial law, and the institutionalization of fear and distrust, neither citizenship nor a pristine record of civic duty were enough to ensure an individual of escaping the FBI's dragnet. In such circumstances, it is the responsibility of each and every one of us who cherish our democratic freedoms to break the silence—to speak out in defense of those whose voices have been muted and in support of the values we cherish. ❖

Notes

1. Gary Okihiro (1992) takes the added step of indicating the location of the hearing board transcripts in his endnotes to *Cane Fires: The Anti-Japanese Movement in Hawai'i, 1865–1945*, but he does not provide any discussion of individual cases.

2. These figures were originally provided by W. F. Kelly, assistant commander of Hoover's "Alien Enemy Control" program (Kashima 2003:124). This total does not include an additional 120,000 people of Japanese descent who were forcibly "relocated" into War Relocation Authority camps.

3. Hundreds of internee hearing board transcripts from the Territory of Hawai'i can be found in National Archives and Records Administration II in College Park, MD, Record Group 389, Entry 461, Boxes 2605–2646, 1941–1943 and in Record Group 494, Entry 19, Boxes 194–272, 1941–1943. Each transcript begins with the names of the hearing board members.

4. Examples of this can be found in individual hearing board transcripts of Celia Iaculli Ventrella (1942) and Minosuke Hanabusa (1942).

5. One rare exception can be found in the case of Yasutaro Soga, editor and publisher of the *Nippu Jiji* newspaper. Although the three civilian members of Soga's board recommended that Soga be paroled, the FBI/MID/ONI reviewers sided with the lone dissenting voice of the board's army officer and ruled in favor of continued internment. Soga's hearing board transcript can be found in Soga (1942).

6. I have compiled a master list of 139 "German" and "Italian" internees in Hawai'i based on archival records. Of these 139, I was able to cross-check all but four people whose names appeared in records only once. The complete list, entitled "Hawai'i Internment: Caucasian Internee Database," is available at the Japanese Cultural Center of Hawai'i Resource Center.

7. The three exceptions include (1) Friedel Kuehn, who was shipped to the continental United States immediately after the opening of the Honouliuli site, (2) Norwegian composer Alf Hurum, and (3) Alexander Varis, who had obtained US citizenship using an assumed name and a stolen birth certificate. For camp reports, see especially Military Police (1941–1945).

References

Allen, Gwenfread. 1950. *Hawaii's War Years: 1941–1945*. Honolulu: University of Hawai'i Press. Reprinted by Pacific Monographs, 1999.

Anthony, J. Garner. 1943. "Martial Law, Military Government and the Writ of Habeas Corpus in Hawaii." *California Law Review* 31(5):477–514.

———. 1975. *Hawaii under Army Rule*. Honolulu: The University Press of Hawai'i.

Armfelt, Carl Magnus Torsten Jr. 1941. Transcript of the Hearings of a Board of Officers and Civilians in the Case of Carl Magnus Torsten Armfelt Jr., December. Record Group 389, Entry 461, Box 2607, File: Records Pertaining to the Internment of Carl Magnus Torsten Armfelt Jr. National Archives and Records Administration II, College Park, Maryland.

———. 1943. Individual Pay Data Record for Count Magnus Armfelt. Record Group 389, Entry 461, Box 2607. 1943, File: Records Pertaining to the Internment of Carl Magnus Torsten Armfelt Jr. National Archives and Records Administration II, College Park, Maryland.

Coffman, Tom. 2003. *The Island Edge of America: A Political History of Hawai'i*. Honolulu: University of Hawai'i Press.

Commission of Wartime Internment and Relocation of Civilians. 1997. *Personal Justice Denied: Report of the Commission on Wartime Relocation and Internment of Civilians*. Seattle: Civil Liberties Public Education Fund and University of Washington Press. Originally published in two volumes by the US Government Printing Office, 1982–1983.

Daniels, Roger. 1993. *Prisoners Without Trial: Japanese Americans in World War II*. New York: Hill and Wang.

DiStasi, Lawrence. 2001. *Una Storia Segreta: The Secret History of Italian American Evacuation and Internment during World War II*. Berkeley, CA: Heyday Books.

Fox, Stephen. 1988. "General John DeWitt and the Proposed Internment of German and Italian Aliens during World War II." *Pacific Historical Review* 57(4):407–438.

———. 2000a. *America's Invisible Gulag: A Biography of German American Internment and Exclusion in World War II*. New York: Peter Lang.

———. 2000b. *Uncivil Liberties: Italian Americans Under Siege during World War II*. Parkland, FL: Universal Publishers.

———. 2007. *Fear Itself: Inside the FBI Roundup of German Americans During World War II*. New York: iUniverse.

Furuya, Kaetsu. 1982. Interview by Japanese-American Resource Center, Honolulu, HI, November 11. Japanese Internment and Relocation Experience Collection, No. 233, Hawai'i War Records Depository, University of Hawai'i at Mānoa, Hamilton Library, Honolulu, Hawai'i.

Hanabusa, Minosuke. 1942. Transcript of the Hearings of a Board of Officers and Civilians in the Case of Minosuke Hanabusa, January–April. Record Group 494, Entry 19, Box 194, File: Records Pertaining to the Internment of Minosuke Hanabusa. National Archives and Records Administration II, College Park, Maryland.

Harada, Umeno. 1942. Transcript of the Hearings of a Board of Officers and Civilians in the Case of Umeno Harada, January–March. Record Group 389, Entry 461, Box 2610, File: Records Pertaining to the Internment of Umeno Harada. National Archives and Records Administration II, College Park, Maryland.

Hayashi, Brian Masaru. 2004. *Democratizing the Enemy: The Japanese American Internment.* Princeton, NJ: Princeton University Press.

Holian, Timothy. 1998. *The German-Americans and World War II.* New York: Peter Lang.

Hoover, John Edgar. 1941. Memoranda to Mr. L. M. C. Smith, Chief of Special Defense Unit, December 18. Federal Bureau of Investigation, Freedom of Information and Privacy Acts file 100-2-20, "Subject: Custodial Detention—Honolulu Division."

———. 1943–1944. "Alien Enemy Control." *Iowa Law Review* 29(4):396–408.

Inouye, Jukichi. 1982. Interview by Japanese-American Resource Center, ʻEleʻele, HI, November 12. Hawaiʻi War Records Depository, Japanese Internment and Relocation Experience Collection, No. 236, Hawaiʻi War Records Depository, University of Hawaiʻi at Mānoa, Hamilton Library, Honolulu, Hawaiʻi.

Internee Hearing Boards and Procedure in Hawaiʻi, May 15. 1942. Archival Collection 19, Box 1, File 42. Japanese Cultural Center of Hawaiʻi, Resource Center.

Jeffreys-Jones, Rhodri. 2007. *FBI: A History.* New Haven, CT: Yale University Press.

Kashima, Tetsuden. 2003. *Judgment Without Trial: Japanese American Internment during World War II.* Seattle: University of Washington Press.

———. 2008. "Introduction." Pp. 1–16 in *Life behind Barbed Wire: The World War II Internment Memoirs of a Hawaiʻi Issei,* by Yasutaro Soga. Honolulu: University of Hawaiʻi Press.

Krammer, Arnold. 1997. *Undue Process: The Untold Story of America's German Alien Internees.* Lanham, MD: Rowman & Littlefield Publishers.

Ludders, Clara. 1942. Transcript of the Hearings of a Board of Officers and Civilians in the Case of Clara Ludders, March. Record Group 389, Entry 461, Box 2623, File: Records Pertaining to the Internment of Clara Ludders. National Archives and Records Administration II, College Park, Maryland.

Ludders, William Carl (Ensign, US Naval Training Station, Farragut, Idaho). 1943. Letter to the Commanding General of the Hawaiian Department, January 10. Record Group 389, Entry 461, Box 2623, File: Records Pertaining to the Internment of Hugo Ludders. National Archives and Records Administration II, College Park, Maryland.

Mehnert, Klaus. 1983. *Ein Deutscher auf Hawaii, 1936–1941.*

Military Police Company Daily Reports from the Sand Island and Honouliuli Camps. 1941–1945. Record Group 494, Entry 25, Boxes 334–337. National Archives and Records Administration II, College Park, Maryland.

Moderow, Margaret Herder. 1942. Transcript of the Hearings of a Board of Officers and Civilians in the Case of Margaret Herder Moderow, March–April. Record Group 389, Entry 461, Box 2626, File: Records Pertaining to the Internment of Margaret Herder Moderow. National Archives and Records Administration II, College Park, Maryland.

Morrison, Susan, and Peter Knerr. 1990. "Forgotten Internees." *Honolulu Magazine* November:76–79, 106–112.

Muller, Eric. L. 2007. *American Inquisition: The Hunt for Japanese American Disloyalty in World War II.* Chapel Hill, NC: University of North Carolina Press.

Nishigaya, Linda, and Ernest Oshiro. 2014. "Reviving the Lotus: Japanese Buddhism and World War II Internment." In this issue.

Nye, Doris Berg. 2009a. Interview by Alan Rosenfeld and Susan Adler, Kapolei, HI. December 5.

———. 2009b. Interview by Brian Niiya, Japanese Cultural Center, Honolulu, HI. March 4.

Okihiro, Gary Y. 1992. *Cane Fires: The Anti-Japanese Movement in Hawaii, 1865–1945.* Philadelphia: Temple University Press.

Orenstein, Otto. 1942. Signed Release Waiver, April 30. Record Group 494, Entry 19, Box 272, File: Records Pertaining to the Internment of Otto Orenstein. National Archives and Records Administration II, College Park, Maryland.

Orenstein, Zdenka. 1942a. Transcript of the Hearings of a Board of Officers and Civilians in the Case of Zdenka Orenstein, December 1941–April 1942. Record Group 494, Entry 19, Box 272, File: Records Pertaining to the Internment of Zdenka Orenstein. National Archives and Records Administration II, College Park, Maryland.

———. 1942b. Signed Release Waiver, April 29. Record Group 494, Entry 19, Box 272. 1942b, File: Records Pertaining to the Internment of Zdenka Orenstein. National Archives and Records Administration II, College Park, Maryland.

Pacific, Joe. 1994. Interview by Joe Rossi, Honolulu, HI. March 18. Pp. 163–189 in *Era of Change: Oral Histories of Civilians in World War II Hawai'i,* edited by Center for Oral History. Honolulu: University of Hawai'i, Social Science Research Institute.

Robinson, Greg. 2001. *By Order of the President: FDR and the Internment of Japanese Americans.* Cambridge, MA: Harvard University Press.

———. 2009. *A Tragedy of Democracy: Japanese Confinement in North America.* New York: Columbia University Press.

Rosenfeld, Alan. 2011a. "Barbed-Wire Beaches: Martial Law and Civilian Internment in Wartime Hawai'i." *World History Connected* 8(3). Retrieved June 14, 2013 (http://worldhistoryconnected.press.illinois.edu/8.3/forum_rosenfeld.html).

———. 2011b. "'An Everlasting Scar': Civilian Internment on Wartime Kaua'i." *The Hawaiian Journal of History* 45:123–145.

Rossiter, Clinton Lawrence. 1976. *The Supreme Court and the Commander-in-Chief.* Ithaca, NY: Cornell University Press.

Scheiber, Harry N., and Jane L. Scheiber. 1990. "Constitutional Liberty in World War II: Army Rule and Martial Law in Hawaii, 1941–1946." *Western Legal History* 3(2):341–378.

———. 1997. "Bayonets in Paradise: A Half-Century Retrospect on Martial Law in Hawai'i, 1941–1946." *University of Hawai'i Law Review* 19(4):477–648.

Scheiber, Harry N., Jane L. Scheiber, and Benjamin Jones. 2009. "Hawai'i's Kibei under Martial Law: A Hidden Chapter in the History of World War II Internments." *Western Legal History* 22(1–2):1–102.

Shivers, Robert L. (Special Agent in Charge, Honolulu, T. H.) 1941. Letter to J. Edgar Hoover, Director, Federal Bureau of Investigation, December 4. Federal Bureau of Investigation, obtained from Arthur Jacobs via Freedom of Information and Privacy Acts file 100-2-20, "Subject: Custodial Detention—Honolulu Division."

———. 1942. Letter to J. Edgar Hoover, Director, Federal Bureau of Investigation, February 6. Federal Bureau of Investigation, Freedom of Information and Privacy Acts file 100-2-20, "Subject: Custodial Detention—Honolulu Division."

Soga, Yasutaro. 1942. Transcript of the Hearings of a Board of Officers and Civilians in the Case of Yasutaro Soga, January–April. Record Group 389, Entry 461, Box 2637, File: Records Pertaining to the Internment of Yasutaro Soga. National Archives and Records Administration II, College Park, Maryland.

Stimson, Henry J. (Secretary of War). 1942. Memorandum to President Franklin D. Roosevelt, April 15. Japanese Internment and Relocation Experience Collection, Box 1, Hawai'i War Records Depository, University of Hawai'i at Mānoa, Hamilton Library, Honolulu, Hawai'i.

Theoharis, Athan G. and John Stuart Cox. 1988. *The Boss: J. Edgar Hoover and the Great American Inquisition.* Philadelphia: Temple University Press.

Valdastri, Mario. 1942. Transcript of the Hearings of a Board of Officers and Civilians in the Case of Mario Valdastri, December 1941–February 1942. Record Group 389, Entry 461, Box 2643, File: Records Pertaining to the Internment of Mario Valdastri. National Archives and Records Administration II, College Park, Maryland.

Valdastri, Mario Jr. 2001. "Two Men in Suits." Pp. 153–155 in *Una Storia Segreta: The Secret History of Italian American Evacuation and Internment during World War II*, edited by Lawrence DiStasi. Berkeley, CA: Heyday Books.

Ventrella, Celia Iaculli. 1942. Transcript of the Hearings of a Board of Officers and Civilians in the Case of Celia Iaculli Ventrella, December 1941–March 1942. Record Group 389, Entry 461, Box 2643, File: Records Pertaining to the Internment of

Celia Iaculli Ventrella. National Archives and Records Administration II, College Park, Maryland.

Walther, Anna Phillipsen. 1942. Transcript of the Hearings of a Board of Officers and Civilians in the Case of Anna Walther, December 1941–April 1942. Record Group 389, Entry 461, Box 2643, File: Records Pertaining to the Internment of Anna Phillipsen Walther. National Archives and Records Administration II, College Park, Maryland.

Walther, Gunther Herbert. 1942. Letter to International Red Cross, March 25. Record Group 389, Entry missing, German Civilian Internees, Box 84, File: Records Pertaining to the Internment of Gunther Herbert Walther. National Archives and Records Administration II, College Park, Maryland.

Wasserstein, Bernard. 1999. *Secret War in Shanghai: An Untold Story of Espionage, Intrigue, and Treason in World War II*. Boston: Houghton Mifflin.

Weglyn, Michi. 1976. *Years of Infamy: The Untold Story of America's Concentration Camps*. New York: William Morrow.

Honouliuli's POWs:
Making Connections, Generating Changes

Suzanne Falgout

ABSTRACT

Immediately adjacent to Honouliuli's internment camp was Hawai'i's largest prisoner of war camp. It housed as many as 4,000 or more Japanese, Okinawans, Koreans, and Filipinos sent from various locations in the Pacific Theater, plus Italians picked up from the Atlantic Theater. The Camp served as an important base camp and also as a main transit point for those sent to destinations on the US mainland.

Although framed within wider Geneva Convention and US military guidelines for the humane treatment of prisoners, conditions of imprisonment differed significantly from one group to another and also changed over time. Those differences were largely dependent on ethnic backgrounds, wartime political statuses, and the reputations of various POW groups. They were also significantly affected by connections made between POWs and the US military, some with internees of their own ethnic groups in the camp, and especially with members of the local community.

This paper examines those varying conditions of imprisonment. It also describes the significance of transnational, national, and local connections made by Honouliuli's POWs.

Suzanne Falgout, Professor of Anthropology, University of Hawai'i–West O'ahu; 91-1001 Farrington Highway; Kapolei, HI 96707. This material is based upon work assisted by a grant from the Department of the Interior, National Park Service. Any opinions, findings, and conclusions or recommendations expressed in this material are those of the author and do not necessarily reflect the views of the Department of the Interior. The author may be reached at falgout@hawaii.edu.

The bombing of Pearl Harbor in Hawai'i—the surprise military strike by the Japanese Imperial Navy against this United States naval base on the morning of December 7, 1941—came as a profound shock to the American people and led directly to their entry into World War II in both the Atlantic and Pacific Theaters. The lack of any formal advance warning, furthermore, led President Franklin D. Roosevelt to proclaim December 7, 1941, as "a date which will live in infamy." Over the years, this event has indeed been immortalized in a wide variety of representations, with the result that Pearl Harbor has become an important part of American history and has gained a very prominent place in global memories of World War II. For Americans, Pearl Harbor is where World War II began, and it is the major symbol of that war itself.

Pearl Harbor's prominence, however, has long overshadowed other important wartime events and sites within Hawai'i, which until recently have been given very little recognition. The internment of those classified as enemy aliens, or even suspected as sympathizers, residing in Hawai'i had been planned for years and even decades earlier than the outbreak of World War II, and those plans began to be carried out later that same day on December 7. US wartime internment activities, then, actually began in Hawai'i. That fact, and Hawai'i's different rationale for, and patterns of, internment, the locations and types of camps that were set up, the ethnic groups held, and the various impacts of internment, however, are only now coming to be fully known. And, only recently has the major internment site in Hawai'i, Honouliuli Camp, been identified (see Kurahara, Niiya, and Young 2014; Burton et al. 2014) and been given state and national recognition.

The existence of prisoners of war in Hawai'i and at Honouliuli has been almost entirely unrecognized until now. While the first-ever Japanese POW, Ensign Kazuo Sakamaki, captured on December 7 from a disabled Japanese midget submarine, is often given recognition (Office of the Chief of Military History [hereafter OCMH] 1955; Krammer 1983), little has been known of the large numbers of POWs shipped to Hawai'i from both the Atlantic and Pacific Theaters. In fact, Hawai'i became an important outpost and transition point of national and transnational significance for POWs in World War II.

At the beginning of World War II, the United States had only very limited information about the geographic areas, peoples, and cultures they would encounter as enemies during the war. They also had little prior experience dealing with POWs, with only very limited numbers received in World

War I and with an original World War II plan to retain captives within actual war zones or to send them to other Allied nations. It was only in the middle of 1942, when mounting numbers of POWs began to exceed capacities and also the value of POWs as a crucially needed labor source was realized, that the War Department began to make its first plans to bring them to the United States. The earliest efforts involved the redesignation of six internment camps. However, it was quickly realized that hundreds of other POW camps in the United States would be needed, leading to the development of more than 500 main and branch camps. Whenever possible, they were located near existing military bases (Keefer 1992; Krammer 1983), spread throughout the nation, but with more than half located in the southern and southwestern regions (Keefer 1992). Eventually, the United States would hold some 425,000 POWs—mostly Germans, Italians, and some Japanese (Krammer 1983), but there were many others as well. Important US "overseas" POW camps were also established in Hawai'i, the Marianas, and the Philippines.

The need for accurate information about our enemies was especially the case for the little-known Pacific Theater, and particularly for the various "Oriental" (Asian) peoples found throughout much of the region. The pressing need for this information produced a heyday for American anthropology (Kiste and Marshall 1999; Kiste and Falgout 1999), fostering new studies relying on a new research method and funded by the Office of Naval Research, called "culture at a distance" and spearheaded by prominent leaders in American anthropology (Mead and Metraux 1953). This method entailed interviews with expatriates and searches of often scant archival, library, and media sources to develop country profiles and "national characters" of places and people involved in the war. That information was also used by anthropologists who worked for the US Office of Strategic Services (OSS) in their training of US military officers expected to assume command of liberated areas (Kiste and Falgout 1999); anthropologists also acted as advisers to the military administration for several internment camps (Guerrier 2007; Starn 1986).

In this "total war," Fujitani (2011) points out, both sides experienced an acute need not only to understand but also to mobilize every available human and material resource. She argues that these material demands produced adjustments in the ways both the United States and Japan managed their national minorities and/or colonial subjects—in order to gain their help to win the war, as well as their support for their possible postwar regional or global hegemony. In response, both sides disavowed racism, or at least made a massive shift over the course of the war from vulgar exclusionary racism to a more polite inclusionary racism[1] (Fujitani 2011). This major change in policy, she reveals, unleashed changes in practice within both nations in egalitarian directions. In addition, this may have contributed to a more in-depth understanding and somewhat less restrictive treatment of some categories of POWs by the United States over time. This change of tactic was of value to US global propaganda efforts, as well.

This article aims to reveal other very important sources of information about our World War II enemies—those connections made "on the ground" that fostered important shifts in US policy and treatment of POWs. Over time, the US military's ethnic group categorizations of POWs became differentiated, stereotypes became more nuanced, prejudices lessened, and treatments relaxed. One very important source of information came from the US military's own direct interactions with POWs. We will see those connections were of great help to the US military in determining the political statuses and treatments of various ethnic groups; ongoing deliberations led to several significant changes over the course of the war. On the mainland United States, this was especially true for Italian POWs. The Territory of Hawai'i and its POW camps were especially significant for Asians—Japanese, Okinawans, Koreans, and Filipinos, and a few others.

Hawai'i's century old practice of importing plantation laborers had produced a very multicultural society with a largely Asian local population. POWs brought to Hawai'i during World War II from the Pacific Theater, then, often shared their ethnic backgrounds with local civilian residents. Interactions between POWs and locals in the Hawai'i community were definitely limited and controlled by the US military; nevertheless, the direct and indirect connections made between them proved very important. They provided the POWs with a great deal of comfort and often incidental, but much appreciated, supplies. Not only did it help the US military better understand those ethnic groups, both in and out of the camps, but it also helped to normalize the military's relationships with them. In the case of Koreans, that exposure led the US military's re-evaluation of, and major changes in, the wartime political status of Koreans in the US military, with Korean citizens and resident aliens (hereafter residents), and also to a more favorable treatment of the Korean prisoner population.

The connections made by POWs with the US military in the camps and residents in the Hawai'i community also provided, in varying ways, opportunities to experience a measure of democracy in action. Of course, those experiences of POWs were not ordinary ones—those experiences were within a wartime context in which they had been imprisoned as enemies. And, at Hawai'i's Honouliuli Camp, some POWs discovered that residents of their own ethnic group had been interned within the very same camp.

Hawai'i's POW Camps

The organization for handling POWs in Hawai'i varied somewhat over time, in order to meet the changing conditions (Hawai'i, Office of the Military Governor [hereafter OMG] n.d.). At first, the POWs were held at the Immigration Station and at Sand Island Detention Camp, until the Honouliuli Camp (also referred to by the military as the Alien Internment Camp) was opened in March 1943. The move was due to limitations of existing space and also the fear of a direct attack by an enemy landing (Hawai'i, OMG n.d.). Early

Table 1
POW Compounds in Hawai'i

Compound Number	Compound Name	Date Opened
1	East Range Schofield	July 1944
2	Kalihi Valley	September 1944
3	Sand Island	September 1944
4	Kaneohe	July 1944
5	Fort Hase	August 1944
6	Honouliuli	March 1943
7	Sand Island	March 1944
8	Honouliuli	December 1944
9	Honouiliuli (same area as 6)	August 1945
10	Hauula	August 1945
11	Hilo	August 1944
12	Kilauea Military Camp	August 1944
13	Waikakaula	August 1945

Source: History of Hawaiian Department, USAFCPA, USAFPOA, USAFMIDPAC, 1945a.

on, the POWs were administered under the Office of the Military Governor (MilGov), with custodial responsibility under the Provost Marshall. From 1944, Hawai'i's POW camps were under the control of the US Navy, and for most of that period under Commander H. K. Howell. Eventually, there were at least 13 POW compounds in Hawai'i, with three at Honouliuli (Table 1).[2]

There were many regularities in the daily life of POWs at camps located throughout the United States, and these were also followed in Hawai'i. Most camps were designed to hold an average of 2,500–3,000 prisoners and followed Geneva Convention rules for overall layout, food, sanitation, and health services, which were to be identical to those for the American armed forces (Krammer 1983). The camps were also run according to guidelines set by the Geneva Convention and with further directives from the US War Department. In Hawai'i, there were regular staff conferences that developed standard operating procedures for camp life (Headquarters Army Port and

Processing POWs at Honouliuli Camp. Photo 111-SC-237776. Here prisoners remove their clothing, which are fumigated and then used for other prisoners that are captured. Everything is taken from the prisoner, except his personal belongings. Signal Corps Photo #CPA-45-8832 (Ellner) (3116) restricted by BPR 4/16/1946, Lot 11886, esmed; National Archives and Records Administration II, College Park, MD.

Service Command [hereafter HAPSC] 1944a, 1944b; Headquarters Prisoner of War Camp [hereafter HPWP] 1944a, 1944b, 1944c, 1944d, 1944e).

Accommodations for POWs were designed to meet only basic needs. In Hawai'i, most lived in small six- to eight-man pyramidal tents, used pit latrines, and took cold-water showers. However, the food and supplies given to them were, in fact, the same as for US soldiers and internees. They were also given standard clothing and other supplies (HAPSC 1944a, 1944b). As for Asian internees, it was determined that they required less food overall, but more rice, and the diet was adjusted accordingly (Hawai'i, OMG n.d.). Also, like the internees, POWs grew their own vegetable gardens to supplement camp rations with items they preferred. At regular intervals, the Swedish vice consulate provided inspections and sent reports to the Japanese Embassy. A Swiss delegation also made a report in late 1944–early 1945 (Cardinaux 1945). Facilities were kept clean. The POWs were disinfected upon their arrival, laundry was done three times per week, and bedsheets were changed every fifteen days (Hawai'i, OMG n.d.).

POWs working in the garden. Photo by R. H. Lodge. Courtesy of Hawai'i's Plantation Village and the Japanese Cultural Center of Hawai'i, Honolulu.

The main motive for bringing POWs to Hawai'i was the acute wartime labor shortage (Allen 1950; Lewis and Mewha 1955). The types and conditions of work appropriate for POWs in Hawai'i were also clearly specified with adherence to the Geneva Convention, and detailed records were kept (HAPSC 1944a). Prisoners should be properly clothed, and marked with PW badges. No POWs should be asked to do military-related work. Officers were exempt from mandatory work detail. Enlisted men were required to do some basic work within the camps, and they could volunteer for other work assignments. However, they were to work for only 8 hours a day, not including transportation. Outside of the compound, they could work 12 hours a day (HAPSC 1944a, 1944b).

Medical treatment was offered at the camps, with required immunizations and monthly inspections. Two hospitals were available—one in the North Sector General Hospital at Schofield Army Barracks and one at Tripler Army Hospital (HAPSC 1944a, 1944b).

Mail service was available, with free postage. POWs were limited to two letters and four postcards from family and friends per month. Packages of approved materials were limited to up to 11 pounds, needed customs declarations, and followed specified wrapping and addressing rules. Of course, the mail was censored (Postal Bulletin 1942; HAPSC 1944a, 1944b).

Recreation and athletics were encouraged (HAPSC 1944a, 1944b). Canteens were operated in each camp. Catholic and Protestant chaplain and church services were provided. Movies were shown once a week. Sports included the American game of baseball, the international sport of soccer, and other competitive sports (HAPSC 1944a, 1944b). And, there was some interaction between POWs of different ethnic backgrounds, and even from different camps. At Sand Island, Italian and Japanese POWs exchanged rice for wheat. Some Italian POWs at Sand Island belonged to the soccer squad; at one point, someone arranged an Olympic Games competition in which the Italians participated (Keefer 1992). Koreans were also known to enjoy the game of soccer, and the local newspaper, the *Honolulu Advertiser*, reported on their competition against the Italians in late November 1945 (Ch'oe 2009). English classes, mostly popular with Korean POWs, were also offered (*Honolulu Advertiser* [hereafter *HA*] 1945).

Reportedly, the Hawai'i camps maintained very good social control, with little discord, practically no homicides (OCMH 1955), and not one suicide (Salzar 1942). There were reports of some POWs who passed notes at work, and of occasional underground campaigns and strikes. Official military reports state that no POWs were ever beaten; however, detention facilities were located at the Immigration Station and at Honouliuli. Commander Howell reported that when POWs occasionally became belligerent about their work, they were given the "cooking treatment"—they were confined and given no food for several days, and their hunger usually drove them back to work (*HA* 1945). Escapes were rare; there were only two or three instances involving Italians. Military Governor General Richardson said these were trivial ones, in which the escapees were quickly apprehended (OCMH 1955). There were very few recorded deaths of POWs at Honouliuli and elsewhere in Hawai'i. Most POWs who were still at Honouliuli at the end of the war were repatriated in 1946—first the Italians and Koreans, then the Japanese (Allen 1950).

Honouliuli's POWs

It is difficult to obtain an accurate accounting of the POWs in Hawai'i and at Honouliuli Camp. With prisoners coming and going, their numbers varied over time. This is further complicated by different methods of reporting, as well as by missing records. Furthermore, some ethnic groups were referred to by different labels during the wartime period (see discussion below). Table 2 shows the approximate numbers according to ethnic group membership.

Table 2
Approximate Numbers of POWs in Hawai'i, by Ethnic Group[4]

Ethnic Group	Number of POWs
Italian (nearly 1/3 of all prisoners)	5,000
Japanese	4,766
Okinawan	3,723
Korean	2,692
Others (Formosan, Southeast Asian, Chinese, Filipino, etc.)	36
Total Number of POWs Received	16,217

Source: History of Hawaiian Department, USAFCPA, USAFPOA, USAFMIDPAC (1945b).

The estimated total number of POWs received in Hawai'i over the course of the war was 16,217 (History of Hawaiian Department 1945b).

The Honouliuli Camp was somewhat unusual in that from the beginning it was specifically designed to hold both internees and POWs.[3] The Camp was originally envisioned to house some 3,000 civilian internees and POWs, with the two main sections of the camp divided by the pre-existing Waiāhole Stream aqueduct. Upon entrance into the gulch, the first and smaller section of the camp housed the internees; the much larger section located at the back of the gulch was for the POWs. Each section of the POW camp was furthermore internally divided into barbed-wire enclosures for various types of occupants and their military status (officers, enlisted, noncombatants) (Hawai'i, OMG n.d.).

Although the ethnic composition of Italian, Japanese, and Okinawan POWs overlapped with internees held at Honouliuli, interaction between them was highly controlled, limited, and rare. However, the Swiss International Red Cross expressed their concern about the close proximity of the POWs at Honouliuli, saying it was detrimental to children in the internment portion of the camp (Cardinaux 1945). At Honouliuli, there are known instances of bilingual Japanese internees who provided needed translations for POWs. Hanako Hashimoto recalled her visits to her husband, Koji, who had worked at the Libby MacNeil Company Laboratory and also as a principal

Table 3
Numbers of POWs at Honouliuli,
Provided for Different Compounds and Dates

Compound Number	Number of POWs	Date Counted
6	1,500	March 1, 1943
	500	January 1, 1945
8	3,000	January 1, 1945 and September 2, 1945
9 (same as 6)	1,000	September 2, 1945

Source: History of Hawaiian Department, USAFCPA, USAFPOA, USAFMIDPAC (1945a).

and teacher at a Japanese language school, and was interned at Honouliuli. While in the camp, Koji Hashimoto was first asked by some of the other internees to teach them English; later the American dentist there asked him to translate for the Japanese POWs. Through his work as a translator, he also received some information about conditions in the POW camp (Hashimoto 2010). The total numbers of POWs at Honouliuli varied over time, for reasons discussed below. Table 3 shows the number of POWs at different compounds in censuses from 1943–1945.

This table suggests that in January and September 1945, the number of actual prisoners held at Honouliuli may have exceeded planned capacity, reaching 4,000 or even more. This expansion over time may have led to some later-arriving POWs being housed near the entrance to the Honouliuli Camp.

Table 4 shows the population of different ethnic groups and in which compounds they were located at Honouliuli at different points in time when censuses were conducted.[5]

Table 4
Dates and Ethnic Compositions of POW Compounds at Honouliuli[6]

Compound Number	Date Counted	Number of POWs	Ethnic Group
6	1943	250	Italian
		200	Korean
	1945	87	Italian
8	January 1945	320	Japanese
		752	Korean
		15	Formosan
	September 1945	337	Japanese
		2,426	Okinawan
		15	Formosan
9 (same as 6)	September 1945	6	Italian
		154	Korean
		1,035	Okinawan

Source: History of Hawaiian Department, USAFCPA, USAFPOA, USAFMIDPAC (1945a).

Taking these numbers at face value, the largest group of POWs at the Honouliuli Camp over time was Okinawans; the Korean POWs were next in size. The number of Japanese who were held at the camp remains unclear, for reasons discussed below. Italians and especially Formosans (now called Taiwanese) held at Honouliuli were smaller groups.

The military statuses of POWs at Honouliuli were similar to the entire population of POWs held in Hawai'i as a whole. Relatively few POWs at Honouliuli were officers (only a few Japanese and Italians, at less than 1 percent), and the camp also had slightly fewer enlisted men than at other camps in Hawai'i (mostly Japanese and Italians, at about 7 percent). The overwhelming majority of POWs were noncombatants (all categories of POWs, especially the Okinawans and Koreans, at about 92 percent) (Statistical Data Report 1945).

Initially, administrative orders prohibited any visitors to POW camps, except on official business and even then only with official clearance from the director of intelligence, arrangements made with the commanding officer for each visit, and the completion of official forms (HAPSC 1944a). Irma Loo, then a young girl of Chinese ancestry who lived on a truck farm in the Honouliuli area, remembers a "concentration camp" located nearby, but recalls "it was so secure, you couldn't even get into the road going into the place. It's inside a sugarcane field.... [Y]ou couldn't see it, because there was sugarcane all around it" (Loo, Irma 2010). This was likely the nearby Honouliuli Camp, although she and her older brother, Calvin Loo, knew it as Kunia Camp. Calvin Loo recalled occasionally seeing Military Police near the entrance to the road that led to the camp, but he never saw the camp itself. Calvin Loo did visit the Schofield POW Camp on one occasion, however. While working for the US Air Force at the age of 16, he accompanied a corporal who visited the Japanese POWs there. He recalls the area surrounded by a big fence that was further patrolled by guards; the POWs were located at the fence. The corporal had befriended one of the Japanese POWs, and he delivered cigarettes and other small items to him that day (Loo, Calvin 2010).

Unlike the internees at Honouliuli, non-Japanese POWs were allowed outside the camp, mainly for work on various projects (Lewis and Mewha 1955). Initially, the POW compounds were divided into two main categories—A (trustworthy) and B (untrustworthy)—and the number of guards stationed varied according to their perceived security risk (Lewis and Mewha 1955). However, security concerns over all enemy prisoners decreased over time.

Hawaiʻi's military governor, General Robert C. Richardson, stated that the ratio of guards to prisoners decreased over the course of the war—with POWs going from being closely guarded to more relaxed. At Schofield Barracks later in the war, prisoners were put on the honor system—still behind barbed wire, but without guards (OCMH 1955).

Also later in the war, POW fraternization with locals of the same ethnicity, especially for Okinawans and Koreans, increased dramatically. This became known as a "local fraternization problem," and eventually led the military to set up a Visitors Bureau to help regulate visits to POWs in the camps (OCMH 1955) (see discussion below).

Despite these regularities found in Hawaiʻi's POW camps, conditions were varied according to prisoner ethnic differences and political statuses. We will now examine the types and degrees of connections these various groups of POWs made and how those impacted their treatment by the US military over the wartime period.

Making Connections: Transnational, National, and Local

The Atlantic Theater

The Italians ("The Fascists")

The largest ethnic group of POWs to arrive in Hawaiʻi were from the Atlantic Theater—they were Italians, with the first 1,000 arriving in July 1944 (Hawaiʻi, OMG n.d.; Lewis and Mewha 1955), and eventually reaching approximately 5,000 (Table 2). However, as Table 4 reveals, their numbers were relatively small at the Honouliuli Camp.

The Italians had been picked up in the 1943 surrender with Rommel in various parts of North Africa (particularly Egypt, Libya, and Tunisia). Other Allied victories in Sicily and other parts of southern Italy had resulted in more than 500,000 Italian POWs (Keefer 1992; Calamandrei 2001). Shortages of space and supplies within the war zone and in British camps led to some 50,000 Italian POWs being eventually transported to the United States. Most arrived by ship, within a limited six-month period, usually two to three months after their capture in 1943, from the summer until the end of the year. With most captured before the overthrow of Mussolini, they were initially regarded as "fascists" and designated as "enemy aliens," and they were carefully guarded and spread over 27 camps in 23 states in the United States (Keefer 1992).

Once in US mainland camps, some Italian POWs worked inside the camps on routine maintenance assignments, or later outside the camps in the private sector as farmers, cowboys, cooks, carpenters, and engineers (Keefer 1992). In March 1944, the US government established Italian Service Units (ISUs), and those that volunteered earned them the status of "collaborators" that granted them additional privileges outside the camps (Keefer 1992). Outside the camps, they found Italians to be the largest foreign born population in the United States, especially on the northeastern coast and in California (Keefer 1992). In connecting with Italians outside the camp, some of those Italian POWs would find a few sympathetic friends, and occasionally romantic partners or even wives in unauthorized marriages. Based on those wartime connections made, some of the POWs decided to return to the United States in the postwar period (Calamandrei 2001; Keefer 1992).

Of the large number of Italian POWs found on the US mainland, some 5,000 were later sent from various mainland camps to several ports on the West Coast and then on to Hawai'i beginning in the summer of 1944 (Allen 1950; Keefer 1992; OCMH 1955; Lewis and Mewha 1955). Some resented the move to Hawai'i, feeling it was a deportation because they had refused to cooperate with the US military. In fact, some of those sent to Hawai'i early on had indeed been labeled "non-collaborators," and most still pledged allegiance to the Italian Fascist Republic (Cardinaux 1945). Although most non-collaborative officers had been sent to the POW camp located at Hereford, Texas (Calamandrei 2001), a few officers were among those Italians sent to Hawai'i. Those officers, in particular, were said to have an intransigent attitude, to be unmovable, uncooperative, and very influential over the enlisted men (Cardinaux 1945). Some of the Italian POWs wrote booklets on the wonders of fascism; the guards waited until the booklets were finished so that they could tell which prisoners had been involved (HA 1945). In fact, compound commanders submitted lists of names of those believed to be fascists to the camp commanders. Howell indicated that the pro-Nazi Italian fascists were the most difficult to control, stating "Their fascism is almost an insanity" (HA 1945); despite punishment, they gave only the fascist salute. In addition, the earlier Italian non-collaboratives had to be separated from the later Italian Service Unit (ISU) collaboratives that followed (HPWC 1944c).

Although there were many incidents when Italian POWs in Hawai'i refused to work, engaged in work slowdowns, or committed minor acts of sabotage (Allen 1950) because they considered their assignments to be connected to the war effort, a visiting Swiss delegation found most of their complaints to be unjustified (Cardinaux 1945). Eventually, most of the Italian enlisted men became willing workers in Hawai'i, especially on agricultural projects or on the maintenance of the post, and this helped to improve relations. One of the principal places where Italians worked was at 'Iolani Palace (Allen 1950), which during the war served as the temporary headquarters for MilGov Hawai'i. Other Italian POWs helped to replant 5,000 acres of burned or damaged forest land used as firing ranges or maneuver grounds; others removed bomb shelters (Allen 1950). In September 1945, Howell told *Honolulu Advertiser* reporters that the Italian POWs, along with the Koreans, were the most easily managed and cleanest of all. However, some of the Italian POWs were considered dangerous (Allen 1950), including one who claimed to have been one of Mussolini's guards (*HA* 1945).

The Italian camps in Hawai'i were reported to be excellent, with all the facilities available to POWs on the mainland, and in some ways the material conditions were actually better (Cardinaux 1945). The Italian POWs in Hawai'i, although recognized to present some difficulties for the US military, were also clearly admired by them. Commander Howell told the newspaper reporters, "[E]very meal the Italians prepare is a banquet." He regarded them as articulate and stated that they provided their own entertainment "on a high plane," citing their radio broadcasts and their enjoyment of classical phonographic records (provided by the International Red Cross) (*HA* 1945). Clearly, they were generally thought to be civilized, some were considered to be very well-educated, and a few were judged artistic. As on the US mainland, there were several Italian POWs who were noted artists in Hawai'i. Frequently mentioned is Alfredo Giusti, a former landscape architect from Buenos Aires, who had been told to return to Italy when the war began, and eventually became a POW at Sand Island. Giusti is noted for his sculptures "Bathing Beauty" and "Hula Maids" that bore the faces of his Italian and Hawaiian girlfriends, which he "dedicated to give hope to those without hope" (*HA* 1945). Another noted work is the Mother Cabrini Chapel at Wheeler Air Force Base, designed and built by Astori Rebate of Venice on his off-duty hours on Sundays during 1944 and 1945 (Keefer 1992; *HA* 1946.) After the end of the war, the chapel was occupied by Japanese POWs (*HA* 1946).

Despite the relatively favorable conditions for Italians in Hawai'i's POW camps, they were noted for their very low morale (Cardinaux 1945). The relationships between Italian POWs and the local Italian community did not form as they had on the mainland. Indeed, most of the local Italians had been targeted for internment, with some housed at Honouliuli. Furthermore, some of the Italian POWs had been held as prisoners for nearly four years. Throughout their stay in the United States and then even farther away from home in Hawai'i, they felt isolated and abandoned. They had been given very little information about the progress of the war or even news of their families. In addition, there was very little early repatriation of Italian POWs, even for those who were eligible. At the end of the war, some of the Italian POWs did express their appreciation for their good treatment while in Hawai'i's camps (Cardinaux 1945). However, there are no recorded instances of Italian POWs returning to live in Hawai'i after the war, as was often the case on the US mainland.

The Pacific Theater

Most of the POWs sent to Hawai'i were captured in the Pacific Theater—a combination of Japanese, Okinawans, Koreans, Filipinos, and a few others. Most were picked up after late 1943 from several locations in nearby Micronesia. With thousands of small islands in this crucial region, only a few, but very notable, land battles were fought on the edges of the region—in the Gilberts (now called Kiribati), especially in Tarawa and Makin; in some of the Japanese-held colonial possessions (Nany'ō) in atolls in the Marshall Islands on the eastern edge of the region; plus some on the larger continental areas to the western and northern areas close to Japan itself, notably in Saipan in the Marianas and in Palau (Morison 1968a, 1968b; Poyer, Falgout, and Carucci 2001; Falgout, Poyer, and Carucci 2009). It was from these land battles—especially ones in the Gilberts/Kiribati and in Saipan—that Japanese military and Korean and Okinawan noncombatant laborers and even some civilians were picked up and brought to Hawai'i as POWs.

The Japanese ("The Enemy")

Although all POWs held by the United States during World War II were technically considered to be enemies, the bombing of Pearl Harbor resulted in the ethnic Japanese being considered "the enemy" in the Pacific Theater, by both the US military and many members of the local population in Hawai'i. Over the course of the war, approximately 1.5 million Japanese became POWs, housed in camps located in Russia, China, Britain, and the United States. Far fewer Japanese sailors and soldiers were held in the United States than other groups of POWs (Lewis and Mewha 1955)—only about 5,424 in total, due in part to the Japanese preference for death to surrender and the deep shame felt by those captured in battle (Krammer 1983). Indeed, many Japanese prisoners refused to file their names with the International Red Cross Prisoner Information Bureau or to fill out the required postal card to let their families know of their safety; they preferred to let their families think them dead rather than dishonored by surrender. This was combined with some fear of treachery of Japanese troops by American soldiers, leading to their reluctance to take them as prisoners (Krammer 1983; Lewis and Mewha 1955). Early in the war, only dozens of Japanese were captured as compared to the thousands who were killed. The numbers of captured increased, however, after the campaign in the Philippines during October 1944, less than a year before the war's end (Krammer 1983; Lewis and Mewha 1955). In addition, the United States preferred to turn Japanese prisoners over to its Allies, particularly to Australia, promising to share costs and to assume the responsibility for their final disposal after the war. Those brought to the United States, then, were only those who were designated for special interrogation or whose capture was from a region closer to the United States than to Australia or New Zealand (Krammer 1983).

Angel Island in San Francisco Bay, California, is usually thought of as the main entry and temporary transit center for incoming Japanese captives (see Krammer 1983). From there, some were sent for further interrogation at a few other US mainland camps. Interrogation techniques were developed from observed patterns in interviews with Japanese prisoners, conducted by American intelligence officers, many of whom were Japanese American specialists from the army's Military Intelligence Service (MIS) Language School. Anthropological analyses of Japanese national character also drew upon and used that knowledge (Benedict 1946; Krammer 1983). Their small numbers were then spread across various mainland camps. The largest concentration, some 3,000, was at Camp McCoy, Wisconsin (Krammer 1983).

Largely unreported, however, were the more than 4,700 Japanese POWs who were first sent to Hawai'i (see Table 2) from the Pacific Theater, before being sent on to the mainland United States. After the capture of Sakamaki on December 7, 1941, the next Japanese captives to arrive in Hawai'i were 37 sailors from the carrier *A. Kaji*, picked up after the Battle of Midway in June 1942 (OCMH 1955). Most were sent from the battles of Tarawa and Makin in the Gilberts/Kiribati in 1944 (OCMH 1955); others were from Iwo Jima, Okinawa, Guam, and other Pacific Island battlefields (*Honolulu Star-Bulletin* [hereafter *HSB*] 1946). Over time, Japanese POWs would become the second largest group sent to Hawai'i (Table 2), although their numbers held at the Honouliuli Camp were relatively small (Table 4).

Like those sent to the mainland US camps, Japanese POWs in Hawai'i reportedly felt disgraced (Office of the Chief of Military History, 1955). Strongly influenced by their own leaders, they were labeled as "untrustworthy" by the US military (Lewis and Mewha 1955). Among them, there was tension between those who had been in the army vs. the navy, and between those who had been wounded and others who had not. The *Honolulu Star-Bulletin* reported the wounded "wear their scars as badges of distinction—evidence that they did not give up without a fight" (1947). In Hawai'i camps, the Japanese POW section was separated from the Italians and the Koreans; it was itself internally divided according to military rank—officers, enlisted, noncombatants. Most Japanese POWs sent to Hawai'i were evacuated to the US mainland after their clearance. By the end of the war in September 1945, only 342 remained in Hawai'i, with most housed at Honouliuli Camp (see Table 4).

As the war's end neared, US Secretary of War Henry Stimson launched a six-month democracy indoctrination project for 205 potential Japanese POW converts at three "re-orientation centers" on the mainland. This was in violation of the Geneva Convention (Krammer 1983). This brush with democracy is not known to have occurred for Japanese POWs in Hawai'i, however.

The Japanese POWs in Hawai'i, as "untrustworthy" sorts, were not granted permission to work outside the camps; however, they had occasional visits in the camps from friends (see Loo, Calvin 2010), and they were sometimes transported to other camps for work details. Thomas Shiroma, of Okinawan descent and originally from the Big Island of Hawai'i, enlisted in the US Army after the war ended, at the beginning of 1946. Based on his knowledge of Japanese language, the US military assigned him to supervise 16 of the Japanese POWs then housed at Sand Island to work at Ft. Shafter. Shiroma remembers:

> So they [the Japanese POWs] approach me and say, "Eh, you Japanese?" I say, "Yeah." "You know what, give us rice, we do whatever you want." Okay, I do it. I knew the cooks. Get rice? [The Japanese POWs] tell me, "You know what, don't worry." I ask, "How many buckets, or how many cans, how many rice do you need every day?" And, then they [say], "Please two. Two buckets." And, "No problem," I tell them. All of them my friends anyway. So long you give them rice, they do whatever you want. (2011)

While working with the Japanese POWs, Shiroma said he reflected on what it must have been like to be in that position and he took care to not abuse his wards (Shiroma 2011). The cordial relations he established with them apparently persisted after the war. Shiroma tells a story of a postwar trip to Okinawa, when a cancelled leg of his flight stranded him in Tokyo.

> So, since it was cancelled, I might as well walk around. I might as well visit Tokyo, see what get. Then, one guy point at me, "Eh, you Shiroma?" "Yeah," I tell, "How I know you?" "I was one of your prisoners, in Honolulu." I tell him, "Really? Wow. Come, we go lunch, I take you lunch. Tell me the story." They had a misery was really hard, you know. No job, no money. They took a long time before the recovery of Japan, before people get job and money. But he told me the hardship they went through. Then later on, I feel kind of sorry for him, all what he went through. But, that's war. See? And you have a defeated country, and you meet a guy like that, what they went through? You know, you got a lot of pity. You know you were angry at one time, but when you hear that kind of story, you get a little compassion. (2011)

The Okinawans ("Enemy Japanese," or What?)

Possibly the third largest group of POWs in Hawai'i, and the largest group held at Honouliuli, was Okinawans. This is somewhat difficult to determine, however, due to the US military's confusion regarding their ethnicity as well as their political status.

Okinawan history is itself complex, and therefore surrounds the identity of its people with a measure of ambiguity. The ancient settlement and subsequent history and culture of the Ryūkyū Islands of Okinawa included ties to both China and Japan. However, Okinawa became an official prefecture of Japan in 1879.

Perhaps for this reason, then, Okinawan residents in Hawai'i were lumped by the US military into the category of "Japanese." However, as Gwenfread Allen (1950) points out, neither the local Japanese nor Okinawans in Hawai'i thought of them as Japanese. Those who had been picked up for questioning clearly identified themselves as "Okinawan." And, the Okinawans' objection to this misidentification as "Japanese" was a factor in the Office of Strategic Services (OSS) in Honolulu's ability to recruit a large group of them during the war. Holding responsibility for analysis of the islands and its inhabitants to the west, one of this office's major wartime projects was a detailed study of Okinawa. Later, Okinawans in Hawai'i also provided significant support for American landing forces in the Battle of Okinawa (Allen 1950).

It is possible that some of the early Okinawan POWs sent to Hawai'i were also designated by the US military as "Japanese." As the end of the war neared, however, POWs who were by then labeled as "Okinawan" came to Hawai'i and to Honouliuli in large numbers. They first appeared in Hawai'i under this designation in the September 1945 survey (see Tables 2 and 4). Many were sent to Hawai'i following the Battle of Saipan that ended in the summer of 1944 after a period of incarceration in Saipan within slum-like barracks quickly hammered together from wartime debris by the US Navy, called Camp Susupe (Embree 1946). In fact, of the approximately 13,500 "Japanese" survivors of the Battle of Saipan, the majority were actually former civilian sugar plantation laborers of Okinawan ancestry; however, some may also have been young Okinawan boys who had been recruited or otherwise pressed into Japanese military service. Reportedly, almost half of the Japanese and Okinawans held at Camp Susupe were under the age of 16 (Meller 1999). Another camp, smaller and with somewhat better conditions, was later established on nearby Tinian, named Camp Churro (Embree 1946). In addition, other Okinawan POWs may have been sent directly to Hawai'i from the Battle of Okinawa that ended in mid-June 1945 (US Army Forces 1944–1945 and 9/1946b). Military Governor Richardson commented particularly on the young Okinawan boys, ages 14 and 15 years old, housed in Hawai'i's POW camps, saying they were "pathetic in lack of comprehension of what they were supposed to do and why they were classed as POWs" (OCMH 1955).

Those labeled as Okinawan POWs in Hawai'i were clearly not favored by the American military; in fact, there was a significant amount of prejudice against their traditional customs and behavior. Commander Howell described the Okinawan food as "miserable," always containing lots of onions and garlic, and lamented that they were not as neat or as clean as the Japanese or Italian POWs. He also found them to be stubborn, and disloyal to each other; furthermore, he stated that most of them were illiterate in Japanese (*HA* 1945).

The Okinawan POWs had the greatest amount of contact with the local Hawai'i population. Reportedly, nearly all of them had relatives in the islands. This was the source of the US military's biggest "local fraternization problem." In a *Honolulu Advertiser* article dated September 26, 1945, Commander Howell discussed his reluctance to discontinue this fraternization, so instead he halted the Okinawan POWs' work on Thomas Square and at Punahou School. Howell reported, "Locals came in carloads, with kids, bearing cigarettes, candy, fruit, money, etc." Howell said, "It's just like Christmas." Reviewing wartime records in her book *Hawaii's War Years*, Gwenfread Allen wrote:

Many were seeking information concerning other relatives and friends in the Orient of whom they heard nothing since before the war. So disruptive to the work and so full of potentialities for escape and other difficulties were these contacts that the Okinawans were withdrawn from Thomas Square. Thereafter, most work outside of military reservations was entrusted to Italians, as they had few countrymen in Hawaii. (1950:221–222)

In an attempt to better handle the fraternization problem, the military's Visitors Bureau directed visits by locals within the POW camps. The local response was robust; the military received some 380 applications on the very first day. They thronged to the Immigration Station before daylight, and slept on the grass while waiting in line. It became necessary for the military to check licenses, so other visitors would have a chance. It also became necessary to place one guard for every ten men, and to limit visits to two per month (*HA* 1945). While these measures apparently helped the military to control the problem, there were also a number of infractions. Those Okinawan POWs who exceeded the limit on visitations via their aiding and abetting the visitors were penalized—the military took away two-thirds of their monthly allowance, confined them, and put them on a bread-and-water diet for two weeks. Even with these new measures in place, one Okinawan prisoner was recorded as having numerous offenses, and twenty-two others had five convictions each (*HA* 1945).

This connection to local Okinawans in Hawai'i proved very significant for the POWs. Although the US military did occasionally question their political status as "enemy aliens" but in the end did not modify it, still by the end of the war Commander Howell reported that most Okinawan POWs wanted to remain in Hawai'i. However, US immigration law forbade them to do so (*HA* 1945).

The Koreans ("Enemy Aliens," "Friendly Aliens," or What?)
Korea also had a complex history of relations with Japan, leading to some US military confusion about their identity and political status during World War II. Japan had declared the region as a protectorate in 1905, and the Japan-Korea Annexation Treaty ceding all rights to the Emperor of Japan was signed in 1910.

As the largest Japanese colonial possession, Korea held great potential for civilian and military labor. Beginning in 1938, the Japanese Army allowed small numbers of carefully screened and trained Koreans to volunteer for duty.

Efforts were accelerated during the war, and in 1943 Korean men were subject to mass conscription. For that largely uneducated and unskilled population, they were assigned primarily as laborers in noncombatant units and some as soldiers. The estimated total of Koreans serving in the Japanese military was more than 214,000, which meant they played an extremely large role in the Japanese war effort (Fujitani 2011).

Summarizing results from other researchers as well as her own oral interviews with Korean veterans of the war, Fujitani (2011) writes:

> Korean attitudes toward Japanese military service cannot be reduced to any simple categorization, such as the conventional nationalist one that seeks to place every individual into the neat rubrics of collaborator or resister, with all but a few Koreans emerging as essentially resistant to Japanese rule. (243)

While some Korean veterans spoke of tremendous pressure, others were more ambiguous and uncertain about their involvement in the Japanese military, and still others felt strong patriotism toward the Japanese. Nevertheless, in their official testimonies and informal conversations with the US military, most Korean POWs expressed their dislike of Japan, saying they were either coerced or enticed into their service (Fujitani 2011).

Many Koreans held as POWs in US mainland camps stated that they felt their allegiance was more to Korea than to Japan, and they continued to voice their strong desire for independence. This position was strongly reinforced by the Korean community in America, and especially by some Korean societies in Hawai'i (US Army Forces 1944–1945 and 9/1946a) (see discussion below). The US military clearly understood this desire although they continued to struggle to define the political status of Koreans in the United States and its territories—as Korean members of the US military, as Korean resident aliens, and as Korean POWs.

From the very beginning of the war, the United States signaled a positive position regarding the Koreans in the military. Attorney General Francis Biddle and the Department of Justice made a distinction between the citizens vs. the subjects of the enemy nations of Germany, Italy, or Japan. In January 1942, Biddle declared those Austrians, Austro-Hungarians, and Koreans who had registered as native citizens under the Alien Registration Act of 1940 were exempt from restrictions, as long as they had not since that time voluntarily become a citizen or subject of the mother country's colonizing state. This stopped short of granting them "friendly alien" status, however

(Kim 2007). Reports of continued harassment of Koreans in the US military also resulted in Secretary of War Stimson issuing further instructions to all field commanders in May 1942. Added to the earlier Department of Justice ruling, he instructed that soldiers of Korean parentage and Korean nationals enlisted or inducted into the US Army were to be treated in the same manner as soldiers whose parents were from nations friendly to the United States (War Department 1942).

Although the War Department's instructions had clarified the status of Koreans in the US military, it remained somewhat unclear for Korean residents on the US mainland and in Hawai'i. However, in Hawai'i, no Koreans had been interned. The practice of treating local Koreans as "friendly aliens," exempt from some minor restrictions (possession of cameras or shortwave radios, or from work on the waterfront), and on that basis considering individual cases on their own merits, was noted (Hawai'i, Office of Strategic Services [hereafter OSS] 1943; B. 1942). However, local Koreans remained as "enemy aliens" in some regards—they were subject to an early curfew law; they were restricted from the possession of explosives, arms, ammunition, radio transmitting; and they had to obtain a special permit to purchase liquor, drugs, and medical supplies. A pressing need for a more definite policy was recognized by both the US military and the local population.

For the most part, Korean residents in Hawai'i, as on the US mainland, were very careful to abide by those restrictions. However, Hawai'i provided two important court cases for local Koreans who violated the curfew law—cases that became prominent in continued local and national deliberations over Korean residents' wartime status. One case was eventually considered at the highest levels of government and aided in the wartime redesignation of resident Koreans.

The first case was heard in January 1943—that of Ko Duck Wha (nee Kang Won Do), a citizen of Korea who came to Hawai'i in 1904 when Korea was an independent country, on a Korean passport as a plantation laborer (Wha 1943). Although the case received relatively little local press coverage, it attracted considerable protest from the local Korean community in Hawai'i, and it was accompanied by appeals to Secretary of War Stimson for a clarification of Korean status (Kim 2007). Y. K. Kim of the United Korean Committee in America located in Honolulu and editor of the *National Herald Pacific Weekly* wrote to Roosevelt (Kim 1943), asking him to modify or amend the blackout law exempting Koreans living in Hawai'i from being charged as enemy aliens.

The second case in March 1943 was that of Syung Woon Sohn, who came to Hawai'i in 1905 as a citizen of Korea, again some five to six years before Japan seized Korea, who was arrested on curfew violation (*HSB* 1943b). The military provost court ruled against Sohn, imposing and then suspending a $10 payment. The judge argued that Attorney General Biddle's ruling on Koreans in the United States was not applicable in Hawai'i because the territory was under the War Department and martial law (Kim 1943). This ruling triggered a ripple of protests from both the local Koreans and the wider community in Hawai'i and led to an appeal of the case (Hawai'i, OSS 1943).

Honolulu newspapers, the *Honolulu Advertiser* and the *Honolulu Star-Bulletin*, began an urgent call for the reclassification of resident Koreans. The *Star-Bulletin* reported it was "time to correct an injustice" (1943a). The *Star-Bulletin* argued, "Here is a situation which Congress, if necessary, should move to change. Here is an injustice being visited on a people who, suffering for more than 30 years under the harsh Japanese yoke, have never given up faith and hope of eventual freedom" (1943a).

Nodi Sohn, the wife of Syung Woon Sohn, wired Syngman Rhee (Hawai'i, OSS 1943), first president of the Korean Provisional Government (in exile) and chairman of the Korean Commission in Washington, DC, who used Hawai'i as his home base during the war (Ch'oe 2007). Rhee, in turn, telegraphed his comments about the case to Hawai'i's governor, Ingram Stainback, and Honolulu's tax collector, William Borthwick. Although the case had by then quieted down in Hawai'i, this would be the beginning of repercussions being heard in Washington (Hawai'i, OSS 1943). Hawai'i's Sohn case would be used as a "test case," making resident Korean status a capital issue (Hawai'i, OSS 1943; Richardson 1943).

Other influential people who were visiting in Washington, DC or permanently located on the US mainland helped to advance the cause. Hung Wai Ching, the head of the University YMCA and the head of the morale committee of the Office of the Military Governor of Hawai'i, while on a trip to Washington, DC was received at the White House. It was believed by some that he may have influenced Mrs. Roosevelt "in stirring up the question of the 'enemy alien' status of the Koreans" (Hawai'i, OSS 1943). Senator Guy Gillette also made an appeal to President Roosevelt "to correct a United States Provost Court ruling in Hawai'i that Koreans are subject to consideration as enemy aliens" (Gillette 1943; *HSB* 1943b).

An article in the *Honolulu Star-Bulletin* called upon Franklin D. Roosevelt to correct the ruling on Koreans residing in the United States (1943b). Kilsoo Haan, representative of the Korean National Federation Front, Sino-Korean Peoples' League, wrote to Roosevelt as well, pointing out the contradiction with the earlier ruling by the Alien Registration Bureau that had changed resident Korean status to "friendly aliens" (Haan 1943). Both Rhee (1943) and Roosevelt (1943) next wrote to Secretary of War Stimson, asking that he give consideration to the matter.

The avalanche of appeals for a more positive reconsideration of the status of Korean residents in Hawai'i drew a strong reaction from MilGov in Hawai'i. As the end of May 1943 neared, the status of Koreans residing in Hawai'i was placed in Military Governor General Delos Emmons's hands (*HSB* 1943c), who ruled that Koreans in Hawai'i would remain as "enemy aliens" (*HSB* 1943d). General Robert Richardson, who replaced Emmons, sent a letter to Stimson providing a long list of justifications for Koreans to remain classified as such. Among the many reasons given in his letter was his concern that the Okinawans and Formosans (Taiwanese), who also had an unwilling association with Japan, might also petition to become friendly aliens if Koreans led the way (Richardson 1943).

All of these efforts, originating in Hawai'i and with the support of others on the US mainland, had the desired effect of reevaluating the status of resident Koreans in Hawai'i. By July 1943, Governor Ingram Stainback stated that the category "enemy alien" did not include any Koreans, and he lifted the restrictions on Koreans from purchasing drugs or photographic supplies (*HSB* 1943e). By December, the blackout and curfew restrictions as previously applied to local Koreans, which had come to symbolize Korean enemy-alien status itself, were lifted (General Orders No. 45) (Kim 2007). Six months later, on May 6, 1944, resident Koreans in Hawai'i were officially recognized as "friendly aliens" under General Orders No. 59 (Kim 2007).

The question of wartime political status still remained for Korean POWs, however. Those Koreans who were sent to Hawai'i as prisoners of war were primarily noncombatant laborers from various Pacific Islands—from the islands of Makin and Tarawa in the Gilberts/Kiribati beginning in late 1943, even more from Guam and Saipan in the Marianas in 1944, as well as from other islands in Micronesia (Ch'oe 2009). In Saipan, some 1,350 had been held at a small compound adjoining, but separated by barbed wire from, the Japanese/Okinawan one at Camp Susupe (Meller 1999; Russell 1983).

Korean POWs in Saipan were tended to by the Reverend Noah K. Cho, a minister of St. Luke's Korean Mission in Honolulu. Reverend Cho, a native of Korea and son of a Korean Army sergeant and grandson of a colonel, having served for 14 years as church vicar in Honolulu, was one of three Koreans invited by Admiral Nimitz to accompany the 2nd and 4th Marine Divisions. Cho was with the US Marines as they hit the beach in Saipan on June 15, 1944. At first, the Koreans feared the Americans, but Rev. Cho comforted those in the camp, telling them the Americans were their friends and wanted to make them free. At the camp, he became a "virtual mayor" of the native Korean community. He helped the hundreds of wounded, sick, and starving in prison compounds, most of whom had been workers for the Japanese Navy. He stayed with the Koreans in the camp in Saipan for 53 days (Lucas 1945); later, some of them were transferred to camps in Hawai'i.

Also brought to Hawai'i and held at Honouliuli were three Korean fishermen, picked up by a US submarine off of the southern coast of Korea in April 1945 and brought to Pearl Harbor for interrogation. Shortly after the end of the war, three Korean college draftees were also sent to Honouliuli; they had been conscripted into the Japanese Military Army while enrolled in colleges in Japan (Ch'oe 2009).

But what exactly was the wartime political status of Korean POWs? Throughout the wartime period, this topic received much discussion and debate among the US government and various military officials, both at the national and local Hawai'i levels.

In many ways, the Korean POWs in Hawai'i seemed to the US military to be decidedly different than other POWs. As was reported for Korean POWs in US mainland camps (Krammer 1983), many who arrived in Hawai'i strongly objected when they were termed by the American military as "Japanese" and then had their names reported to Japan (Cardinaux 1945). Like many of their counterparts in the US military and in the civilian community, many Korean POWs in Hawai'i professed strong anti-Japanese and strong pro-American sentiments. They clearly maintained that their country had been invaded by Japan. The Swiss International Red Cross' 1943–1944 report for Korean POWs in Hawai'i stated, "They show at all times great respect and devotion for the American officers with whom they come into contact, and the American Flag, as a sign of faith and friendship, flies in the camps" (Cardinaux 1945).

Those Korean POWs sent to the Honouliuli Camp were invited to a meeting with Colonel Howell, who expressed his sympathy with them (Ch'oe 2009). At Honouliuli, the Korean POWs were separated from the compounds of the Japanese and the Italians (who were sometimes referred to as the "whites") by a barbed-wire fence. Reportedly, the Korean compound was of a lower standard than for Italians; however, there were no complaints. Indeed, their morale was reported to be excellent, with their "willingness to cooperate apparent everywhere" (Cardinaux 1945). The exception was for the two camps located on the Big Island of Hawai'i that had proven too small for the numbers of POWs held there (Cardinaux 1945).

Korean POWs in the Hawai'i camps also engaged in a variety of political activities. They built a stage in the camp from scrap lumber, which they used in occasional plays and nationalistic political campaigns (*HA* 1945). They developed their own provincial and country associations based on clan lineages; although these displayed some factional strife, they also helped to forge a measure of unity among them. They also developed a political club, Han Chu Dang, one with reported democratic tendencies (Ch'oe 2009). Another organization, the Kanshu (Korean Eagle) Party, was formed to "repay at least in some slight measure the favors of our benefactors, the UNITED STATES ... and, the formation ... of a movement for the independence of our native land" (US Army Forces 1944–1945 and 9/1946b). Howell also encouraged the development of a program of "self-reliance and self-governance toward building a democratic country" (Ch'oe 2009). A handwritten and mimeographed Korean-language newsletter, *Chayu Han'in-bo* (Free Press for Liberated Korea) was also produced by the three former Korean agents in the Office of Strategic Services (OSS); in addition to providing world news translated from English into Korean, this newsletter also attempted to instill the ideas of independence and freedom. However, the newsletter was apparently little read (Ch'oe 2009).

Given their various nationalistic efforts, the United States had decided early in the war that the Korean POWs should be given the opportunity to do their part during the war for the liberation of their country. Korean POWs clearly expected to be given an opportunity to work to win the war against Japan.[7] By early 1945, issues were being raised about the establishment of Korean Service Units (KSUs) and also the possible removal of the PW designation from their clothing (Taylor 1945). In fact, the visiting Swiss delegation had recommended switching the Italian and Korean work assignments (Cardinaux 1945), and the Korean POWs even mounted a demonstration asking to be formed into KSUs. Their request was denied, however, due to the additional administrative overhead it would have required, as well as the military's fear of adverse publicity for "pampering" prisoners of war (as it had for the creation of ISUs on the US mainland) (US Army Forces 1944–1945 and 9/1946a).

The Korean POWs in Hawai'i also engaged in considerable fraternization with the locals who had friends and family back in Korea, although on a lesser scale than did the Okinawan POWs. They talked to resident Koreans when they were sent to work in public areas. The US military also approved of requests from Y. K. Kim for local Korean community members to send Christmas gifts (of approved types and after a thorough inspection) to the Korean POWs, in order to convey their "aloha" (Goldsmith 1943). In addition, the Korean POWs were often visited in the camps by various Christian church groups. As for the Okinawan POWs, those visits eventually came under the control of the Visitors Bureau.

Clearly, the very pro-American stance and generally cooperative attitude of Korean POWs in Hawai'i resulted in them being favored by the American military. But, despite their favored status, the Korean POWs in Hawai'i remained as "enemy aliens" and were held as POWs for the duration of the war. Indeed, they were so favored that most were retained in Hawai'i for use as critically needed labor for the duration of the war, a situation the military deemed "highly desirable." They were transferred to mainland POW camps only upon specific direction of headquarters in Hawai'i (War Department 1942).

The Filipinos ("Allies"?)

The Philippines was an overseas territory of the United States at the outbreak of World War II, with control transferred from Spain at the end of the Spanish-American War in 1898. Civil government was instituted in 1901, commonwealth status had been granted in 1935, and complete independence from the United States was planned for 1946. This was interrupted by the Japanese occupation during World War II, however.

Although Philippine nationals were considered to be US allies, four were picked up in the islands during the war and brought to Hawai'i, and were placed in the Honouliuli POW camp. For all of these rather unlikely POWs, the US military in Hawai'i seemed rather unsure about how to either officially classify or handle them.

Korean POWs in Hawai'i commemorate the death of President Franklin D. Roosevelt. Photo SC 207920. Korean national anthem is sung by the prisoners of war at the memorial service for the late President Franklin D. Roosevelt at the Korean prisoner of war compound, Sand Island. Signal Corps Photo, O'ahu, TH, 15 April 1945; National Archives and Records Administration II, College Park, MD.

Three of them had been fishermen who were picked up at sea near the Philippines in 1943. After a short stay at Honouliuli, they were paroled to work at the US Engineers, Mills Division, Construction Service; they were sponsored by and lived with one of their supervisors, who was required to make regular reports on their conduct. Over the war period, all changed jobs and/or residences; one married a local woman. One, in particular, frequently complained about his sponsor and his low wages; he was cited for frequent unauthorized work absences, a gambling offense, and was even once arrested. Although the authorities kept track of him, he remained outside the Honouliuli Camp for the duration of the war (Arcilla 1946; Gurrobat 1946; Tablate 1946).

The fourth man presented a very puzzling case for the military. At the outbreak of the war, he had volunteered in the 101st Infantry Regiment of the Philippines, and in the spring of 1942 he had asked for and received permission from his company commander to take leave to evacuate his wife from Mindanao to Leyte. While he was away, the American forces on Leyte had surrendered, so he remained at home. Then he joined guerilla forces there, which were well staffed by American officers, and continued to fight with them until February 1944, when he was picked up by an American submarine and brought to O'ahu. While his story was checked and proven truthful, the US military in Hawai'i felt there was no rush to provide an answer regarding his status; instead, he was given his freedom, worked on odd jobs, and made regular reports. He was judged to be very friendly. In July, the decision was made that he could not be considered either a POW or an internee, but instead a Filipino national, lawfully residing in the Territory of Hawai'i (although under the circumstances, he did not enter Hawai'i in accordance with im-migration laws). Still, it was decided it was appropriate to continue to keep a regular account of him and his whereabouts. Finally, in March 1945, he was released and turned over for transportation to the Philippines (Cabugao 1946).

Hawai'i's POWs: Generating Changes

Of course, neither military forces nor their wars are organized according to democratic principles, nor are they particularly concerned with extending social justice to their captives. Nevertheless, the Geneva Convention does pro-vide a baseline for prisoners' humanitarian treatment. Furthermore, through their interactions with the US military within the camps and especially with locals of their own ethnic backgrounds out in the wider community, Hawai'i's prisoners of war did experience a measure of both.

At the beginning of the war, the US government and its military forces knew little about the global locations, peoples, and cultures they would fight during World War II. Along with the wartime research and advice of anthropologists and other social scientists, the US military's day-to-day administration of POWs in the camps provided them with a deeper, and more nuanced, understanding of them. In Hawai'i, this was especially the case for "Orientals" (Asians) from the Pacific Theater. Initially, most Asians captured from the Pacific region were labeled "Japanese." Over the course of the war, Hawai'i's military began to better understand the historical, political, and cultural differences between them, as well as the unique circumstances that had led them to participate in the war and to be captured.

Accommodations for POWs in Hawai'i and at Honouliuli Camp were limited; in addition, they were also carefully guarded, especially at the outset of the war, and particularly for "untrustworthy" ethnic Japanese POWs. However, the high demand for wartime labor in Hawai'i resulted in the non-Japanese POWs being allowed to work outside of their own camps, and even in the local community. This allowed them to make very important connections with people residing in the local Hawai'i community, and even some with members of their own ethnic groups, who later began to also visit them within the camps. In the case of Okinawans and Koreans, these visits were in very high frequency. POWs' interactions with members of their own ethnic groups in Hawai'i furthered the US military's understanding of them; it gave POWs important forms of support, helped to normalize them in the military's eyes, and contributed to the United States' continued deliberations about their political statuses over the wartime period.[8]

Military documents provide ample evidence of continued animosity, fear, and/or prejudice against POWs throughout the wartime period. But, it is also clear that over the course of the war, the POWs in Hawai'i and at Honouliuli went from being the unknown to the known, and that in the process their treatment was modified in significant, positive ways. Overall, their supervision went from very strict to somewhat more relaxed. For non-Japanese groups of POWs, it is also clear that the military developed a measure of appreciation of their cultural characteristics, hard work, and/or unique talents. In the case of the US military's interactions with Koreans, those connections led to continued re-evaluations of their wartime political status, with those in the military and residents eventually considered to be "friendly aliens." Still, by the end of the war, the official political status of all POWs initially considered to be "enemy aliens" was not changed. In the case of the four Filipino allies brought as POWs to Honouliuli, they were allowed near–freedom of work, residence, and activities, and one was even returned home.

Regularities in the conditions of imprisonment for all POWs in Hawai'i must surely have produced some similarities in their experiences—feelings of fear, confinement, discomfort, tedium, boredom, homesickness, loneliness, and loss. The war's end must have brought another set of similar emotions—welcome release from the hardships of war and imprisonment and the anticipation of happy reunions at home, as well as anxieties about their return to their war-devastated homelands, communities, and/or families, and to uncertain futures. Given the differences in the POWs cultural backgrounds, political circumstances, interactions with the local community, and their treatment by the US military, however, one can also speculate in very general ways about the differences in their postwar experiences, as well. For many of those Italian and Japanese POWs who had been in the military, their primary motivation for participation in the war was patriotic; as a result, their capture and imprisonment must have been surrounded with feelings of anxiety and shame that would stigmatize them in the eyes of their countrymen, especially upon their return to their vanquished nations. For many of the noncombatant Okinawans and Koreans, their capture meant an end to their conscription and wartime hardships under the Japanese military. For young Okinawan boys, especially, their incarceration was also a time of confusion with much relief coming from their connections with those in the local Hawai'i community; these sentiments were reflected in their postwar desires to remain in Hawai'i, a familiar and safe place. For many Koreans, their imprisonment involved a quest for justice against the Japanese colonists; their work in the camps was regarded as a means to a new future; and the war's end was a signal of that new beginning.

There is no evidence of any formal attempts at democracy training of POWs by the US military in Hawai'i. Any such efforts initiated by the military themselves would have been in violation of the Geneva Convention; yet, those undertaken by some of the Korean POWs were definitely encouraged. Still, POWs' interactions with the US military in the camps and with locals in the wider Hawai'i community provided them with opportunities to experience the workings of democracy. Although those experiences differed from one group of POWs to another, all became exposed to ideas and possibilities that could provide models for what their countries could offer after the war ended.

In the case of POWs held at Honouliuli, however, that context also included exposure to the US government's unjust internment of citizens and resident aliens—and even of some who were members of their own ethnic groups. ❖

Notes

1. Fujitani (2011) describes vulgar racism as a particularistic, inhumane, naturalistic understanding of difference, antihistoricist in its denial of the possibility of assimilation, unconcerned about their health and well-being, collectivist in understanding groups of individuals in a racial group, etc. In contrast, polite racism is humane, relativist and more culturalist, historicist in its affirmation of possible assimilation, somewhat concerned about health and well-being, still collectivist in understanding groups of individuals within a cultural group, etc.

2. Gwenfread Allen (1950) lists the Army's first prison camp near Wahiawā. It had only 56 occupants in 1942 and 179 in 1943; these prisoners were only briefly held pending transfer to the mainland. Conversations with interviewees suggest that there may have been other locations early in the war where POWs were held for a limited time.

3. Sand Island continued to hold some internees and even POWs over time. During the war, these included those en route to camps on the US mainland; after the end of the war, it included some who would eventually be repatriated.

4. Gwenfread Allen (1950) lists the total of POWs in Hawai'i at the end of the war as 16,493 (Italians: 4,841, Japanese: 320, Formosan (Taiwanese): 230, Indochinese (Southeast Asian): 7, Chinese: 3). The Office of the Chief of Military History (1955) indicates a total of 17,124 internees and POWs in Hawai'i; the maximum number in Hawai'i at any one time was estimated to be 11,351.

5. Several questions remain, however. Are those POWs that were added to the Honouliuli Camp at later times "additional"? Or are some or all of them holdovers from an earlier time? How many were moved elsewhere (within Hawai'i or to the mainland) in the interim?

6. Dates for the arrival of the first Italian and Korean POWs vary in military documents and reports. Most indicate the first Italians began to arrive in the summer of 1944.

7. Some records indicate not all Korean POWs in Hawai'i willingly worked in support of the war effort. The US military maintained lists of those who were to be punished for wrongfully refusing to work. In addition, in March 1945 some Korean POWs from Compound 8 refused to work because their leader, Kim Chuyong, had been removed and punished. They stated they would not return to work unless ordered to do so by their POW leaders.

8. Much effort, in this issue and elsewhere, has been devoted to examining the wartime and lasting impacts of internment, especially of the Japanese, on resident popula-

tions. This is especially highlighted in the literature surrounding the famous World War II 442nd Infantry Regiment, comprised of Nisei from the US mainland and Hawai'i that very valiantly fought in Italy. What remains to be known, however, is how the interactions with POWs affected local residents, especially of the various Asian ethnic groups in Hawai'i.

References

Allen, Gwenfread. 1950. *Hawaii's War Years: 1941–1945*. Honolulu: University of Hawai'i Press. Reprinted by Pacific Monographs, 1999.

Arcilla. 1946. Record Group 494, Entry 19, Box 179—Arcilla, File: Military Government of Hawai'i, Office of Internal Security, Alien Processing Center, Records of the US Armed Forces in the Middle Pacific, Internee Case Files, 1942–1946. National Archives and Records Administration II, College Park, Maryland.

B., G. W. 1942. Letter to the Office of the Military Governor. Status of the Korean Aliens, September 2. Record Group 389, Records of the POW Division, 1941–1945, File: Aliens. National Archives and Records Administration II, College Park, Maryland.

Benedict, Ruth. 1946. *The Chrysanthemum and the Sword: Patterns of Japanese Culture*. New York: New American Library.

Burton, Jeff, Mary Farrell, Linda Kaneko, Linda Maldonato, and Kelly Altenhofen. 2014. "Hell Valley: Uncovering a Prison Camp in Paradise." In this issue.

Cabugao. 1946. Record Group 494, Entry 19, Box 184—Cabugao, File: Military Government of Hawai'i, Office of Internal Security, Alien Processing Center, Records of the US Armed Forces in the Middle Pacific, Internee Case Files, 1942–1946. National Archives and Records Administration II, College Park, Maryland.

Calamandrei, Camilla. 2001. *Prisoners in Paradise*. DVD. Directed by Camilla Calamandrei and edited by Nancy Kennedy. (http://www.prisonersinparadise.com)

Cardinaux, Alfred L. 1945. Report on the POW Camp in the Territory of Hawaii visited by Mr. Alfred L. Cardinaux during December 1944 and February 1, 1945. International Committee of the Red Cross, Geneva, Switzerland. Delegation to the USA. February 1. Prisoner of War Files. Japanese Cultural Center of Hawai'i, Resource Center, Archival Collection, Honolulu, Hawai'i.

Ch'oe, Yong-Ho. 2007. "Syngman Rhee in Hawai'i: His Activities in the Early Years, 1913-1915." Pp. 53–88 in *From the Land of Hibiscus: Koreans in Hawai'i*, edited by Yong-Ho Ch'oe. Honolulu: University of Hawai'i Press.

———. 2009. "Korean Prisoners-of-War in Hawaii during World War II and the Case of US Navy Abduction of Three Korean Fishermen." *Asia-Pacific Journal: Japan Focus* 49(2).

Embree, John F. 1946. "Military Government in Saipan and Tinian; A Report on the Organization of Susupe and Churo, together with Notes on the Attitudes of the People Involved." *Applied Anthropology* 5(1): 1–39.

Falgout, Suzanne, Lin Poyer, and Laurence M. Carucci. 2009. *Memories of War: Micronesians in the Pacific War.* Honolulu: University of Hawai'i Press.

Fujitani, Takashi. 2011. *Race for Empire: Koreans as Japanese and Japanese as Americans during World War II.* Berkeley and Los Angeles: University of California Press.

Gillette, Gary M. (Senator). 1943. Letter to Mr. President [Roosevelt]. May 11. Record Group 389, Records of the POW Division, 1941–1945, File: Aliens. National Archives and Records Administration II, College Park, Maryland.

Goldsmith, (Lieutenant Colonel, Field Artillery). 1943. Memo, December 21. Record Group 389, Records of the POW Division, 1941–1945, File: Aliens. National Archives and Records Administration II, College Park, Maryland.

Guerrier, Elizabeth. 2007. "Anthropology in the Interest of the State." Pp. 199–222 in *Histories of Anthropology*, edited by Regna Darnell and Frederick W. Gleach. Volume 3. Lincoln: University of Nebraska Press.

Gurrobat. 1946. Record Group 494, Entry 19, Box 192—Gurrobat, File: Military Government of Hawai'i, Office of Internal Security, Alien Processing Center, Records of the US Armed Forces in the Middle Pacific, Internee Case Files, 1942–1946. National Archives and Records Administration II, College Park, Maryland.

Haan, Kilsoo. 1943. Letter to Franklin D. Roosevelt. May 8. Record Group 389, Records of the POW Division, 1941–1945, File: Aliens. National Archives and Records Administration II, College Park, Maryland.

Hashimoto, Hanako. 2010. Interview by Garyn Tsuru, Kaimukī, HI. September 9.

Hawai'i (Territory), Office of Strategic Services (OSS). 1943. The Sohn Case and the Status of Koreans in Hawai'i, May 13. Record Group 389, Records of the POW Division, 1941–1945, File: Aliens. National Archives and Records Administration II, College Park, Maryland.

Hawai'i (Territory), Office of the Military Governor (OMG). N.d. Control of Civilian Internees and Prisoners of War in the Central Pacific Area. Prisoner of War Files. Japanese Cultural Center of Hawai'i, Resource Center, Archival Collection, Honolulu, Hawai'i.

Headquarters Army Port and Service Command (HAPSC), APO 455. 1944a. Information for Proper Utilization of POW Labor. September 9. Prisoner of War Files. Japanese Cultural Center of Hawai'i, Resource Center, Archival Collection, Honolulu, Hawai'i.

———. 1944b. Annex No. 30 to Administrative Order No. 1. Prisoners of War, August 15. Prisoner of War Files. Japanese Cultural Center of Hawai'i, Resource Center, Archival Collection, Honolulu, Hawai'i.

Headquarters Prisoner of War Camp (HPWC), APO 950. 1944a. PW Camp Officers Conference, September 17. Prisoner of War Files. Japanese Cultural Center of Hawai'i, Resource Center, Archival Collection, Honolulu, Hawai'i.

———. 1944b. Prisoner of War Camp Staff Officers Conference, September 24. Prisoner of War Files. Japanese Cultural Center of Hawai'i, Resource Center, Archival Collection, Honolulu, Hawai'i.

———. 1944c. Staff Officers Conference, October 5. Prisoner of War Files. Japanese Cultural Center of Hawai'i, Resource Center, Archival Collection, Honolulu, Hawai'i.

———. 1944d. Staff Officers Conference, October 12. Prisoner of War Files. Japanese Cultural Center of Hawai'i, Resource Center, Archival Collection, Honolulu, Hawai'i.

———. 1944e. Staff Officers Conference, October 22. Prisoner of War Files. Japanese Cultural Center of Hawai'i, Resource Center, Archival Collection, Honolulu, Hawai'i.

History of Hawaiian Department, USFCPA, USAFPOA, USAFMIDPAC, Provost Marshall Section. 1945a. Chapter IX. Prisoners of War and Internees. Vital Statistics. Prisoner of War Compounds, and Internees in Hawaiian Islands (All Data Approximate), (Period December 7, 1941–September 2, 1945). Prisoner of War Files. Japanese Cultural Center of Hawai'i, Resource Center, Archival Collection, Honolulu, Hawai'i.

———. 1945b. Chapter IX. Prisoners of War and Internees. Approximate Racial Totals, on Dates Shown of POWs and Internees in the Hawaiian Islands (Period December 7, 1941–September 2, 1945). Prisoner of War Files. Japanese Cultural Center of Hawai'i, Resource Center, Archival Collection, Honolulu, Hawai'i.

Honolulu Advertiser. 1945. "Japanese POWs and Local Fraternization Problem." September 28.

———. 1946. "Italian PWs Built Church—Monument to Mother Cabrini." May 27.

Honolulu Star-Bulletin. 1943a. "Time to Correct an Injustice." May 6.

———. 1943b. "Gillette Asks FDR to Correct Rule on Koreans." May 13.

———. 1943c. "Korean Status Here in General Emmons' Hands." May 20.

———. 1943d. "Koreans Here to Remain as Enemy Aliens." June 2.

———. 1943e. "Koreans Allowed to Purchase Drugs." July 2.

———. 1946. "Liberty Ship Carries Last of Japanese POWs in Hawaii Home." December 13.

———. 1947. "War Still Going on for Japanese POWs Held on Oahu." August 26.

Keefer, Louis E. 1992. *Italian Prisoners of War in America, 1942-1946: Captives or Allies?* New York: Praeger.

Kim, Lili M. 2007. "How Koreans Repealed Their 'Enemy Alien' Status: Korean Americans' Identity, Culture, and National Pride." Pp. 195–219 in *From the Land of Hibiscus: Koreans in Hawaii*, edited by Yong-Ho Ch'oe. Honolulu: University of Hawai'i Press.

Kim, Y. K. 1943. Letter to President Franklin D. Roosevelt. May 8. Record Group 389, Records of the POW Division, 1941–1945, File: Aliens. National Archives and Records Administration II, College Park, Maryland.

Kiste, Robert C., and Suzanne Falgout. 1999. "Anthropology and Micronesia: The Context." Pp. 11–51 in *American Anthropology in Micronesia: An Assessment*, edited by Robert C. Kiste and Mac Marshall. Honolulu: University of Hawai'i Press.

Kiste, Robert C., and Mac Marshall, eds. 1999. *American Anthropology in Micronesia: An Assessment*. Honolulu: University of Hawai'i Press.

Krammer, Arnold. 1983. "Japanese Prisoners of War in America." *Pacific Historical Review* 52(1): 67–91.

Kurahara, Jane, Brian Niiya, and Betsy Young. 2014. "Finding Honouliuli: The Japanese Cultural Center of Hawai'i and Preserving the Hawai'i Internment Story." In this issue.

Lewis, George G., and John Mewha. 1955. *History of Prisoner of War Utilization by the US Army, 1776–1945*. Pamphlet No. 20-213. Washington, DC: US Department of the Army. June.

Loo, Calvin. 2010. Interview by Suzanne Falgout, Mililani, HI. October 21.

Loo, Irma. 2010. Interview by Suzanne Falgout, Mililani, HI, on October 21.

Lucas, Jim G. (Second Lieutenant). 1945. "Even the Marines Were Impressed." *Forth* (May): 18–21. Hawai'i War Records Depository, University of Hawai'i at Mānoa, Hamilton Library, Honolulu, Hawai'i. Card catalog.

Mead, Margaret, and Rhoda B. Metraux. 1953. *The Study of Culture at a Distance*. Chicago: University of Chicago Press.

Meller, Norman. 1999. *Saipan's Camp Susupe*. Occasional Paper 42. Honolulu: Center for Pacific Islands Studies.

Morison, Samuel Eliot. 1968a. *History of the United Stated Naval Operations in World War II*. Volume VII, *Aleutians, Gilberts and Marshalls, June 1942–April 1944*. An Atlantic Monthly Press Book. Boston: Little, Brown and Company.

———. 1968b. *History of the United Stated Naval Operations in World War II*. Volume VIII, *New Guinea and the Marianas, March 1944–August 1944*. An Atlantic Monthly Press Book. Boston: Little, Brown and Company.

Office of the Chief of Military History (OCMH), Special Staff. 1955. US Army Historical Manuscript File. United States Armed Forces Middle Pacific and Predecessor Commands during World War II, 7 December 1941–2 September 1945. *History of Provost Marshall's Office*. Stamped declassified September 1955. Richardson Files. Ft. Shafter, Office of the Historian, Honolulu, Hawai'i. (Available on CD.)

Postal Bulletin, Excerpts. 1942. *Mails and Parcels for Prisoners of War and for Detailed or Interned Civilians*. Vol. LXIII, No. 18433. Washington. Wedn. May 6. Prisoner of War Files. Japanese Cultural Center of Hawai'i, Resource Center, Archival Collection, Honolulu, Hawai'i.

Poyer, Lin, Suzanne Falgout, and Laurence M. Carucci. 2001. *The Typhoon of War: Micronesian Experiences of the Pacific War*. Honolulu: University of Hawai'i Press.

Rhee, Syngman. 1943. Letter to Secretary of War Stimson. May 17. Record Group 389, Records of the POW Division, 1941–1945. File: Aliens. National Archives and Records Administration II, College Park, Maryland.

Richardson, Robert C. 1943. Letter to Assistant Chief of Staff, G-2, War Department. June 7. Record Group 389, Records of the POW Division, 1941–1945. File: Aliens. National Archives and Records Administration II, College Park, Maryland.

Roosevelt, Franklin D. 1943. Letter to Secretary of War Stimson. May 25. Record Group 389, Records of the POW Division, 1941–1945. File: Aliens. National Archives and Records Administration II, College Park, Maryland.

Russell, Scott. 1983. "Camp Susupe: Postwar Internment on Saipan." *Pacific Magazine* 21–23.

Salzar, John Rudolph. 1942. Total Civilian Prisoners and Civilian Internees at Sand Island and Immigration Station, Honouliuli. September 9. Prisoner of War Files. Japanese Cultural Center of Hawai'i, Resource Center, Archival Collection, Honolulu, Hawai'i.

Shiroma, Thomas. 2011. Interview by Suzanne Falgout, Hilo, HI. March 23.

Starn, Orin. 1986. "Engineering Internment: Anthropologists and the War Relocation Authority." *American Ethnologist* 13(4): 700–720.

Statistical Data Report for Prisoner of War Base Camp APO 950. 1945. July 28. Hawai'i War Records Depository, University of Hawai'i at Mānoa, Hamilton Library, Honolulu, Hawai'i. Card catalog.

Tablate. 1946. Record Group 494, Entry 19, Box 292—Tablate, File: Military Government of Hawai'i, Office of Internal Security, Alien Processing Center, Records of the US Armed Forces in the Middle Pacific, Internee Case Files, 1942–1946. National Archives and Records Administration II, College Park, Maryland.

Taylor, Angus (Major). 1945. Letter to General Morrison on Korean POWs. March. Record Group 389, Records of the POW Division, 1941–1945. File: Aliens. National Archives and Records Administration II, College Park, Maryland.

US Army Forces Middle Pacific and Predecessor Commands, G2 Historical Section. 1944–1945 and 9/1946a. File: War Department Histories, The Army in Pacific Ocean Areas, Prepared by Historical Sub-section G2, HUSAFMIDPAC. Record Group 494, Entry 8. Box 10. File: Administration of Manpower. Volume 14, Chapter 5. National Archives and Records Administration II, College Park, Maryland.

———. 1944–1945 and 9/1946b. File: War Department Histories, The Army in Pacific Ocean Areas, Prepared by Historical Sub-section G2, HUSAFMIDPAC. Record Group 494, Entry 8. Box 23. Provost Marshall. History of Provost Marshall's Office, Operations, Chapter 9. National Archives and Records Administration II, College Park, Maryland.

War Department. 1942. Message to CGCPBC. August 26. Prisoner of War Files. Japanese Cultural Center of Hawai'i, Resource Center, Archival Collection, Honolulu, Hawai'i.

Wha, Ko Duck. 1943. Letter to the Office of the Military Governor. January 14. Record Group 389, Records of the POW Division, 1941–1945. File: Aliens. National Archives and Records Administration II, College Park, Maryland.

Transnational Identities, Communities, and the Experiences of Okinawan Internees and Prisoners of War

JOYCE N. CHINEN

ABSTRACT

Okinawans, people from Japan's poorest and last to be incorporated prefecture, faced unique challenges during World War II. Regarded as racially and culturally "different" from the rest of the Japanese population, but officially categorized as "Japanese" by Americans, Okinawans in Hawai'i inhabited a social space of shifting transnational identities and experiences. Depending upon the parsing, at least two broad and different subgroups of Okinawans experienced detention and imprisonment in Hawai'i. In the first group were local Okinawans, either Issei (first generation immigrants carrying Japanese passports) or Kibei (American-born offspring of the Okinawan immigrants who had been raised in Okinawa or on the main islands of Japan); in the second group were prisoners of war (POWs or PWs) taken in the Pacific Theater or as a result of the Battle of Okinawa. Since Okinawan experiences varied noticeably from other Japanese internees and other POWs, this article explores some of the factors contributing to their detention and eventual imprisonment, and the responses of the local Okinawan community.

Joyce N. Chinen, Professor of Sociology; University of Hawai'i–West O'ahu, 91-1001 Farrington Highway, Kapolei, HI 96707. This work is based upon material assisted by a grant from the Department of the Interior, National Park Service. Any opinions, findings, and conclusions or recommendations expressed in this material are those of the author and do not necessarily reflect the views of the Department of the Interior. The author can be reached at chinen@hawaii.edu.

Okinawans occupied a liminal space between being Japanese, and not-Japanese; being American, and not-American; being Hawai'i-born, but not being Local. This was especially the case for those who were Kibei (the children of the immigrants from Okinawa and Japan—thereby birthright American citizens—but who had spent their childhood years in Okinawa or Japan). "Citizenship" for Okinawans was, therefore, a problematic state of being, and this contributed to their unique set of experiences before, during, and after the Pacific War (or "World War II" to Americans).

This article will explore some of the conditions that led to the internment of ethnic Okinawans, some of whom were American citizens, some dual citizens, and some simply citizens of Japan. It will also explore the experiences of Okinawans who were brought to Hawai'i as prisoners of war (POWs or PWs) resulting from their capture in the islands of Micronesia, as well as a result of the bloody Battle of Okinawa. These groups of Okinawans—American citizens in some cases, Japanese nationals in others, and even dual citizens—although incarcerated under different conditions, nevertheless had experiences that were unique compared to others imprisoned in Honouliuli and other Department of the Army internment sites, both in Hawai'i and on the continental United States. Additionally, with a number of sizeable Okinawan communities scattered across the Hawaiian Islands as a result of the industrial sugar and pineapple plantation economy, significant interactions occurred between the prisoners and Okinawans in the community, as well as with those who guarded over them. These features suggest that Okinawan experiences of imprisonment varied somewhat from the other Japanese internees and POWs and are worthy of special attention because of the varying forms of treatment of and agency exhibited by them.

After a brief discussion of Okinawa's unique relationship to Japan, to Hawai'i, and to the United States, an explanation of the methods used to investigate the Okinawan imprisonment experiences will follow. Next, an exploration of the imprisonment of Okinawan internees will take place. This will be followed by a discussion of the prisoners of war captured in the Pacific and especially as a result of the Battle of Okinawa. The responses of the Okinawan community in Hawai'i (as well as those of their Okinawan captives) will also be explored. Finally, some thoughts on the significance of the social category of "Okinawan" and of internment or imprisonment will be discussed.

Background on Okinawa and Okinawans

Sociologists Michael Omi and Howard Winant's (1989/1994) notion of *racial formation* is useful in understanding how Okinawans became uniquely embroiled in the international and intra-national politics of the Pacific War. Omi and Winant note that "race" is socially "formed." That is, it is "created" via socially constructed hierarchies and through the establishment and institutionalization of cultural, social, economic, political "difference." Through various social conventions or practices, *nominal* characteristics (i.e., differences in name only) are transformed into *ordinal* differences (or inequalities in value), and varieties of hierarchies can become socially constructed. Thus, through political, legal, symbolic, and common everyday social practices and imaginaries, racial hierarchies become infused and institutionalized throughout societies. In addition, feminist sociologists such as Evelyn Nakano Glenn (2002) note that concepts like "citizenship" benefit from an integrative analysis of race, class, gender, and other forms of difference, and that particular locales or social spaces matter in the constructed configurations of stratification systems; in this case I would argue, the implementation of wartime incarceration was so affected. Finally, within the structural limits posed by internment or incarceration, Okinawans exercised a degree of *agency* that is noteworthy. As James Scott (1985) has noted, it is in the margins that the weak often exercise their resistance, however minor it may appear to be, to the oppressive conditions with which they are faced.

Prior to its incorporation as the 47th and last prefecture of Japan in 1879, Okinawa was known as Liu Ch'iu (Ryūkyū being the Japanized pronunciation of Liu Ch'iu), a small kingdom whose realm spanned the archipelago stretching from the Amami Islands in the north to Yonaguni in the south (Kerr 1958/2000:40). For approximately four centuries, its population lived mostly village-based lives, engaged in subsistence agriculture, fishing and crafts, largely isolated from the lives of their kings and members of the court in Shuri. The kingdom of Liu Ch'iu's affluence was built on its far-flung entrepôt trading throughout Southeast Asia and parts of East Asia, supported by the tributary relationship it had established with imperial China.

All of that changed in 1609, when the Satsuma clan of southern Japan, in a move sanctioned by the Tokugawa Shogunate, invaded Liu Ch'iu and set up a suzerain government within it. The kingdom of Ryūkyū continued for more than two centuries, but under the surreptitious control of Satsuma.

This arrangement enhanced the status and power of the Satsuma domain, but accelerated the process of the island kingdom's increasing impoverishment. Furthermore, when the Meiji government came to power in 1868, the disposition of Ryūkyū was confusing and economically disastrous; Ryūkyū was transformed from a kingdom to a *han* or domain, and eventually into a prefecture. The diplomatic relationships that the Ryūkyū Kingdom had established with other countries had to be disassembled. The aristocracy, which had resided in Shuri, was dispersed throughout the island and these families were compelled to make their own way. Ryūkyū, after this period known as the *Ryūkyū Shobun* (Ryūkyū Disposition), became "Okinawa," the 47th and last prefecture incorporated into the modernizing Japanese nation.

While other prefectures' incorporation into the emergent nation of Japan were difficult, those processes were far more gradual, less complicated, and less traumatic than it was for Okinawa. Okinawa's physical distance and separation from the Japanese "mainland" were accompanied by linguistic and other cultural differences. These differences were coded as inferiority, and the "other-ing" meant that the central government in *hondo* (mainland) Japan aggressively took control. It appointed Okinawa prefecture's governor (Shigeru Narahara from Kagoshima, formerly the Satsuma domain), imposed heavy taxes to develop the governmental infrastructure, and established an educational system based in "standard" Japanese language and cultural practices. The lateness of Okinawa's incorporation into Japan meant that these required changes occurred at a faster pace and resulted in more social dislocations than in other prefectures.

While social activists such as Noboru Jahana within Okinawa struggled against the Narahara government for social reforms, their efforts largely fell on deaf ears. Activists' appeals to emigrate were also ignored, because the leaders of a modernizing Japan wanted to avoid being embarrassed by what they regarded to be substandard subjects representing the new nation of Japan on the world's stage. Okinawans persisted in petitioning for permission to emigrate in spite of their language "deficiencies." Finally, in 1899, the appeals were granted. Kyuzo Toyama, a young activist, student of Jahana, and entrepreneur was able to convince Okinawa prefecture's appointed governor to grant permission to organize a small group of thirty men to emigrate to Hawai'i to work in its expanding sugar industry. Twenty-six men survived the ocean passage and the physical exams to work in Hawai'i in 1900. They were followed by even more Okinawans, and when the Gentlemen's Agreement was signed in

1907 by women and children, it fueled the natural increase in the Okinawan population. Most families were composed of parents and often eight or more children (Ethnic Studies 1981).

On the eve of the attack on Pearl Harbor, most Okinawans in Hawai'i were either Issei (immigrants) from Okinawa, or Nisei (the offspring of immigrants), including a subset of the Nisei (called Kibei, children of immigrants raised in Okinawa or the main islands of Japan). Okinawans had arrived in Hawai'i beginning in 1900, at least a decade and a half after the Kanyaku Imin (government-sponsored immigration) from Japan, and some thirty-plus years or so after the Gannen Mono (earliest contract labor migration from Japan). Okinawans, as a result, were incorporated into an already existing Japanese ethnic community, most of which were from the Chugoku or south-central area of mainland Japan (Kimura 1988).

Okinawans were a double minority on the plantations and in the urban areas of Hawai'i—they were an ethnic minority in relationship to the larger society as citizens of Japan, but they were also a minority in relation to the existing Japanese population in Hawai'i (Toyama and Ikeda 1950/1981). The level of discrimination against Okinawans in both urban and rural areas was palpable, and many elderly Okinawans in Hawai'i still recall epithets and taunts leveled at them in their youth such as, "Okinawa-ken ken, *buta kaukau!*" or "Big Rope!" The first saying is a combination of Japanese and creole terminologies (*buta* = pig and *kaukau* = food) referred to the fact that Okinawans were disproportionately represented among pig farmers, and the dominant source of feed for their pigs was composed of the food scraps they routinely collected from households and restaurants in the neighborhoods, and then cooked into a puree. Thus, Okinawan-ness was often conflated with garbage for pigs. The notion, "Big Rope" was a play on words—*ōki* meaning "big" and *nawa* meaning "rope"—hence the reference of "Big Rope" to Okinawa.

Additionally, family strategies differed. While mainland Japanese (*naichi*) families who could afford it often sent their children to Japan to be formally educated and retain their Japanese *cultural* identity, Okinawans in Hawai'i often sent their offspring to grandparents and other extended kin back in Okinawa for *economic* reasons—to care for children, to permit the immigrant parents to devote more time to wage earning (Maehara Yamazato 2007). When these offspring returned to Hawai'i, many of them more than a decade later, they found themselves awkwardly reintegrating into families with cousins or even siblings who had become Americanized in the interim. The Kibei, by virtue of their education in the Japanese educational system, which often integrated military and imperial ideological components, were less fluent in English, more formal than their other Nisei counterparts, and thus could be more easily identified and differentiated from other local Japanese and Okinawan residents. This made them more likely to be targets of suspicion, especially on the eve of the attack on Pearl Harbor.

Research Methods

The remainder of this article used a multi-method approach to investigate the Okinawan experience in Honouliuli and the various confinement sites throughout Hawaiʻi and the continental United States. It relied on data retrieved from official records retained at the National Archives and Records Administration II (NARA II), official histories, newspaper accounts, personal essays, and interviews. The NARA II material included interrogation transcripts, policy and protocol memoranda, daily reports (somewhat incomplete), lists of prisoners entering or exiting facilities, etc.

Since Okinawan residents in Hawaiʻi prior to the attack on Pearl Harbor were officially considered "Japanese," there was no official census designation of "Okinawan" internees in Honouliuli or any other confinement sites. On the other hand, when Okinawans entered Honouliuli and other confinement sites as POWs, they were designated as "Okinawan." Consequently, the following procedures were developed and used to "estimate" the situation of Okinawan internees. First, in narrative reports, some individuals identified themselves as Okinawan or "Uchinanchu." These self-reports were taken as validation of Okinawan identity. Second, when examining official reports and/or lists, the "narrator," or writer/official, may designate individuals or groups as "Okinawan" or "from Okinawa." In such cases, the designation was taken to indicate Okinawan identity of those individuals. Finally, and most problematic, when examining narratives and/or lists of Japanese names, Okinawan names and persons were identified by what might be "commonly considered" Okinawan names. To best systematize the process, the list of immigrants to Hawaiʻi in the centennial booklet, *To Our Issei: Okage Sama De* was used (Hawaii United Okinawa Association) . While that list is incomplete, it provided a rudimentary method to code Okinawan names, and thus to estimate what percentage of the "Japanese" population who were detained might have been ethnic Okinawan. However, those names are in Romanized (*Romaji*) form and the Chinese (*kanji*) characters would provide a more accurate determination of Okinawan identity.

Finally, narratives of various individuals both in Hawai'i and in Okinawa provide supplemental first-person accounts or stories of the period,
either of events here or in Okinawa. Often, they are spliced between other
larger narratives that may only indirectly touch upon Honouliuli. However,
the triangulation of the different stories or accounts often provide points in
time and space that, when viewed collectively, help "connect the dots" and
construct a composite picture of the Okinawan experience during this period.

Okinawan Internees

Although it was impossible to determine the exact number, using the
methodology described above, it was determined that approximately 12–15
percent of those with Japanese surnames who were interned/imprisoned were
probably ethnic Okinawans. Detention centers were to be found across the
island chain. After interrogation, the detainees were either held or shipped
to the continental United States. Prior to the construction and opening of
Honouliuli Camp in 1943, detention on O'ahu was primarily at the Immigration Station and at Sand Island Camp. In this section, the cases of five
individuals will be described to provide a picture of the range of Okinawan
internee experiences—why they were arrested, what happened to them, and
what they tell us about the internee experiences.

Ten ships carried people (including Okinawans) from Hawai'i who
were arrested/detained and taken to the internment camps administered by
the Department of the Army and/or the Department of Justice on the continental United States between February 17, 1942, and December 2, 1943.
The distinction between these kinds of camps and those administered by the
War Relocation Authority (WRA) is significant; they should not be conflated,
although they often have been. As Tetsuden Kashima notes in his introduction to Yasutaro Soga's *Life behind Barbed Wire* (2008), it reminds us that
just "knowing people before a shattering event occurs can affect the process
generated to deal with difficult situations (Soga 2008:15). Being apprehended
when others of one's community are not, takes a heavier psychic and social
toll. Okinawans fit this profile. Furthermore, as Ueunten (2007) points out
individuals held in Justice Department and army administered camps were
detained for possible prisoner exchanges (this was especially true of those sent
to Crystal City in Texas where Peruvians and other Latin American Nikkei
[overseas Japanese] were held).

Some of the ethnic Okinawans who were eventually interned were picked up almost immediately; certainly a number of internees were arrested within a month of the attack on Pearl Harbor, and they were transported to the continental United States shortly thereafter. Ryosen Yonahara was one of those. An Issei from Shuri, Okinawa, he was arrested on January 7, 1942, a month after the imposition of martial law, and after being detained at Sand Island, was sent out on the first ship on February 17, 1942. He eventually ended up in Santa Fe, New Mexico. In a college theme written in 1947, Roy Yonahara recalled his father's arrest and eventual internment:

> ... three FBI men came and searched our house. They couldn't find what they came to look for, but they took my father with them. My Mother and sisters cried as he said, "Don't worry, I'll be back soon." I stood by the door and nonchalantly said "goodby." I guess I was a mere youngster for I didn't realize what they were going to do to him.... Days of worrying lapsed into weeks, but Father didn't come home. We later found out that he had been interned at Sand Island. Only then did I realize that he wouldn't be home for some time. (Yonahara 1947:1)

Why was Ryosen Yonahara, a Japanese school teacher, apprehended? The transcript of his interrogation hearing held on January 12, 1942, at Fort Shafter is quite revealing. In a highly scripted hearing, the "evidence" was presented. Yonahara, an Issei (first generation) from the Shuri area of Okinawa, was a well-respected Japanese language teacher. As noted earlier, Shuri was the former seat of the Ryūkyū Kingdom and Yonahara's ancestors were high-ranking figures in the Ryūkyūan court. He had been asked, and therefore consented, to serve as a consular officer in rural Maui for the two years prior to moving his family to Honolulu in 1940. In that capacity, he was notified of births in the remote areas of Haʻikū–Paʻuwela, and had assisted parents to fill out and then send applications for dual citizenship to the Japanese Consulate office in Honolulu.

In spite of his insistence that his children were American citizens and that his own position on the war was one of neutrality, the transcript, like so many others, concludes with the finding: "The Board having carefully considered the evidence before them finds: 1) that the internee is a subject of the Empire of Japan; 2) is loyal to Japan; 3) has not engaged in any subversive activities." Nevertheless, the interrogators' decision was "internment for the duration of the war" (Yonahara 1947). From the Sand Island Internment Camp, Ryosen Yonahara and other Okinawan internees like Ryosei Aka and Kenjitsu Tsuha were taken to various other Department of Justice camps on the continental

United States eventually ending up in Santa Fe, New Mexico, the designated "enemy alien" camp where he and they remained for the duration of the war.

When his son, Roy, returned after serving with the American Occupation forces in Japan and the Philippines, he recalled:

> I saw my father for the first time in five years. He looked very old and thin, but had that same warm smile that I had missed all those years. The thought that I had somebody to father me again made me very happy.... The war had been unkind to many people and my father was one of these unfortunates. He had to suffer all those years for reasons I don't know. (Yonahara 1947:2)

Unlike Yonahara, Kenjitsu Tsuha was a birthright American citizen, but he was a Kibei. Although born in Hawai'i, he was taken back to Okinawa by his father to be raised by his grandparents because his mother had died while he was a young child. His father had decided that the family would be better off if he concentrated on wage earning while his parents took care of the younger Tsuha (Saiki 1982). As mentioned earlier, Kinuko Maehara Yamazato's work (2007) points out that this was especially common among Okinawans in Hawai'i. After nearly a decade and a half, the 17-year-old Kenjitsu Tsuha returned to his birthplace, in 'Ewa, O'ahu, but Hawai'i was in the midst of the Great Depression. He took on employment as a Japanese language teacher and as an assistant to a Buddhist priest. As Nishigaya and Oshiro point out in this volume, because people in these occupations were more likely to be targeted, Tsuha was arrested and interned. He eventually ended up at Santa Fe with other teachers and priests, most of these men at least twice his age. Young, frustrated, and impulsive, he became one of the "no-no boys" who answered "no" and "no" to both questions #27 and #28 (i.e., willingness to serve in the armed forces and pledging unqualified allegiance to the United States, even when it had interned them), refused to serve in the US military, renounced his American citizenship, and became a man without a country for the next 50 years (Saiki 1982). Unlike those with dual citizenship, Tsuha was a birthright American; when he renounced his citizenship, he was essentially country-less. When he eventually returned "home" to O'ahu, he became a visiting Buddhist priest (*nembutsu-do*), visiting Okinawan families and administering the memorial rites for their ancestors in their homes.

Masakichi Sesoko (aka Shoichi Sezoko), another Kibei, also renounced his American citizenship after being incarcerated in Honouliuli. A printer for the *Nippu Jiji* newspaper (later renamed the *Hawaii Times*), Sesoko also taught Japanese language classes at Wai'alae Baptist Church. He was born in

1918 in 'Ewa and, like his brother and sister, held dual citizenship. They were taken back to Japan where he was educated to become a teacher, but, in order to avoid conscription into the Japanese Imperial Army, returned to Hawai'i in 1938. His late return from Japan meant that his English language skills were limited, but without funds, he could only afford ten months of English language instruction. The very occupations he could fill (i.e., Japanese language teacher and newpaper printer) made him a target for detention. In the hearing held at Fort Shafter to determine his loyalty to the United States, he was asked questions such as: "Where is Sacramento located? How many stripes on the Japanese flag?" Since he could not answer the first question accurately, but answered the second correctly, Sesoko was deemed a security risk. What cinched the Review Board's decision was "His answers seem to be truthful and with little hesitancy, but there was an air of his being peeved at his detention. The Board feels he is dangerous to the public peace, safety and internal security of the United States" (Sesoko 1945). In other words, he was uppity and had a bad attitude about being maltreated. On the other hand, by the time he was arrested, detained, and then interned, Honouliuli had already been built, so he was able to remain in Hawai'i. Still, the trauma of being an educated man and receiving such treatment must have been devastating. Although she was aware of his internment, his niece, Jean Fujita, knew little of his experiences because he never talked about it; she only knew he was very bitter about it.

Probably the government's most curiously reasoned case for internment was the one that they made for Chinyei Kinjo, who was the publisher of the *Yoen Jiho Sha*, a weekly Japanese language paper based in Hanapēpē, Kaua'i. According to the hearing transcript, Chinyei Kinjo was a Christian Issei who had resided in Hawai'i for over twenty years, and who had planned to remain in Hawai'i. His newspaper was published with Ginjiro Arashiro, who served as its editor. Together these two figures were "considered the most important leaders of the incipient communistic movement among the Okinawans in the Territory," according to the information shared by John Harold Hughes of the Federal Bureau of Investigation (Kinjo March 19, 1942). Despite the recognition of this fact, in the decision to intern Kinjo, the findings were:

> The Board, having carefully considered the evidence before it, finds: 1) That the internee, CHINYEI KINJO, is a subject of the Empire of Japan, 2) That he is loyal to Japan, 3) That he is not engaged in any subversive activity, And recommended that in view of the above findings, the Board recommends that the internee: CHINYEI KINJO be interned for the duration of the war. (Kinjo 1942)

How leadership in a "communistic movement" might not be considered subversive is certainly contorted reasoning; nevertheless, the recommendation was the same as it was for the many others—internment. Kinjo departed on the third ship, May 23, 1942.

These interrogations and detainments continued well into 1943. Dr. Henry Shimpuku Gima, a naturopathic physician who had been practicing in Honolulu for some years, was arrested in 1943. Like the others mentioned above, he declined to avail himself of a lawyer because he felt he had done nothing wrong. However, in his initial interrogation hearing, he took advantage of the opportunity to call a character witness; a week later he had to report that the person he had expected to call to testify on his behalf had himself been arrested and interned (Gima 1945). After being incarcerated at Honouliuli, he was then sent on the tenth ship, and eventually to Crystal City, Texas, a Justice Department camp which also held Peruvian and other Latin American detainees who could be used for prisoner exchanges. After the war, he returned to Honolulu, resumed his practice, and became a leader in the community. That included being the first president of the Hawaii Okinawa-jin Rengo Kai, the forerunner of the current Hawaii United Okinawa Association. It is noteworthy that the organization's name would have to be the Hawaii United Organization of Okinawan People because, after the war, Okinawa initially remained under US military occupation, and subsequently, under the US Civil Administration of the Ryūkyū Islands (USCAR); it would not return to its status as a prefecture of Japan until 1972.

The cases above provide some insight into how individuals in the Okinawan community were swept up into the internment experience. The whirlwind speed from arrest to hearing, the inability to contact family members, together with the sense of bewilderment, given their belief that they had done nothing wrong, that they were upstanding members of their ethnic communities, probably contributed to their being considered suspicious. Their loss of rights, and their subsequent segregation from the rest of the population created a vacuum into which new leadership eventually emerged.

Okinawan Prisoners of War

Two distinct waves of Okinawan prisoners of war (POWs) were brought to Hawai'i. The first were those captured during the various battles in the South Pacific islands. Another group of POWs who were held in Hawai'i came after the fierce Battle of Okinawa, the only site of direct land battles in Japan proper, which produced over 250,000 casualties, immeasurable suffering, and large numbers of prisoners of war.

As American forces advanced across the Pacific, hard fought battle after bloody battle, they took as prisoners of war those Japanese officers and enlisted personnel as well as noncombatants who were part of Japan's colonial Nanyō project—its managers and workers. In this initial period Okinawans and Koreans who were skilled laborers were considered and designated "Japanese POWs" since they carried Japanese passports. As the tide changed and Allied forces advanced westward toward the final battles in Okinawa, these prisoners were more differentially identified "Okinawan" and "Korean" and separately designated by rank—officers, enlisted, and noncombatants (see Falgout's article in this volume). The vast majority of the Okinawan POWs were noncombatants.

The operations of the Honouliuli internment and POW camp in 1943 roughly coincide with the turning of the tides in the Pacific War. In fact, after completing their training at Camp Savage, some of the Military Intelligence Service (MIS) units actually spent a few days of training at Honouliuli before embarking on their Pacific mission (Higa 2011). They practiced their Japanese interrogation techniques, "name, rank, serial number, unit, etc.," on the Japanese POWs held at Honouliuli.

This section concentrates on the aftermath of "Operation Iceberg," the code name for what became the bloody Battle of Okinawa. While it is lesser known than Iwo Jima, the Battle of Okinawa, spanning only about three months, nearly decimated the island and inflicted enormous casualties (Feifer 1992; Ota 1984). Many of the prisoners of war from the Battle of Okinawa were interrogated by MIS soldiers, some of whom were of Okinawan ancestry and Kibei (Ota 1984; Higa 2011). POWs were also processed though the various base camps constructed throughout the Hawaiian Islands. Memoranda and reports from the NARA II files of the western and middle Pacific show an elaborate infrastructure and military posts, arrangements, and trans-Pacific movements of people (see articles by Falgout and by Rosenfeld in this volume). In Hawai'i, many "camps" were created to temporarily house, interrogate, and process these POWs before they could be released.

In Okinawa, the largest POW camp by far was Yaka Camp in Kin town on the northeast coast of the central part of the island. Until recently, most references to POWs, or PWs as was more commonly used in Okinawa, had disappeared. Indeed, the site of the Yaka POW Camp was demolished and redeveloped. No reminders of it exist, save for a small marker next to a city bus stop. That is not entirely surprising, since the human condition tends toward ridding itself of unpleasant memories rather than preserving them. Consequently, only a few traces remain—one of the best known is in a song. The composer of "Yaka Bushi" (or "Song of Yaka") is unknown, although several names have been associated with it. However, this folk song resonated with enough of the population that it has persisted, and been passed on from one *uta-sanshin* teacher/performer to another (*sanshin* being an Okinawan three-string plucked musical instrument resembling a banjo, always with vocal accompaniment). "Yaka Bushi" makes reference to the near total destruction of Okinawa, where the ordinarily lush tropical landscape was leveled, left denuded, trees merely bare branches. It also refers to wives and family members held in yet another camp across the Onna Mountains—this one a refugee camp in central Okinawa: Ishikawa Camp on the other side of the mountains, which was the largest of the refugee camps in Okinawa (see photos of Yaka Camp and Ishikawa Camp).

Though mournful, the song ends with a metaphor of hope, that the dried-up tree will have another chance, and its flowers (and metaphorically, its people) will again be able to bloom and thrive. Anthropologist James Roberson (n.d.) cites another blue song about being a POW, not necessarily at Yaka, and notes in the final verse of PW Mujō:

If only there had not been this thing, war
This pitiful figure, I [we] would not have become
How pitiful is a PW

So, who were these prisoners of war? Many were ordinary Okinawans caught in the Japanese empire's drumbeat of hyper-nationalism and patriotism. The Japanese Imperial military forces fostered such fervor, instituted conscription, and recruited via the school system. The Blood and Iron Loyalist Troop of high school male students, the Himeyuri (Student Corps) nursing students were all assigned and attached to support Japanese military units.

Masahide Ota, previously the governor of Okinawa and now a staunch pacifist, was one such student conscript. In a conversation with me in March 2012, Governor Ota described how the patriotic fervor in the high school system persuaded many young Okinawan youth like himself to join the Blood and Iron Scouts for the emperor. After being captured, he and other PWs were

Yaka Bushi

Author Unknown; translated by W. Ueunten

Nachikashi ya uchinaa	なちかしや沖縄	How sad, my Okinawa
Ikusaba ni nayai	戦場になやい	You are a battlefield
Shikin umanchu nu	世間御万人ぬ	All the people of the world—
Nagasu namida	流す涙	tears are flowing.
Namida nudi wamiya	涙ぬでぃ我身や	I drink my tears
Unna yama nubuti	恩納山上てぃ	And climb Unna Yama
Umanchu tu tumu ni	御万人とぅ共に	With all the people
Ikusa shinuji	戦凌じ	I wait for the war to end
Awari yaka mura nu	哀り屋嘉村ぬ	A crow is crying in the dark night
Yami nu yu nu garashi	闇ぬ夜ぬがらし	In pitiful Yaka Village
Uya uran wami nu	親うらん我身ぬ	I no longer have family
Nakan uchumi	泣かんうちゅみ	Can't help but cry?
Njo ya Ishichaa mura	んぞや石川村	You are held in Ishikawa Village
Kayabuchi nu nagaya	茅葺ぬ長屋	In one of the many long grass-roof houses
Wami ya Yaka mura nu	我身や屋嘉村ぬ	while I am held in Yaka Village
Shinaji makura	砂地枕	My pillow is the sand
Kukuru isamiyuru	心勇みゆる	Four C-ration cigarettes
Shifun iri tabaku	四本入り煙草	Make me feel a little better
Sabishisaya chichi ni	寂しさや月に	I am letting my sadness
Nagachi ichusa	流ち行ちゅさ	Fly up to the moon with the smoke
Nunchi [nundi] kugaritoga	ぬんち[ぬんでぃ]焦がりとが	How is it I feel restless?
Yaka mura nu kariki	屋嘉村ぬ枯り木	The dried up tree in Yaka Village
Yagati hana sachuru	やがてぃ花咲ちゅる	Is going to get a season
Shichin ayusa	節んあゆさ	When its flowers will bloom

Yaka POW Camp. Photograph courtesy of Okinawa Prefectural Peace Museum.

Ishikawa Refugee Camp. Photograph courtesy of Okinawa Prefectural Peace Museum.

shaved and sprayed with DDT for delousing purposes. Unlike others who were sent to Yaka Camp, he was sent to a smaller camp near Kadena town. Because he had attended high school and could read, write, calculate, and had some English proficiency, he was given a job and was able to earn a bit of money. He remained in Okinawa until the US military government began to recruit students to study abroad.

Another POW, one who spent a little time in Honouliuli, was the late historian Michael Mitsugu Sakihara, who retired from the faculty of the University of Hawai'i at Mānoa. He was also one of the pioneers of the contemporary field of Ryūkyūan and Okinawan studies. Sakihara also joined up to be part of the Iron and Blood Loyalist Troop, in his words, "an impressive name for an unimpressive group of middle school boys who had volunteered to serve in a support capacity in the Japanese military during the Battle of Okinawa in 1945" (2009:187). After the surrender in late June, he and 53 others of the Troop who were captured were sent to Honouliuli, Sand Island, and then via Washington state, south to Angel Island, California. In an essay reflecting on his POW days at Angel Island, the late Mitsugu Sakihara noted :

> Apart from the KP duty, it was very much like we had already experienced at the prisoner-of-war camp in Honouliuli, on the Hawaiian island of O'ahu. . . . Here on Angel Island the food was a little simpler than at Honouliuli, but it was still good: toast, jam, butter, fried eggs, bacon, cereal, milk, and coffee. That was our first breakfast. . . . (2009:187)

Sakihara noted that he and other POWs at Honouliuli were fed three times a day, and they were able to purchase items with scrip. Sakihara recalled he bought a copy of Sanseido's *Japanese-English Dictionary* with his dollar scrip and tried to learn some English words. But his English language abilities really developed during his stay at Angel Island.

Sakihara did not describe much of his journey to Hawai'i. For that we must rely on the accounts of others discovered and documented by Dr. Masanori Nakahodo. Nakahodo notes that while stories of the MIS soldiers such as Takejiro Higa and Taro Higa using their *Uchināguchi* (Okinawan language) skills to persuade Okinawans to come out of the caves, thereby saving hundreds of lives, are now better known, less is known of the POWs. Examining the memoirs of POWs (which are still available only in Japanese), Nakahodo provides a window into their chaotic, fearful experiences. One of those sent to Hawai'i was Seiki Miyazato who left behind a record in "My Memo" (n.d.).

On July 8(?), 1945 we left Okinawa, arrived at the Saipan port on the fourth day. The ship was an infamous "naked carrier" since they were stripped of their clothes and plunged into oil stained "dumbles" or compartment. The note starts by describing it as a "ship of hell," landing at island of Oahu on July 24(?) The prisoners were confined at Honouliuli Camp. Someone named the place "Red Clay Girls School."

Moreover, Mr. Miyazato (and other POWs) was moved frequently—from Honouliuli to Kāne'ohe, and Fort Hase Camp, then to Sand Island, and via a ship named *Comet*, to Hawai'i island, and then back to Kalihi on O'ahu. Miyazato worked outside the camps on several projects, before being returned to Okinawa in December. This account provides one confirmation of a pattern of frequent POW movements, which is noticeable in the NARA II documents (Nakahodo 2012).

Other POW accounts discovered by Nakahodo, including one by Chosho Tokuyama, suggest that the direction of movement of POWs from Okinawa was first to Honouliuli, and, subsequently, to Sand Island (Nakahodo 2012:3). There is mention of frequent visitors to Sand Island, individuals seeking information about their family members in Okinawa. The POWs were ministered by a Rev. Shiroma from Hilo who promoted a Southern Baptist ministry; but through his travels, he was able to share information about individuals with various family members. Shiroma, an Okinawan, somehow managed to escape internment, possibly because he was a Christian minister.

Occasionally, there were some "miracles." A mother met her son, Noboru Gima, after many years of separation. He had been born on Maui, but had been taken to Okinawa as a young child, and was not able to return. When the war began, he had been assigned to Japanese soldiers and had been captured in Okinawa by American forces, and then transported to Hawai'i as a POW. His mother heard about his status as a POW in Hawai'i and was able to reunite with her son after many years (Nakahodo 2012).

The frenetic comings and goings of POWs from Okinawa and other parts of the Pacific quickly came to an end within two years. Often, the Okinawan POWs were conflated with the Japanese POWs. The *Honolulu Star-Bulletin* of May 21, 1946, reported that "Four hundred Japanese prisoners of war who have been working on Oahu and will be transferred permanently to Guam and Saipan aboard the Marine Wolf…. The Japanese are all skilled laborers from Okinawa according to the report and will be used for construction and maintenance work there" (Epstein 1946a).

Marching POWs down. Photograph courtesy of Okinawa Prefectural Peace Museum.

POWs at docks awaiting transport. Photograph courtesy of Okinawa Prefectural Peace Museum.

Trucks POWs for Hawaii. Photograph courtesy of Okinawa Prefectural Peace Museum.

JPOWs trucks. Photograph courtesy of Okinawa Prefectural Peace Museum.

By December 13, 1946, the *Honolulu Star-Bulletin* reported the last of the remaining 1,733 Japanese POWs in Hawai'i left for their homes in Japan, Okinawa, and Korea. "Although Hawaii is now free of the prisoners of war, there still are more than 100,000 being held in the Philippines, Okinawa and the Carolines, Marianas and other Pacific Islands" (Epstein 1946b).

Okinawan Community Responses

On December 7, when Pearl Harbor was bombed, most Okinawans reacted as other Hawai'i residents—with shock and fear. Some lost their homes as stray bombs reduced their homes to rubble. Artist Seikichi "Chick" Takara recalled bombs destroying his family home in the McCully area of Honolulu. It was later determined that his neighborhood was destroyed by errant anti-aircraft fire returned by the American forces.

Student conscripts. Photograph courtesy of Okinawa Prefectural Peace Museum.

Many Okinawans eventually entered military service. Okinawans in the existing Hawaii National Guard who were draftees became part of the segregated unit 100th Battalion who, after training on the continental United States, were sent to the European Theater. After a stellar performance, but with their ranks severely decimated, the Purple Heart Battalion was incorporated into the 442nd Regimental Combat Team, volunteers whose combat record still stands unchallenged for a unit of its size and duration. Okinawans also played important roles in the Military Intelligence Service, which operated in the Pacific Theater (Higa 2011).

As the Allied victories increased in the Pacific, detention facilities were constructed across the Hawaiian Islands to process the POWs that flowed through. Some facilities like Honouliuli were planned, while others were more makeshift. In places like Honouliuli and Sand Island, regular visits by clergy and family were sanctioned certain days. Nakahodo (2012) mentions clergy such as a Reverend Shiroma who "visited the camp on Sunday to talk about Christ and, at the same time, he told us about Okinawa and of any recent information."

At Honouliuli and other POW camps, visits and exchanges were so frequent, that on February 12, 1946, an article appeared in the *Hawaii Hochi* quoting Captain H. R. Howell, commander of the Engineering Unit, stating that talking to the POWs and giving money or gifts were prohibited and should be stopped. Nevertheless they continued. Often the items were brought to the POWs and were culturally expressive or significant (e.g., sweets and treats wrapped in the traditional manner in the leaf of a banana plant: *ka-sa bento*). In fact, "Chick" Takara also recalls accompanying his mother to a detention area in Kapi'olani Park near the Honolulu Zoo to visit a relative or family friend. He recalls his mother packing a bento (lunchbox) of prepared foods for the visit and a trolley car ride, and the visit conducted through the wire fence. Most of all, he recalls that the guard gazed away just long enough to let Takara's mother slip the *bento* under/through the fence to the relative held in the POW camp. This was, of course, not officially permitted, but was routinely practiced.

The ambivalence of soldiers guarding the POWs stands in stark contrast to the volumes of regulations on how POWs were to be treated. Writer-playwright Jon Shirota, a Nisei Okinawan from Maui, captured this ambivalence. More often, however, Okinawan POWs were simply being greeted and socialized for a few minutes while they were out on work details. Jon Shirota, who was assigned to Kīlauea Military Camp describes how on at least several occasions, Okinawan women would gather along the roadside when he and other guards transported the POWs for work details in ʻŌlaʻa. Stops before intersections netted questions about their relatives in Okinawa, and warm exchanges between the prisoners and the residents were commonplace. One young POW was given some money by a woman at one of those stops; he asked Shirota to purchase some a supplies for him, and with some trepidation, Shirota complied with the request (Shirota 2009).

Summary and Conclusion

Okinawans—Issei, Nisei, Kibei, and prisoners of war—were people who were "caught in between"—and therefore were likely to be ensnared in the nets of suspicion. As the latecomers of the Japanese immigrant population in Hawaiʻi, the Okinawan Issei and Kibei were visibly less acculturated to Hawaiʻi and American societies than the larger "mainland" Japanese population who had immigrated at least some 15 to 25 years earlier.

Additionally, last to be incorporated into the modernizing Japanese "nation," their citizenship in Japan was subject to question. This meant they often overcompensated to demonstrate their loyalty and identification with Japan, even more visibly than other *naichi* Japanese. Okinawan community leaders were therefore those who could best reproduce the persona of respectable Japanese—speak "proper" Japanese and circulate in those leadership circles because their Japanese education and experiences provided that kind of human and cultural capital.

Okinawan Kibei, although born in Hawaiʻi, had been raised in Okinawa or mainland Japan. Furthermore, the colonization of the Ryūkyū Kingdom and its subsequent incorporation into Japan as Okinawa prefecture, meant that the "neo-Japanese citizens," especially the males, were conscripted and caught in the defense of the Japanese nation. They became prisoners of war on their home island, or POWs as a result of becoming enlisted or noncombatants on distant battlefields on faraway Pacific islands, or in their own island home.

In conclusion, Okinawans in the context of the Pacific War, were not only internees who were incarcerated, but also prisoners of war from battles in the Pacific and the Battle of Okinawa. Some resisted military service and were sent to higher security camps on the continental United States. Ironically, even some of the soldiers who captured and interrogated these Okinawan POWs were themselves of Okinawan descent. Moreover, the staff in some of the POW camps in Hawai'i, like some of those who worked in the mess halls or even the guards were of Okinawan descent. Consequently, although their formal "citizenship" designations or social roles may have diverged, Okinawan cultural identities served to bridge the chasms of the nation-states, or of suspected loyalties. Finally, the larger community of Okinawans in Hawai'i, through the informal extended-kin networks, provided moral and material support to the prisoners. In short, the situations faced by Okinawans, were troubling, extraordinarily confusing, and resistant to simple categorization as either aggressors or as victims. They serve as a reminder of the human capacity of agency even in the midst of extraordinary oppressive structure. ❖

Acknowledgments

I wish to thank Hiroshi Kunugi and Makoto Arakaki of the Okinawa Prefectural Peace Museum for permission to use the photos of Yaka POW Camp, Ishikawa Refugee Camp, POWs on a truck destined for Hawai'i. I also acknowledge the assistance of Kazuhiko Nakamoto and Yuko Kakinohana of the Okinawa Prefectural Archives in accessing materials on Okinawan prisoners of war and other records on the US Occupation of Okinawa. Former Okinawa prefecture Governor Masahide Ota generously shared his memories of his POW experiences and post–Battle of Okinawa experiences. Dr. Wesley Ueunten generously translated the lyrics for "Yaka Bushi," and Lynette Teruya read an earlier draft of this and reviewed Okinawan names and terminology. Finally, I appreciate and acknowledge the patience and detailed work of the editors of this issue, Drs. Suzanne Falgout and Linda Nishigaya, and Mark Nakamura.

References

Epstein, Moray. 1946a. "400 Japanese Prisoners To Be Moved From Hawaii." *Honolulu Star-Bulletin*, May 21. File 36 #140.

———. 1946b. "Liberty Ship Carries Last of Japanese POWs in Hawaii Home." *Honolulu Star-Bulletin*, Dec. 13. File 36 #140.

Ethnic Studies Oral History Project and United Okinawan Association of Hawaii. 1981. *Uchinanchu: A History of Okinawans in Hawaii*. Honolulu, HI: Ethnic Studies Oral History Project, Ethnic Studies Program, University of Hawai'i.

Falgout, Suzanne. 2014. "Honouliuli's POWs: Making Connections, Generating Changes." In this issue.

Feifer, George. 1992. *Tennozan: The Battle of Okinawa and the Atomic Bomb*. New York: Ticknor & Fields.

Gima, Henry Shimpuku. 1945. Record Group 494, Entry ISN-HUS-869-CI, Box 2635. Records of the Military Government of Hawaii. National Archives and Records Administration II, College Park, Maryland.

Glenn, Evelyn Nakano. 2002. *Unequal Freedom: How Race and Gender Shaped American Citizenship and Labor.* Cambridge, MA: Harvard University Press.

Hawaii United Okinawa Association, Okinawan Centennial Celebration Issei Commemorative Booklet Committee. 2000. *To Our Issei…Our Heartfelt Gratitude.* Waipahu, HI.

Higa, Warren T. 2011. Interview by Joyce N. Chinen. July 7.

Kashima, Tetsudan. 2008. "Introduction." Pp. 1–16 in *Life behind Barbed Wire: The World War II Internment Memoirs of a Hawai'i Issei*, by Yasutaro Soga. Honolulu: University of Hawai'i Press.

Kerr, George H. 1958/2000. *Okinawa: The History of an Island People.* Revised edition with an afterword by Mitsugu Sakihara. Boston: Tuttle Publishing.

Kimura, Yukiko. 1988. *Issei: Japanese Immigrants in Hawaii.* Honolulu: University of Hawai'i Press.

Kinjo, Chinyei. 1942 (Feb. 13 and March 19). Record Group 389, Entry ISN-HJ-276-CI, Box 2620. National Archives and Records Administration II, College Park, Maryland.

Maehara Yamazato, Kinuko. 2007. "To Okinawa and Back Again: Life Stories of Okinawan Kibei Nisei in Hawai'i." Pp. 83–96 in *Uchinaanchu Diaspora: Memories, Continuities, and Constructions.* Social Process in Hawai'i, 42. Honolulu: University of Hawai'i Press.

Miyazato, Seiki. N.d. "My Memo" In "Okinawan Prisoners of War in Hawaii POW Camp," by Tomonori Nakahodo. Presentation to the Okinawan Genealogical Society of Hawaii, October 12, Hawaii Okinawa Center, Hawai'i. Nakahodo, Tomonori. 2012. "Okinawan Prisoners of War in Hawaii POW Camp," translated by Robert Kishaba and edited by Nancy Tome.

Nishigaya, Linda, and Ernest Oshiro. 2014. "Reviving the Lotus: Japanese Buddhism and World War II Internment." In this issue.

Omi, Michael, and Howard Winant. 1989/1994. *Racial Formation in America.* 2nd ed. New York: Routledge.

Ota, Masahide. 1984. *The Battle of Okinawa: The Typhoon of Steel and Bombs.* Tokyo: Kume Publishing Co.

Roberson, James E. N.d. Songs of War and Peace: Music and Memory in Okinawa. Asia Pacific Journal: Japan Focus. Retrieved 6/10/2012.

Rosenfeld, Alan. 2014. "Neither Aliens nor Enemies: The Hearings of 'German' and 'Italian' Internees in Wartime Hawai'i." In this issue.

Saiki, Patsy Sumie. 1982. *Gambare! An Example of Japanese Spirit.* Honolulu: Mutual Publishing.

Sakihara, Mitsugu. 2009. "Sparrows of Angel Island: The Experience of a Young Japanese Prisoner of War." In *Voices from Okinawa; Mānoa: A Pacific Journal of International Writing*, edited by Frank Stewart and Katsunori Yamazato. Honolulu: University of Hawai'i Press.

Scott, James C. 1985. *Weapons of the Weak: Everyday Forms of Peasant Resistance.* New Haven: Yale University Press.

Sesoko, Masaichi. 1945. Record Group 494, Entry ISN-HUS-819-CI, Box 2635. Records of the Military Government of Hawaii. National Archives and Records Administration II, College Park, Maryland.

Shirota, Jon. 2009. "The Dawning of an Okinawan." Pp. 157–167 in *Voices from Okinawa; Mānoa: A Pacific Journal of International Writing,* edited by Frank Stewart and Katsunori Yamazato. Honolulu: University of Hawai'i Press.

Soga, Yasutaro. 2008. *Life behind Barbed Wire: The World War II Internment Memoirs of a Hawai'i Issei.* Honolulu: University of Hawai'i Press.

Toyama, Henry, and Kiyoshi Ikeda. 1950. *Social Process in Hawai'i,* 14:51–65. Reprinted in *Uchinanchu: A History of Okinawans in Hawaii,* by Ethnic Studies Oral History Project and United Okinawan Association of Hawaii. Honolulu: Ethnic Studies Oral History Project, Ethnic Studies Program, University of Hawai'i, 1981.

Ueunten, Wesley Iwao. 2007. "Japanese Latin American Internment from an Okinawan Perspective." Pp. 97–120 in *Uchinaanchu Diaspora: Memories, Continuities, and Constructions. Social Process in Hawai'i,* 42. Honolulu: University of Hawai'i Press.

Yonahara, Roy. 1947. "Father." (Feb. 11, Sec. MWF 8:30 Theme 2) Hawai'i War Records Depository, University of Hawai'i at Mānoa, Hamilton Library. W24.01 7965.

Yonahara, Ryosen. 1945. Record Group 389, Entry 461 ISN-HJ-CI, Box 2646. Records of the POW Division, 1941–1945. National Archives and Records Administration II, College Park, Maryland.

Reviving the Lotus: Japanese Buddhism and World War II Internment

LINDA NISHIGAYA
ERNEST OSHIRO

ABSTRACT

The World War II internment of American civilians and resident aliens of Japanese ancestry at Honouliuli Internment and POW Camp in Central O'ahu, Hawai'i included mostly male leaders in the Japanese immigrant community. Religious leaders, especially those identified as Buddhist priests, figured prominently among those detained. The religious designation of Buddhist/Buddhism and the ethnic/racial category of Japanese were commonly viewed as synonymous and membership in either was cause for suspicion and internment. Buddhist priests numbered among the first civilians of Japanese ancestry to be arrested and detained, many until the end of the war. Most of the priests were transferred to one of the internment camps on the US mainland and records indicate that only seven were interned at Honouliuli for any length of time. The internment of the Buddhist priests at Honouliuli and other camps on the US mainland severely curtailed Buddhist religious services and activities in the Hawaiian Islands. On a larger scale, its effects on the future of Buddhism in Hawai'i and the US mainland were institution and life changing. This paper examines Buddhism and World War II internment and the aftermath of the war and uses rational choice theory to clarify the decisions and changes that followed.

Linda Nishigaya and Ernest Oshiro are retired professors of the University of Hawai'i–West O'ahu, 91-1001 Farrington Highway, Kapolei, HI 96707. This work was assisted by a grant from the Department of Interior, National Park Service. Any opinions, findings, and conclusions or recommendations expressed in this material are those of the author(s) and do not necessarily reflect the views of the Department of the Interior. The authors may be contacted at nishigay@hawaii.edu and oshiro@hawaii.edu.

The unearthing of the World War II internment and POW camp at Honouliuli in Central Oʻahu, Hawaiʻi uncovers a dark and painful past of more than 2,000 (Rosenfeld 2011) local American civilians and resident aliens of Japanese ancestry who were interned, as well as an immigrant community left bereft of most of its religious, business, educational, and cultural leaders. Immediately after the bombing of Pearl Harbor, among the first detained by FBI agents were religious leaders, especially Shintō and Buddhist priests, who were targeted as being dangerous and subversive. These ministers were high on the FBI's priority list of potential enemy aliens (Kashima 2003, 2008; Williams 2002, 2003). Their internment changed the structure and practice of Buddhism in Hawaiʻi and the US mainland.

The literature on religion in general and Buddhism, its priests and congregations in particular, in relation to World War II internment is scant. Tangentially and anecdotally, stories of religious activities in the camps and in the Japanese communities in Hawaiʻi during the war years have been told, but serious study of the role of the Buddhist religion as a major institution of the Japanese has been largely bypassed. Thus, our understanding of its influence, evolution, suppression, and revival is limited.

Koda (2003) contends that "While no one theory can explain Japanese religion in Hawaii, theories such as acculturation, assimilation, Americanization, and cultural pluralism all have roots in the Japanese American religious story" (p. 238). Smith and Froese's (2008) connection of Buddhist scholarship to Warner's (1993) "new religious paradigm" juxtaposed with the "old religious paradigm" offers insight into the dynamics of Buddhist religiosity in the lives of its adherents and in an ever-changing society. In brief, the old paradigm assumes that individuals follow cultural and social tradition by taking for granted the religious identity, beliefs, and practices of their social group. In contrast, the new paradigm assumes rational choice, that is, that individuals act by weighing the costs and benefits of religious choices, such as membership and extent of participation. While we do not intend to enter the ongoing debate of the efficacy of the old versus the new paradigm, or the theoretical discussion of which of many perspectives best accounts for the accumulating religious research data, we do recognize the contribution that a conceptual framework that fits the data can make. The discovery of unifying concepts can help to integrate existing religious research data and generate new ways of thinking about and investigating religious behavior.

A retrospective analysis of the history of Buddhism in Hawai'i suggests the relevancy of the new paradigm in helping to explain Buddhism in the early plantation economy and its adaptation to the conditions in the emerging and modern service economy. The rational choice model objectively considers costs and benefits, competition, and constraints in explaining the choices made by suppliers (e.g., ministers) and demanders (e.g., lay followers) of religious and other services on the individual, group, and societal levels (Iannaccone 1995). It provides awareness of and insight into the difficult choices that confronted interned Buddhist priests and their congregations with respect to loyalty, institutional changes, and other critical issues. The tragic experience of World War II internment had far-reaching effects on Japanese Buddhism in Hawai'i and the US mainland. An understanding of its impact illuminates the path taken by Japanese Buddhism from the past to the present and offers insight into its future direction.

The Powerful Influence of Buddhism in Pre–World War II Hawai'i

At the time America was thrust into World War II after the bombing of Pearl Harbor on December 7, 1941, Buddhism in Hawai'i was thriving. There were over 180 temples or shrines on O'ahu and the neighbor islands, ministered by well over 100 active priests from over a dozen different Buddhist traditions (Hunter 1971; Williams 2003). (See Tables 1 and 2). The temple congregations were larger then than they have ever been since. Most of the Japanese immigrants identified themselves as Buddhists, with more than a majority affiliating themselves with the Jōdo Shinshū sect. The Buddhist temples in Hawai'i kept ties with their religious headquarters in Japan and the hierarchical organizational structure with priests at the top was in keeping with Japanese tradition. The Japanese language was spoken at religious services as the congregations were mostly first generation Japanese (Issei) and their bilingual second generation young adult children (Nisei) (Yosemori 2011). Although efforts to convert the Japanese immigrants and their children to Christianity were not lacking in the Hawaiian Islands, most adhered to Buddhism.

The powerful influence of Buddhism in the lives of the Japanese in Hawai'i in the pre– World War II years was duly recognized even by the Office of the Provost Marshal General, Army Service Forces. "While religion was a strong centralizing factor on the Pacific Coast, it was probable [sic] secondary to the Japanese consulate domination of social, political, and semi-military organizations. In Hawai'i the Buddhist Church is a much stronger controlling element" (Office 1946a). More than any other institution, the Buddhist religion played an active and influential role in Japanese immigrant communities. For immigrants in a new and foreign land, Buddhism provided more than spiritual sustenance and support. Especially in the rural sugar plantations, more than simply places of worship, the temples functioned as community centers fulfilling spiritual, economic, social, educational, and cultural needs (Horinouchi 1973; Bloom 1998; Koda 2003; Tanabe n.d.). A priority of most temples was to provide Japanese language instruction to the children of the immigrants who numbered in the tens of thousands (Asato 2012).

From the arrival of the first Buddhist missionary priest in 1889 and into pre–World War II, the prevailing perceptions of Buddhism were clearly nega-

Table 1
Number of Temples and Shrines in Hawai'i in 1941, by Sect and Island

Sect	Hawai'i	Kaua'i	Lāna'i	Maui	Moloka'i	O'ahu	All Islands
Jōdo Shinshū - Higashi	1	1	0	0	0	4	6
Jōdo Shinshū - Nishi	14	7	1	7	0	13	42
Jōdo Shū	9	2	0	3	0	3	17
Kegon	0	0	0	0	0	1	1
Konkyōkō	1	0	0	0	0	3	4
Kurozumikyō	0	1	0	0	0	0	1
Nichiren	1	0	0	2	0	3	6
Shingon	15	1	0	4	0	10	30
Shinshū Kyōkai	0	0	0	0	0	1	1
Shintō	12	7	0	7	0	20	46
Sōtō Zen	2	0	0	1	1	7	11
Tenrikyō	1	1	0	1	0	7	10
Tenshindō	0	0	1	0	0	0	1
Independent	0	0	0	0	0	2	2
Sect not known	1	0	0	0	0	3	4
Total	57	20	2	25	1	77	182

Sources: Hawai'i Hongwanji Ministers' Association (1991); Hayashi (2012); Box 228 (1945); Box 257 (1945); Box 293 (1945); Box 305 (1945); Box 2632 (1945); Soga (2008); and Williams (2003, n.d.- a, n.d.-b, n.d.-c).

tive among the largely Christian population and even some of the Japanese Christians in the Hawaiian Islands. In the minds of the non-Japanese Christian community, Buddhism was associated with and even thought to be synonymous with Shintō. In 1868, after the collapse of Japan's feudal regime, Shintō was made the state religion in an effort to forge a nation with unconditional loyalty to the Emperor who was considered divine. In Hawaiʻi, Japanese Buddhism and its followers were feared to be intimately tied to Japanese nationalism. In addition, being Buddhist was equated to being un-American and therefore a threat to national security (Hunter 1971; Okihiro 1991). Military intelligence

Table 2
Number of Buddhist and Shintō Priests in Hawaiʻi in 1941, by Sect and Island

Sect	Island not known	Hawaiʻi	Kauaʻi	Lānaʻi	Maui	Molokaʻi	Oʻahu	All
Jōdo Shinshū – Higashi	0	0	1	0	0	0	2	3
Jōdo Shinshū – Nishi	0	17	7	2	8	0	27	61
Jōdo Shū	0	9	2	0	3	0	6	20
Kegon	0	0	0	0	0	0	1	1
Konkōkyō	0	1	0	0	0	0	3	4
Kurozumikyō	0	0	0	0	0	0	0	0
Nichiren	0	1	0	0	0	0	3	4
Shingon	0	2	1	0	1	0	4	8
Shinshū Kyōkai	1	0	0	0	0	0	0	1
Shintō	0	2	3	0	3	0	16	24
Sōtō Zen	1	3	0	0	2	1	11	18
Tenrikyō	2	0	0	0	0	0	1	3
Tenshindō	0	0	0	1	0	0	0	1
Independent	0	0	0	0	0	0	1	1
Total	4	35	14	3	17	1	75	149

Sources: Hawaiʻi Hongwanji Ministers' Association (1991); Hayashi (2012); Box 228 (1945); Box 257 (1945); Box 293 (1945); Box 305 (1945); Box 2632 (1945); Soga (2008); and Williams (2003, n.d.- a, n.d.-b, n.d.-c).

reported Buddhism, along with the Japanese government via its consulate, and the Japanese language schools, as primary sources of anti-Americanism at least two decades before America's war with Japan (Okihiro 1991). The unfounded suspicions of espionage, sabotage, and subversion that surrounded Buddhism and especially its priests nevertheless placed them high on the FBI's custodial detention list of threats to the internal security of the United States in the event of war.

Thus, when the United States declared war against Japan after the bombing of Pearl Harbor, all but a handful of Japanese Buddhist priests were taken from their temple communities and interned in Department of Justice (DOJ), US Army, or War Relocation Authority (WRA) camps, leaving Hawai'i's Buddhist congregations stripped of their leaders. Nearly 100 percent of the active Shintō and Buddhist priests as a category, not selectively, were interned. Unbeknownst to these priests in Hawai'i, nearly all of them had been placed on custodial detention lists that were compiled by the FBI and other military intelligence agencies as early as 1938 through 1941 (Daniels 1994; Kashima 2003). The priests were multiply jeopardized: Most were Issei (more than 90 percent were first generation), Japanese citizens (1924 US law denied them citizenship), educated in Japan, spoke Japanese, and found to engage in activities deemed suspicious, for example, donating funds to the Japanese Red Cross or to the Japanese military campaign in Asia (Kashima 2003; Williams 2003). As a result, they were in the vanguard of those arrested, interrogated, and interned.

Under J. Edgar Hoover's nationwide "Alien Enemy Control" program, Japanese, Germans, Italians, and other potential enemies in Hawai'i and the US mainland were apprehended and interned (Rosenfeld 2014). However, unlike the mass internment of Japanese on the US mainland, the Japanese in Hawai'i who were interned were those judged to be security threats, such as religious, business, cultural, and organizational leaders, consular agents, language school officials, newspaper editors, and commercial fishermen. This was less than one percent of American civilians and resident aliens of Japanese ancestry who comprised over 30 percent of the total population of Hawai'i at the time (Allen 1950). Although some politicians pressed for mass incarceration in Hawai'i, "…the nation's highest military commanders successfully resisted the pressure, not because of any concern for the civil rights of the Hawaiian Japanese, but because Japanese labor was crucial to both the civilian and military economies in Hawaii" (Daniels 1994:48).

Dismantling Buddhism:
World War II Internment of Buddhist Priests

Little wonder that the Shintō and Buddhist priests were among the first civilians of Japanese ancestry to be seized by FBI agents within hours, days, or shortly after the December 7 attack on Pearl Harbor and taken to the Sand Island detention camp and other temporary detention centers on the neighbor islands. From there most were shipped to internment camps on the US mainland, often being transferred from camp to camp. Williams (2003) notes that the number and whereabouts of the Buddhist priests were kept from each other for national security reasons. Many of the priests were incarcerated in camps for the duration of the war though some chose to return to Japan. the Honpa Hongwanji Mission of Hawai'i's (HHMH) records show that of its 51 interned priests, 10 chose to repatriate to Japan during the war in 1943 and another 10 did so at the end of the war in 1945 (Hawaii 1991).

Buddhist Priests in Honouliuli Camp

After the closing of Sand Island Camp, which originally housed quarantined immigrants, internees were sent to the Honouliuli Internment and POW Camp which operated from March 1943 through the end of the war. The Honouliuli internment site was a US Army camp typical of other internment camps run by the DOJ, US Army, or WRA. The wooden cabins for internees and canvas tents for prisoners of war were located in the isolated and inhospitable Honouliuli Gulch. The internees referred to the camp as "Jigoku Dani" (Hell Valley) because of the blazing temperatures, swarming insects, and forbidding environment (Burton and Farrell 2008; Rosenfeld 2012).

The Japanese Cultural Center of Hawai'i (JCCH) data bank (Hayashi 2012) lists 114 Shintō and Buddhist priest internees, only seven of whom were incarcerated in the Honouliuli Camp for any length of time. It is not clear exactly how many priests were actually interned at Honouliuli, but in addition to the JCCH list of seven priest internees, other names of priests, priestesses, and a nun appear in National Archives and Records Administration (NARA II) files, Soga's (2008) list of internees departing from Honouliuli to other US mainland camps, and Williams's (2003) list of "The Fourteen Major 'Assembly Centers'" (1942). The names of 11 religious men and women identified from these sources include: Shintō priests Yoshio Akizaki and his son, Takeo Akizaki; Konkokyo sect Shintō priestess Haruko Takahashi; Jōdo Shinshū Buddhist priests Hakuin Isobe, Ryozen Kuwaye, and Ryuten Kashiwa; Tenrikyo sect

Buddhist priest Ichiro Genishi; Buddhist nun Shinsho Hirai; Sōtō Zen Buddhist Bishop Zenkyo Komagata and priest Jisho Yamasaki; and Kegon sect Buddhist priestess Ryuto Tsuda.

Records show that the Reverends Yoshio Akizaki, Takeo Akizaki, Jisho Yamasaki (Williams 2003), Ichiro Genishi, Hakuin Isobe, and Ryuten Kashiwa (Soga 2008) were shipped to internment camps on the US mainland. It appears that Bishop Zenkyo Komagata, the Reverend Ryozen Kuwaye, Priestesses Ryuto Tsuda and Haruko Takahashi, and Buddhist nun Shinsho Hirai, unlike the mass of Hawai'i's Buddhist priests, were not transferred to internment camps on the US mainland. They remained interned in Honouliuli Camp. Unfortunately, little is written about the living conditions or activities of the religious internees during their internment at Honouliuli. Most of what is learned comes from the available transcripts of their interrogation hearings.

The Buddhist priests in Honouliuli Camp were housed in the civilian section, with the women separated from the men. They were closely guarded and most likely did not conduct religious services although they were permitted private altars within their own confines. At her rehearing in November 1943, to determine if she should continue to be interned, Haruko Takahashi is asked: "Now, at the Internment camp, have you and Mrs. Tsuda held any service over there?" She replies: "I have not prayed once since I have been interned and I don't know if Mrs. Tsuda prays or not because she lives in a separate house from me" (Takahashi 1945). In May 1944, Ryuto Tsuda testifies at her rehearing that she gets up at 5:30 a.m. every morning, faces the Fuji shrine and prays for her members' sons who were fighting in Italy (Tsuda 1945). Neither Takahashi nor Tsuda mentions conducting religious services in the Honouliuli Camp.

The sparse information on some of the priests retrieved thus far is gleaned from interrogation hearings of relatively recent unclassified US government records. It is likely that the religious leaders who remained at Honouliuli were arrested later than those who were sent to camps on the US mainland. For example, both Komagata and Tsuda were able to avoid the initial wave of internment of religious leaders. Komagata was arrested three years later (Komagata 2011) and Tsuda was arrested months later (Nakagawa 1945).

Komagata's Sōtō Zen sect was targeted as dangerous because of its "nationalistic tendencies." Komagata himself was implicated among other reasons for his 1940 visit to Japan and its war front in China where he served as a visiting consolation priest for the Japanese military. His brother served as the resident priest of the family's Buddhist temple in Japan (Komagata 1945). When Komagata was interned he left a newly constructed temple on the edge of downtown Honolulu with a congregation of several hundred followers. In his absence, his wife oversaw the temple and conducted services. In Honouliuli Camp, Komagata volunteered to clean toilets, symbolic of cleansing his heart daily (Komagata 2011).

Tsuda was a colorful if not feisty priestess of the Kegon sect. She was divorced, used an alias, claimed to have healing powers, and was described by her ex-husband and other (unidentified) informants as religiously fanatic (Nakagawa 1945; Nishimura 2014). She ministered over a small temple of 40 to 50 loyal members in the McCully district of Honolulu that was later moved to a Pālolo Valley location by her disciple, Helen Shizuko Nakagawa. Although born in Hawaiʻi, Tsuda was suspect because she was educated in Japan and traveled to visit family there. She was accused of praying for Japanese victory in the war but she denied this in her interrogation hearings. While interned, Tsuda admittedly defied camp rules by smuggling letters out through Helen Nakagawa and talking with Buddhist followers in the camp. Despite her absence, her temple members continued to meet, convinced of her healing powers. Although not an ordained priestess, Nakagawa ministered over them. She, too, was later interned (Nakagawa 1945; Tsuda 1945).

Komagata's and Tsuda's responses to being interned might be seen as polar opposites—the former, seemingly resigned and entering deeper into his Buddhist tradition by daily cleansing his heart and the latter, defiantly continuing to minister to her followers even from afar. Both, however, continued to swear allegiance to the United States as did the other Honouliuli religious internees, to no avail. Although from different sects, both clung to their Buddhist religion in internment and returned to their temple congregations upon release. Regardless of their personal or sectarian differences, what they and other Buddhist priests shared in common was their judgment without trial, a breach of justice and their civil rights.

Buddhist Priests in US Mainland Camps

The small group of Buddhist ministers who were detained at Honouliuli was but a fraction of the well over 100 other Shintō and Buddhist priests from Hawaiʻi who were incarcerated in camps on the US mainland (see Table 3). From their respected positions in tight-knit immigrant communities the

Buddhist priests from Hawai'i were thrust into camps in hostile and stifling environments more than an ocean away from all that was familiar. Not much is written about how these priest internees fared under conditions of unlawful imprisonment. Some information is discovered in personal diaries and stories passed on to family members and others but only in some cases are they translated and/or made available to the public. By recapturing some of the experiences of the Hawai'i Buddhist priests in DOJ, US Army, or WRA camps, we gain some idea of the impact of internment not only on their lives

Table 3
Number of Interned Buddhist and Shintō Priests from Hawai'i in 1941, by Sect and Island

Sect	Island not known	Hawai'i	Kaua'i	Lāna'i	Maui	Moloka'i	O'ahu	All
Jōdo Shinshū – Higashi	0	0	1	0	0	0	1	2
Jōdo Shinshū – Nishi	0	15	6	2	7	0	23	53
Jōdo Shū	0	6	0	0	3	0	6	15
Kegon	0	0	0	0	0	0	1	1
Konkōkyō	0	1	0	0	0	0	2	2
Kurozumikyō	0	0	0	0	0	0	0	0
Nichiren	0	1	0	0	0	0	2	3
Shingon	0	1	0	0	1	0	2	4
Shinshū Kyōkai	1	0	0	0	0	0	0	1
Shintō	0	2	3	0	2	0	13	20
Sōtō Zen	1	3	0	0	2	1	8	15
Tenrikyō	2	0	0	0	0	0	1	3
Tenshindō	0	0	0	0	0	0	0	0
Independent	0	0	0	0	0	0	0	0
Sect not known	3	0	0	0	0	0	0	3
Total	7	28	10	2	15	1	59	122

Sources: Hawai'i Hongwanji Ministers' Association (1991); Hayashi (2012); Box 228 (1945); Box 257 (1945); Box 293 (1945); Box 305 (1945); Box 2632 (1945); Soga (2008); and Williams (2003, n.d.- a, n.d.-b, n.d.-c).

but on the institution of the Buddhist religion. In addition, we see Buddhism's influence on its followers' response to the internment trauma and its effect on camp life.

One Hawai'i Jōdo Shinshū Buddhist priest who was interned in several US mainland internment camps is the Reverend Ryoshin Okano. His thriving temple in Pearl City stood precariously close to Pearl Harbor and its nearby military bases. That alone posed a security threat and so he was arrested the night Pearl Harbor was bombed, spent about two months in the Sand Island camp, and was then interned in various camps on the US mainland (Okano 2014). Representative of other active priests ministering to the Japanese Buddhist communities in Hawai'i at the outbreak of the war, Okano came from Japan an educated and ordained minister in the hopes of spreading the teachings of the Hongwanji or Jōdo Shinshū sect. His decision to live his life as a missionary in the Islands was affirmed when he traveled back to Japan and returned to Hawai'i with his bride ready to start a family. When he was interned, he left his wife and two young children behind. In May 1943, they joined him in camp at Crystal City, Texas. Eventually the family repatriated to Japan via a year-and-a-half stay in Singapore and finally all reunited in Hawai'i in 1951 (Okano 1945; Okano 2008). Okano's son, retired Hongwanji Bishop Thomas Okano, recalls little of the internment experience. He remembers his father telling him that ministers were among the least useful in camp because they were not laborers or skilled in a trade but rather "only read scriptures" and so, many were assigned or volunteered to haul trash (Okano 2010).

In his memoirs, Soga (2008) expresses his personal opinion that on the whole, priests and educators behaved in the worst ways in the internment camps. He was disappointed to find that some Buddhist priests were greedy, others avoided work, and still others lacked character and humility. The priests themselves were somewhat critical of their own character flaws or any less than admirable behavior that surfaced during incarceration (Okano 2010; Tana 1976–89). However, for the most part, they stoically embraced Buddhist teachings such as perseverance, nonattachment, and acceptance that brought comfort and solace while enduring the severe physical, mental, and emotional hardships of internment (Fujimura 1985; Tamai 1981).

Most of the ministers were incarcerated in DOJ or US Army camps for enemy aliens. A few, however, were allowed to serve in WRA camps where the non-enemy internees were held. Many resumed their positions as spiritual leaders in the desolate and inhospitable camps that confined them and their captive congregations. The role of the religious leadership included more than spiritual guidance especially because the Buddhist religion was the only major institution of the Japanese that was allowed to operate in the camps. More than half of the Japanese internees declared themselves Buddhist and it is this group of followers that the cadre of Buddhist priests dutifully served, officiating over memorial services, funerals, and weddings and organizing rituals and festivals acknowledging Buddha's birthday, *Obon* (custom of honoring spirits of ancestors), and other annually celebrated traditional events. Hunter (1971) tells of Hawai'i's Rev. Hakuai Oda expertly fashioning cherry blossoms with beet juice–dyed toilet tissue that was used at a festival commemorating Buddha's birth at Camp McCoy in Wisconsin. On this occasion, Hawai'i's Rev. Ninryo Nago addressed the festival goers and reminisced about the prewar celebrations of this same annual event that were held at Kapi'olani Park in Waikīkī, Hawai'i.

"Buddhist life in the camps revolved around the barrack 'churches' (some were mess halls or recreation buildings) that held religious services and education, especially on Sundays" (Williams 2002:195). In this context the Buddhist priests not only provided spiritual support, they also maintained and transmitted Japanese cultural heritage to their followers. "Especially for the Issei, the Buddhist barrack church became a meaningful gathering place not only for the inspirational aspects of religious practice, but also because it was a place where their Japanese heritage was affirmed" (Williams 2003:267).

Hardships in the Hawai'i Buddhist Communities

While the Buddhist congregations in the camps, led by their priests, observed the rituals and practices of their religion, the Buddhist temples in Hawai'i, left abandoned of their priests, struggled in their absence. Many of the temples were closed, but in some cases, the wives of the interned temple priests assumed their duties in a limited capacity as martial law forbade large gatherings of Japanese people. Bishop Shugen Komagata (2011) recalls that his grandmother conducted services such as funerals and weddings when her husband was interned at Honouliuli. Bishop Yoshiaki Fujitani (2005), whose father Rev. Kodo Fujitani left a wife and eight children when he was interned, recalls that his mother conducted religious services. In 1948, Rev. Kodo Fujitani became the first elected Hongwanji bishop in postwar Hawai'i, following acting Bishop Rev. Ryuten Kashiwa.

The hardships imposed upon the wives of abruptly interned temple priests were severe. Many did not speak English, were isolated from their temple communities, and forced to find work of some kind (Umehara 1993). Typical of other ministers' wives, Shigeo Kikuchi, wife of Jōdo Shinshū Rev. Chikyoku Kikuchi, was left in fear and confusion after her husband was taken away without explanation from their rural temple in Nāʻālehu on the Big Island of Hawaiʻi. Although she was told he would return in two or three days, it was three months before she was permitted to meet with him at Kīlauea Military Camp before he was eventually interned on the US mainland. With no access to their frozen bank account, conditions were desperate. In despair, she burned possessions that were associated with Japan including many rare Japanese books, pictures, and diaries. However, she clung tenaciously to her Buddhist heritage (Kikuchi 1991).

Similarly, Yoshiko Tatsuguchi, herself an ordained Buddhist minister and wife of interned Rev. Goki Tatsuguchi, was left with six young children and the responsibilities of the Shinshū Kyōkai Mission on Oʻahu. With the help of temple members and friends she was able to endure the war-long adversity thrust upon her (Suzuki 2009).

The restrictions placed on the practice of the Buddhist religion and the loss of its priests in Hawaiʻi had especially devastating effects on the Issei members. "Without the temples, where they had congregated for years to worship and socialize, and without their priests, whom they had relied on for moral and spiritual guidance, they were deprived of everything that gave meaning to their existence" (Hunter 1971:193). Suzuki (1957) mentions one especially devout Shin member from the coffee farms in Kona on the Big Island of Hawaiʻi. He characterizes her as a *myōkōnin* (a wondrous devout follower of Shin Buddhism) because of her deeply spiritual songs and poems. In a letter to her interned minister, Chiyono Sasaki, who sent four sons to fight for the United States wrote, "After you left us (for the internment camp in 1942), our life was not hard materially but spiritually it was most terrible" (Wells 2012:176).

In order to alleviate the void left by their interned ministers, lay members of Buddhist temples petitioned the Office of the Military Governor for permission to conduct Buddhist services. However, it ruled that "The general policy of this office is to discourage the resumption of Japanese religious activities other than Christian" (Japanese Internment and Relocation Files 1982). The fear of providing opportunity for subversive gatherings was stronger than any inclination to allow for the practice of a foreign religion.

Buddhism and Priests in the Camps:
Choices, Changes, and Challenges

In Honouliuli and in camps scattered in remote inland areas across the United States, Buddhist priests persevered under conditions fraught with ambiguity, conflict, and contradiction. The question of loyalty, the internal sectarian differences, the pressure to "Americanize," the generational (Issei–Nisei) shift in power, and other daunting issues of daily living posed challenges (Bloom 2010). We suggest that the rational choice model provides insight into the difficult decisions and choices made by the Buddhist leadership, priests, and lay internees as individuals and as a community. The choices they made under the constraints and opportunities at that time helped to revitalize Japanese Buddhism in Hawai'i and the US mainland.

The Question of Loyalty

From the beginning of World War II and even before the bombing of Pearl Harbor the communications sent from the Buddhist headquarters in Kyōto, Japan and from the American-based Buddhist leadership to priests and followers on the national and local levels strongly urged loyalty to the United States (Tabrah 1989; Kumata 2007). The Kyōto-based Rev. Abbot Jikai Yamasato sent to each Hawai'i Kyōdan minister a personal letter exhorting patriotic service to the United States. "Bishop Kuchiba received a telegram from the Abbott with the same unmistakable directive, Japanese ministers serving in the Hawaii Mission were to be one hundred per cent [*sic*] loyal to the United States in the conflict that, this fall of 1941, every headline indicated was imminent" (Tabrah 1989:78). Regardless of the pledge of loyalty and the absence of a single incident of sabotage or subversion, Buddhism was suspect and Buddhist priests were automatically judged dangerous enemy aliens.

While the official position of the North American Buddhist Mission (NABM) headquarters located in Camp Topaz, Utah during the war unequivocally called for loyalty and support of the United States, many of the Issei ministers were personally in sympathy with Japan and elated at news of its victories (Fujimura 1985; Tana 1976–89). Bishop Gikyo Kuchiba, a devout and serious scholar of the HHMH had difficulty accepting Japan's final defeat and repatriated to Japan after the war leaving the Hongwanji temporarily without a leader. His earlier prewar messages to the July 1941 Buddhist assembly of ministers and lay delegates in Hawaiʻi publicly and dutifully championed patriotism and loyalty and in September 1941 at the Young Buddhist Association (YBA) annual conference, Bishop Kuchiba challenged, "… now is time for you young people to prove yourselves by being ready to die a martyr to your country of stars and stripes as an American citizen of Japanese ancestry under the Buddhist faith" (Tabrah 1989:78).

As spokespersons and leaders of their congregations, the Issei Buddhist priests pledged allegiance to the United States, the country that denied them citizenship, while also harboring loyal sentiments to their country of birth and citizenship. Such was their dilemma which Williams (2003) referred to as "complex loyalties" noting that "some of the very same priests who exhibited pro-Japanese tendencies also encouraged young Nisei to volunteer for the 100th Infantry Battalion/442nd Regimental Combat Unit, the all-Nisei American unit in the European theater that earned the distinction of being the most highly decorated unit for its bravery in battle" (p. 270).

Among the interned Hawaiʻi Buddhist ministers, Rev. Ryuten Kashiwa's son, Genro Kashiwa, served in the famed 100th Infantry Battalion/442nd Regimental Unit and Rev. Kodo Fujitani's son, Yoshiaki Fujitani, (later to become reverend and bishop), served in the US Military Intelligence Service (MIS). While on active duty, Yoshiaki Fujitani recalls visiting his father in the DOJ Sante Fe camp but remembers only the small talk and little else of the visit (Fujitani 2005). The Buddhist priests were wedged between a forced either-or question of loyalty when in fact they were likely neither or both, so conflicting were their loyalties. Officially, they stood by their decision to remain loyal to the United States.

The Differences among the Buddhist Sects in the Camps

The oppositions facing the ministers were not limited to those they had with their captors; they were internal among the different Buddhist sects as well. While more than the majority was of the Jōdo Shinshū sect, other Buddhist sects were living side by side. The sectarian differences causing tension and disputes among the groups were not only doctrinal, they were financial and political as well, including the distribution of offerings and the loyalty issue (Kashima 1977). However, the involuntary confinement in close and crowded living quarters in the barracks, the ritual and ceremonial needs of the internees, and other desperate conditions of internment compelled collaboration and mutual aid. In addition, "The WRA forced Buddhist sects to cooperate with each other, which meant that doctrinal differences were often ignored in favor of a more common, trans-sectarian Buddhism" (Williams 2002:195). This was reflected in joint services, common chanting, rites, and other customary practices.

The compromises on the part of the different Buddhist sects helped to prevent conflict and maintain harmony in the camps. The general Buddhist doctrines of non-ego, interdependence of all beings, and nonattachment provided a perfectly suited philosophy for adapting to crisis in forced confinement. Buddhist teachings reinforced the benefits of tolerance and cooperation among the internees in enduring wartime adversity in the camps.

The Pressure to "Americanize"

While priests and internees struggled with divided loyalties; religious, ethnic, and cultural identification; and generational differences, the position of the WRA was unmistakable and deliberate—that of "Americanizing" the Japanese. The WRA's program advocated speaking English not Japanese, playing sports like baseball and basketball rather than *sumō* or *jūdō*, joining American organizations like Boy Scouts and Girl Scouts rather than young Buddhist clubs, converting to Christianity rather than practicing Buddhism, and supporting the war cause by buying war bonds, donating blood to the American Red Cross, joining the US Armed Forces, and other displays of loyalty (Williams 2003). The efforts were not in vain, perhaps more so because the Americanization process had already taken root among the Nisei even prior to the war. Embracing the lifestyle and traditions of the United States was less a problem and more an advantage for the Nisei who were US citizens by birth.

However, in an unintended way, the barracks way of life, especially the practice of Buddhism with its traditional celebrations and ceremonies, strengthened identification with Japanese heritage and culture. Services and social gatherings enhanced ethnic solidarity and maintained cultural beliefs and practices despite the pressure to Americanize. The Buddhist religion functioned simultaneously as a means of affirming Japanese heritage and demonstrating cultural and moral resistance to compulsory Americanization (Okihiro 1984; Williams 2003).

The Generational Shift in Power from the Issei to the Nisei

In the internment camps, the Issei Buddhist ministers were relied upon heavily for ritual and moral support and thus they were respected as leaders by their congregations. However, their authority was undermined by WRA policies that demanded dealing with and working through English-speaking Japanese American Nisei in the camps. This transition of power broke with tradition and religious values and beliefs such as filial piety and ancestral worship and threatened to add to the differences dividing the Issei and Nisei. In light of the mass internment divesting the Issei Buddhist ministers of their influence, and to protect the Nisei and their children whose homeland by birth was the United States, the national Buddhist leadership began to answer to the Americanization policies and program in self-preserving ways. The decisions and adaptations they made helped to ensure the future generations of Buddhists a rightful place in the United States.

The process of adapting to the American way of life was not something new. The war amplified and accelerated the changes set in motion earlier. After a series of meetings in April 1944 in the Topaz Camp, Utah, the NABM with Bishop Matsukage at its head was renamed the Buddhist Churches of America (BCA) (Kashima 1977), confirming changes that were brewing years before the war. In July 1944, at a YBA meeting held in Salt Lake City with predominantly Nisei in attendance, the new organizational changes under the name of the BCA were ratified. In his will to all his ministers, Bishop Matsukage acknowledged that "[w]ith the war as the turning point, the Japanese-American society has changed from the Issei to the Nisei era. Accordingly, the Buddhist Churches must, of necessity, also undergo a change" (Sanada 2007:113). The wisdom of investing the Nisei with power over religious matters proved beneficial for the survival and propagation of Buddhism in the United States.

Although the Nisei were thrust into leadership roles by structural institutional changes in the Buddhist church and the policies of the WRA, their assumption into power was not immediate. Bishop Matsukage and Issei Buddhist priests retained their roles as architects and advisers of the newly configured BCA. Furthermore, Okihiro (1984) contends that rather than widening the generational breach between the Issei and Nisei, the forced internment further exposed the historical anti-Japanese prejudice and discrimination that prevented full communion with the American society, thus drawing the Nisei to their roots from which they were drifting away.

Making the Best of Daily Living in the Camps

The daily drudgery, boredom, and restrictions of camp life imposed burdens on the lives of interned ministers and laypersons and at the same time provided opportunities unavailable to those outside the camps. On a personal level, many of the ministers who were formerly serving in isolated rural communities, shouldering the cares and concerns of their congregations, found camaraderie in adversity and time to study and reflect upon the nature of life, Buddhist teachings, and their fate. Williams (2003) observes that "This optimistic approach to incarceration, as an ideal time to reflect on Buddhist teachings on the nature of life, was a consistent theme in many Issei Buddhist sermons" (p. 267).

In Hawai'i where martial law prevailed, most temples were closed; Japanese language schools were shut down and Japanese organizations, clubs, and social groups were disbanded. American civilians and resident aliens of Japanese ancestry were denied assembly in large groups thus prohibiting religious, educational, and social gatherings of any sort. Meanwhile, in the camps, the Buddhist church was involved with or organized Japanese language classes, study groups, cultural clubs and activities, and religious services that maintained Japanese ethnic heritage. These groups and activities helped to make the best of the dire circumstances of internment.

The Revival of Buddhism in Post–World War II Hawai'i

World War II came to an official end on September 1, 1945, when Japan formally surrendered on the USS *Missouri* in Tokyo Bay. Two months later in November 1945, the first Buddhist priests returning to Hawai'i entered Honolulu Harbor aboard an army transport, with others soon to follow (Hunter 1971). The postwar era gave birth to long incubating changes prefiguring the Americanization of Buddhism, thus defining its future in Hawai'i and the US mainland. The BCA and HHMH had already agreed to significant changes that included severing ties with Japan, minimizing relations with the Jōdo Shinshū Kyōto headquarters, electing its own bishop, and relinquishing control to the Nisei (Kashima 1977; Tabrah 1989).

The direction of these changes was not foreign to the Hawai'i Jōdo Shinshū Buddhists. As early as the turn of the twentieth century, Bishop Yemyo Imamura of the HHMH, a highly respected religious and civic leader whose tenure as bishop was from 1899 to his death in 1932, had charted a course that was meant to hasten the Americanization of the Japanese immigrants as well as to universally spread the teachings of the Buddha. Undaunted by the racial and religious bigotry of the period, "He organized Boys Scout troops and worked to universalize Buddhism through the development of hymns, sermons in English, Sunday school programs, and used pews and pulpits in temples" (Bloom 1998:33). In August 1924, in a landmark ceremony in Honolulu at the Honpa Hongwanji, Bishop Imamura invested ordination rites upon Ernest and Dorothy Hunt. An Englishman by birth and Buddhist by choice, Hunt advanced the program of Americanizing and universalizing Buddhism. Through the war years and beyond he remained a spokesperson, defender, and most influential figure in the Buddhist community in Hawai'i. Buddhist leaders like Imamura and Hunt played pivotal roles in the evolution of Buddhism in the Hawaiian Islands, the portal through which Buddhism passed on its journey to the US mainland. The unprecedented developments and events in the early history of Buddhism in Hawai'i were visible precursors of changes that were to come and the war waged in the Pacific and European theaters hastened the arrival.

On the US mainland the Buddhist church was at the forefront in the resettlement of thousands of internees after the camps were closed (Horinouchi 1973). Although many of the temples had been vandalized or destroyed during the war years those that remained were used as hostels in transitioning the internees back into mainstream society. While those who still owned agricultural land or property returned to their home sites, many others relocated to different areas of the country to begin life anew. Despite the uncertainties and challenges of resettlement, post–World War II America was fertile ground for the spread of Buddhism. Davis (1993) claims that the internment experience forced the spread of Buddhism eastward into new territories, new temples, and new congregations.

In Hawai'i the Buddhist priests returned to temple communities that had been left largely adrift. A few of the temples were vandalized but others were ready to welcome back their priests. The trend toward Americanization and changes in the Buddhist church were already in motion. A series of interviews with religious and academic knowledgeable sources of Buddhism in general and in Hawai'i confirmed the institutional changes that were heralded decades before and thrust into action by the war (Bloom 2010; Okano 2010; Komagata 2011; Williams 2011; Yosemori 2011). In post–World War II Hawai'i, included among the many changes were: the local Buddhist church elected its own Bishop; English fluency was the standard; making decisions and setting policies were in the control of lay leaders; and Nisei were encouraged to be priests. The changes were neither immediate nor necessarily easy but they were imminent.

Returning Nisei veterans were among the leaders of a vibrant YBA in post–World War II Hawai'i that worked together with a formerly interned Buddhist priest, the Reverend Newton Ishiura, a Hawai'i-born Nisei from California, to bring attention to and recognition of the religious identity of Nisei soldiers who fought in the war against Japan. In 1948, the Hawai'i YBA erected and dedicated a memorial plaque on the HHMH temple grounds inscribed with the names of 374 American Buddhists who lost their lives in the war. That same year, the YBAs nationwide sent a petition with 100,000 signatures to James Forrestal, secretary of defense, requesting that the letter "B" for Buddhist be included among the Protestant "P", Catholic "C", and Hebrew "H" religious identification tags. Eventually in 1950, Buddhist soldiers fighting in the Korean conflict were allowed to wear temporary plastic tags with the letter "B" provided by the Hawai'i YBA, along with the regulation metal identification tags. With the success of the "B" for Buddhist campaign, Buddhism was finally accepted as a part of the US government's religious identification system. Shortly after, the US War Department approved the *dharmacakra* (Buddhist wheel of life symbolizing the Noble Eightfold Path) as an appropriate grave marker for Buddhist veterans of World War II and future Buddhist veterans. Amid the symbolic eight Bodhi trees planted in 1949 at the request of the Hawai'i YBA, Nisei Buddhist veterans were identified with appropriate grave markers finally granting them a fitting resting place in the National Cemetery of the Pacific (Punchbowl Cemetery) (Hunter 1971; Tabrah 1971; Masatsugu 2004).

In the ensuing years, the Hawai'i Buddhist community extended its educational reach by establishing the first regularly accredited private Buddhist elementary school in the United States in 1949, a Buddhist Study Center modeled after the Institute of Buddhist Studies at Berkeley in 1972 (Tabrah 1989), and the first Buddhist high school in the United States in 2003 (Essoyan 2003). The Americanization of Shin Buddhism in Hawai'i, initiated by Bishop Yemyo Imamura in the early twentieth century, was most evident in Sunday English services in temples with pews and English *gātha* (hymn) books. From policy to practice the Buddhist church experienced change and revival.

Conclusion

What is the significance of Honouliuli to Buddhism, its priests and congregations, and to its future? Honouliuli Internment and POW Camp's importance to the attacks on the First Amendment rights to freedom of speech, press, religion, peaceful assembly, and petitioning the government for the redress of grievance is monumental. Although many people still do not know that an internment camp ever existed on the island of Oʻahu, Hawaiʻi, as the remnants of the physical site and the story of internees are uncovered, there is a growing awareness of and knowledge about the injustices of war. For those resident aliens and American citizens of Japanese ancestry who suffered through the internment debacle of World War II, whether at Honouliuli or another DOJ, US Army, or WRA camp, it has seemingly come full circle. The denial of their civil rights was recognized by the US government through redress. Still, 70-plus years after the bombing of Pearl Harbor and the events that followed, the painful memories of war linger. Understandably, many remaining internees, as well as their family members, choose not to speak about the experience. However, the silence that shields the injustices of war and its collateral destruction must be broken if only to document and preserve historical realities that threaten democracy. Honouliuli is stark evidence of the threats to democracy that accompany threats to national security.

Our research on Buddhism and the internment and the aftermath of World War II followed from an interest in the history of Buddhism in Hawaiʻi from the early days of immigration to the present, with questions about its future. It is likely that no other single event more greatly challenged its existence, authority, or viability. Japanese Buddhism survived the internment experience of World War II and adapted to the many changes moving from a pre-modern plantation economy to a modern service economy. In attempting to move beyond simply describing to explaining the decisions, adaptations, changes, constraints, and opportunities that were faced in the process, we propose that the new paradigm's rational choice theory is useful as a unifying conceptual framework. It assumes that after considering costs and benefits, individuals, groups, and communities choose options that maximize their benefits.

In this paper, rational choice theory is used to help explain individual choices such as members deciding to remain Buddhist or convert to Christianity, priests choosing to stay in the United States or repatriate to Japan, as well as institutional decisions made by the leadership and governing bodies of the BCA, HHMH, and YBA to pledge loyalty to the United States, revamp archaic organizational structures, and "Americanize" religious policies and practices. Whether choices were made freely or under duress simply points to the constraints and opportunities that are considered in rational choice theory. Further, although the old paradigm appears to better fit Buddhism in the early plantation economy assuming that immigrants follow tradition and take on ascribed religious identities, beliefs, and practices, it leaves little to the discretion of the individual. Smith and Froese (2008) suggest that the new paradigm is not confined to capitalist industrial and post-industrial settings but to pre-industrial societies as well and that there are religious options to what appears to be a monopoly. Further, while critics charge that among other concerns rational choice theory is too simple a model of reality, bordering on tautology and explaining the obvious, proponents counter that these same criticisms can be made of alternative theories and the fact is that it does fit the data (Iannaccone 1995).

World War II internment did not abolish Japanese Buddhism. It did accelerate adaptations and accommodations already in process that foreshadowed the "Americanization" of Buddhism. Looking to the future of Buddhism in Hawai'i and the US mainland, it is likely that it will survive and even thrive if Buddhist actors make religious choices that maximize their benefits as rational choice theory predicts. ❖

References

Allen, Gwenfread. 1950. *Hawaii's War Years: 1941–1945*. Honolulu: University of Hawai'i Press. Reprinted by Pacific Monographs, 1999.

Asato, Noriko. 2012. "The Japanese Language School Controversy in Hawai'i." Pp. 45–63 in *Issei Buddhism in the Americas*, edited by Duncan R. Williams and Tomoe Moriya. Chicago: University of Illinois Press.

Bloom, Alfred. 1998. "Shin Buddhism in America." Pp. 12–47 in *The Faces of Buddhism in America*, edited by Charles S. Prebish and Kenneth K. Tanaka. Berkeley and Los Angeles: University of California Press.

———. 2010. Interview by Linda Nishigaya and Ernest Oshiro, Kailua, HI, September 2.

Burton, Jeffery F., and Mary Farrell. 2008. *Jigoku-Dani: An Archaeological Reconnaissance of the Honouliuli Internment Camp, O'ahu, Hawai'i*. Honolulu: Japanese Cultural Center of Hawai'i.

Daniels, Roger. 1994. *Prisoners Without Trial: Japanese Americans in World War II*. New York: Hill and Wang.

Davis, Susan. 1993. "Mountain of Compassion." *Tricycle* 2(4)(Summer).

Essoyan, Susan. 2003. "Buddhist School to Focus on Peace." *Honolulu Star-Bulletin*. February 18. Retrieved December 24, 2012 (archives.starbulletin.com/2003/02/18/news/index1.html).

Fujimura, Bunyu. 1985. *Though I Be Crushed*. Los Angeles: The Nembutsu Press.

Fujitani, Yoshiaki. 2005. Interview by Michi Kodama-Nishimoto and Warren Nishimoto, Mānoa, HI, April 7.

Hawaii Hongwanji Ministers' Association. 1991. *Biographical History of Hawaii Hongwanji Ministers*. Honolulu: Honpa Hongwanji Mission of Hawai'i.

Hayashi, Tatsumi. 2012. "Hawai'i Internees Database." Japanese Cultural Center of Hawai'i. Unpublished manuscript.

Horinouchi, Isao. 1973. "Americanized Buddhism: A Sociological Analysis of a Protestantized Japanese Religion." PhD dissertation, Department of Sociology, University of California, Davis.

Hunter, Louise. 1971. *Buddhism in Hawaii: Its Impact on a Yankee Community*. Honolulu: University of Hawai'i Press.

Iannaccone, Laurence R. 1995. "Voodoo Economics? Reviewing the Rational Choice Approach to Religion." *Journal for the Scientific Study of Religion* 34(1):76–89.

Japanese Internment and Relocation Files: The Hawaii Experience 1942–1982. 1982. (bulk: 1942–1945). Hawai'i War Records Depository, University of Hawai'i at Mānoa, Hamilton Library, Honolulu.

Kashima, Tetsuden. 1977. *Buddhism in America: The Social Organization of an Ethnic Religious Institution*. Connecticut: Greenwood Press.

———. 2003. *Judgment without Trial: Japanese American Imprisonment During World War II*. Seattle: University of Washington Press.

———. 2008. "Introduction." Pp. 1–16 in *Life behind Barbed Wire: The World War II Internment Memoirs of a Hawai'i Issei,* by Yasutaro Soga. Honolulu: University of Hawai'i Press.

Kikuchi, Shigeo. 1991. *Memoirs of a Buddhist Woman Missionary in Hawai'i*. Honolulu: The Buddhist Study Center Press.

Koda, Tara K. 2003. "Aloha with Gassho: Buddhism in the Hawaiian Plantations." *Pacific World* Third Series(5):237–254.

Komagata, Shugen. 2011. Interview by Linda Nishigaya and Ernest Oshiro, Honolulu, May 10.

Komagata, Zenkyo. 1945. Record Group 494, Records of the Military Government of Hawaii, Entry (A1) 19 Alien Processing Center, Box 228, Internee Case Files, 1941–45, File: "Komagata, Zenkyo (ISN-HJ-959-CI)." National Archives and Records Administration II, College Park, Maryland.

Kumata, Kenryo M. 2007. "Letter to Members of Buddhist Churches of United States of America," dated March 5, 1942. P. 5 in *Memories, The Buddhist Church Experience in the Camps 1942–1945*, revised edition, compiled by Eiko Irene Matsuyama. n.p.: Buddhist Churches of America.

Masatsugu, Michael Kenji. 2004. "Reorienting the Pure Land: Japanese Americans, the Beats, and the Making of American Buddhism, 1941–1966." PhD dissertation, Department of History, University of California, Irvine.

Nakagawa, Helen Shizuko. 1945. Record Group 494, Records of the Military Government of Hawaii, Entry (A1) 19 Alien Processing Center, Box 257, Internee Case Files, 1941–45, File "Nakagawa, Helen Shizuko (ISN-HJ-920-CI)." National Archives and Records Administration II, College Park, Maryland.

Nishimura, Amy. 2014. "From Priestesses and Disciples to Witches and Traitors: Internment of Japanese Women at Honouliuli and Narratives of 'Madwomen.'" In this issue.

Office of the Provost Marshal General. 1946a. Record Group 389, Records of the Office of the Provost Marshal General, Entry (A1) 480, Records Relating to Persons of Japanese Ancestry Residing in the United States, 1942–46. Box 1723, File: "Hawaii, Japanese." National Archives and Records Administration II, College Park, Maryland.

————. 1946b. Record Group 389, Records of the Office of the Provost Marshal General Entry (A1) 461, Enemy Prisoner of War Information Bureau. Subject Files, 1942–46. National Archives and Records Administration II, College Park, Maryland.

Okano, Francis. 2008. Ryoshin & Kimiko: A Family Sketch. Honolulu. Unpublished manuscript.

————. 2013. E-mail correspondence with Ernest Oshiro. April 6.

Okano, Ryoshin. 1945. Record Group 494, Records of the Military Government of Hawaii, Entry (A1) 19 Alien Processing Center, Box 2632, Internee Case Files, 1941–45, File: "Hawaii, Civilian Internees: Okano, Ryoshin." National Archives and Records Administration II, College Park, Maryland.

Okano, Thomas. 2010. Interview by Linda Nishigaya and Ernest Oshiro, Honolulu, October 11.

Okihiro, Gary Y. 1984. "Religion and Resistance in America's Concentration Camps." *Phylon* (1960) 45(3)(3rd Qtr.):220–233.

————. Okihiro, Gary Y. 1991. *Cane Fires: The Anti-Japanese Movement in Hawai'i, 1865–1945*. Philadelphia: Temple University Press.

Prebish, Charles S., and Kenneth K. Tanaka. 1998. *The Faces of Buddhism in America*. Berkeley: University of California Press.

Rosenfeld, Alan. 2011. "Barbed-Wire Beaches: Martial Law and Civilian Internment in Wartime Hawai'i." *World History Connected* 8(3). Retrieved May 21, 2013 (http://worldhistoryconnected.press.illinois.edu/8.3/forum_rosenfeld.html).

————. 2012. "Honouliuli Detention Facility" *Densho Encyclopedia*. Retrieved December 31, 2012 (encyclopedia.densho.org).

————. 2014. "Neither Aliens nor Enemies: The Hearings of 'German' and 'Italian' Internees in Wartime Hawai'i." In this issue.

Sanada, Shintatsu. 2007. "Bishop Ryotai Matsukage and the BCA." P. 115 in *Memories, The Buddhist Church Experience in the Camps 1942–1945*, revised edition, compiled by Eiko Irene Matsuyama. n.p.: Buddhist Churches of America.

Smith, Buster G., and Paul Froese. 2008. "The Sociology of Buddhism: Theoretical Implications of Current Scholarship." *Interdisciplinary Journal of Research on Religion* 4(2):1–24.

Soga, Yasutaro. 2008. *Life behind Barbed Wire: The World War II Internment Memoirs of a Hawai'i Issei*. Honolulu: University of Hawai'i Press.

Suzuki, Daisetz Teitaro. 1957. *Mysticism: Christian and Buddhist*. New York: Harper.

Suzuki, Lois Tatsuguchi. 2009. "Kansha–With Deepest Gratitude." *The Hawaii Herald*. November 6:10.

Tabrah, Ruth. 1989. *A Grateful Past, A Promising Future; Honpa Hongwanji Mission of Hawai'i 100 Year History 1889–1989*. Honolulu: Honpa Hongwanji Mission of Hawai'i.

Takahashi, Haruko. 1945. Record Group 494, Records of the Military Government of Hawaii, Entry (A1) 19 Alien Processing Center, Box 293, Internee Case Files, 1941–45, File: "Takahashi, Haruko (ISN-HJ-307-CI)." National Archives and Records Administration II, College Park, Maryland.

Tamai, Yoshitaka. 1981. *Ichinyo*. San Francisco: Heian International Publishing Company.

Tana, Daisho. 1976–89. *Santa Fe, Lordsburg Senji Tekikokujin Yokuryujo,* 4 vols., edited by Tana Tomoe. Tokyo: Sankibo Busshorin.

Tanabe, George Jr. N.d. *The Lotus in Paradise: A Resource Booklet* in conjunction with the exhibition Lotus in Paradise: Buddhism and Japanese American Identity in Hawaii. Through April 2000.

Tsuda, Kiyome. 1945. Record Group 494, Records of the Military Government of Hawaii, Entry (A1) 19 Alien Processing Center, Box 305, Internee Case Files, 1941–45, File: "Tsuda, Kiyome (alias Ryuto) (ISN-HUS-551-CI)." National Archives and Records Administration II, College Park, Maryland.

Umehara, Toku. 1993. Interview by Yoshiaki Fujitani, Honolulu, HI, September 13. Japanese Cultural Center of Hawai'i Oral History Interviews.

Warner, R. Stephen. 1993. "Work in Progress Toward a New Paradigm for the Sociological Study of Religion in the United States." *The American Journal of Sociology* 98(5) (March):1044–1093.

Wells, Keiko. 2012. "The Role of Buddhist Song Culture in International Acculturation." Pp. 164–181 in *Issei Buddhism in the Americas*, edited by Duncan R. Williams and Tomoe Moriya. Chicago: University of Illinois Press.

Williams, Duncan Ryuken. 2002. "Camp Dharma." Pp. 191–200 in *Westward Dharma: Buddhism Beyond Asia*, edited by Martin Baumann and Charles S. Prebish. Berkeley: University of California Press.

————. 2003. "Complex Loyalties: Issei Buddhist Ministers during the Wartime Incarceration." *Pacific World* Third Series(5):255–274.

————. 2011. Interview by Linda Nishigaya and Ernest Oshiro, Berkeley, June 16.

————. N.d.-a "10 U.S. WRA Camps." Personal files. Unpublished manuscript.

————. N.d.-b "Japanese American Buddhist Temples and Shinto Shrines in the Americas (1941)." Personal files. Unpublished manuscript.

————. N.d.-c "The Fourteen Major 'Assembly Centers' (1942)." Personal files. Unpublished manuscript.

Yosemori, Chikai. 2011. Interview by Linda Nishigaya and Ernest Oshiro, Honolulu, October 30.

From Priestesses and Disciples to Witches and Traitors:
Internment of Japanese Women at Honouliuli and Narratives of "Madwomen"

Amy Nishimura

ABSTRACT

This paper will focus on two of the Japanese American women internees who shared a common variable regarding internment: they were Shintō priestesses or disciples studying the religion at the time of their incarceration. One woman in particular was well regarded within her community and had several followers or disciples; based on transcripts from her trial, retrial, and parole hearing, the questions and accusations leveled against her demonstrate social injustice based on the practice of religion. For another Japanese American woman internee, I will examine how she is objectified and subjected not only to unjust treatment but she is cast as social pariah and a triple-threat to society: Japanese, Shintō disciple, and misdiagnosed "madwoman." Her records demonstrate the neglect of government officials to obtain treatment for her and clarify how she was subjugated to humiliating scrutiny by military authorities. What seems particularly poignant about her narrative are the reflective letters and poems that capture her

Amy Nishimura, Associate Professor of English, University of Hawai'i–West O'ahu, 91-1001 Farrington Highway, Kapolei, HI 96707. This material is based upon work assisted by a grant from the Department of the Interior, National Park Service. Any opinions, findings, and conclusions or recommendations expressed in this material are those of the author and do not necessarily reflect the views of the Department of the Interior. The author may be reached at amynn@hawaii.edu.

angst; these letters and documents are addressed to military personnel who seemed to ignore her pleas. This paper will highlight not only civil rights violations endured by these and other women but I aim to argue how they were examined according to a Western patriarchal lens, preventing them from voicing (in their natural tongue) their identities.

In the state of Hawai'i, the prominent marker that historicizes World War II is Pearl Harbor, and the 50th state is often contextualized with stories about this monument; at times, this symbol overshadows individual narratives that remain silenced. The internment of Japanese Americans and some Europeans was an injustice, and scholars continue to strive toward reconciling the irony of a country that heralds principles of civil rights and freedom though it once detained and interned its own citizens. For the purposes of this paper, I use the word internment[1] to describe the situation of the eight Japanese American women (two in particular) who were unjustly arrested, detained, and interned at Honouliuli. The ongoing discussions about appropriate terminology continue: detainment center, relocation site, and internment or concentration camps are a few euphemisms that aim to contextualize the result of Executive Order 9066. Given the recent discovery of Honouliuli, the words internment and concentration hold center, as United States citizens were unjustly imprisoned. According to Alice Yang Murray, there is still much debate about the use of "euphemisms such as evacuation, assembly centers, and relocation centers" (2000:21).

Roger Daniels notes that the anti-Japanese sentiment was steeped in a sense of vehement hatred: "A viper is nonetheless a viper wherever the egg is hatched—so a Japanese, born of Japanese parents—grows up to be a Japanese, not an American" (2000:51). Printed in the *Los Angeles Times*, the propaganda leveled against the Japanese and Japanese Americans was utilized to support the federal government's decision to call for mass action against all Japanese Americans. Probably most interesting is that the "internment of Japanese Americans did not end after the surrender of Japan in 1945" and "more than a year passed before the last concentration camp closed its gates" (75). In "The Decision for Mass Evacuation," Daniels uses the terms concentration and internment interchangeably and while this may seem problematic, he also requests that readers consider the hatred and mass action taken against United States citizens. As Daniels also notes, the shame that accompanies the experience of being interned outweighs the success of many Japanese Americans, "former prisoners opened stores and farms, and sent their children to prestigious colleges and to success in business and professional careers. But the psychic scars of internment remained" (75). Though a myriad of silences remain, various scholars attempt to convey individual experiences or at least communicate how many men, women, and children demonstrated a silhouette of resistance.

This paper will focus on two of the Japanese American women internees at Honouliuli who shared a common variable regarding internment: they were Shintō priestesses or disciples studying the religion at the time of their incarceration. One woman in particular was well regarded within her community and had several followers or disciples; based on transcripts from her trial, retrial, and a parole hearing, the questions and accusations leveled against her demonstrate social injustice based on the practice of religion. Though religious persecution remains a long-standing discriminatory tool to imprison people, the paradox of the American government's "fight for justice" is a primary reason this topic continues to call for research among scholars in various fields. For one Japanese American woman internee, I examine how she was objectified and subjected not only to unjust treatment, and I argue how she was cast as social pariah and a triple threat to society: Japanese, Shintō disciple, and misdiagnosed "madwoman." Her records demonstrate the neglect of government officials to obtain treatment for her and clarify how she was subjugated to humiliating scrutiny by military authorities. What are particularly poignant about her narrative are reflective letters and poems that capture her angst; these documents are addressed to military personnel who ignored her pleas and repeatedly cited her as "ill." This paper will also highlight not only civil rights violations endured by these women but I aim to argue how they were scrutinized and questioned according to a Western patriarchal lens, preventing them from voicing (in their natural tongue) their identities. The eight Japanese and/or Japanese American women who were interned in Honouliuli had several things in common: they were Japanese American, they studied Shintoism, many of them knew one another and studied together, and all of them did not possess a mastery of the English language, though they attempted to make their opinions heard. There are two women in particular that this article will discuss: one was a Shintō priestess, Ryuto Tsuda who held a rather large following and the other, Haruko Takahashi, seemed to have an eccentric background and was subjected to cruel treatment that, in many ways, align with the fictional tale of "Miss Sasagawara," written by Hisaye Yamamoto (2001).

From a literary standpoint, Hisaye Yamamoto's "The Legend of Miss Sasagawara" (2001), serves as an allegory to comprehend complicit silences that unfolded when the American government actively selected to intern US citizens, foreign nationals, and civilians who were living in Hawai'i during the 1930s and 1940s. Yamamoto's short story symbolizes the fear American citizens felt toward the Japanese and, more specifically, toward Japanese Americans. The characters, the internees, ostracize Miss Sasagawara, refer to her as mad, and deny their own duplicity in their treatment of a sensitive human being who desperately seeks to retain her artistic sensibility; her creative endeavors are remarked as "different" from those who conform easily to the expectations of the American government. She is depicted as untraditional, as a woman who values specific aesthetic forms such as dancing, poetry, and painting, and she is not hardened to life within the internment camp, a camp that serves as a microcosm to the larger civilian life of deference and proper hegemonic protocol. As Cheung (1993) notes in her work, *Articulate Silences*, Yamamoto's "The Legend of Miss Sasagawara" is set pointedly in an internment camp and uses the story of a putative madwoman as an "ironic mirror" that magnifies the insidious effects of gossip, rumor, name-calling—those practices that indirectly led to the unjust incarceration of Japanese Americans" (2001:11). Offering a parallel to how many Americans treated Japanese Americans upon internment, Miss Sasagawara symbolizes the complacent attitude that held America at a time when the United States was fighting horror in Europe, the paradox that engaging in social justice abroad while persecuting others at "home," remains a confounding predicament for the United States.

The parallel between the fictional Miss Sasagawara and one of the internees rendered "madwoman" during her time at Honouliuli provokes questions as to how other women who were imprisoned on the continent were also perceived and mistreated as mad. Cheung notes that as a woman or more particularly, as a Japanese unmarried woman, Miss Sasagawara disrupts the normative expectations of a culture that demands deference of the female gender (1993:59). The idle gossip that consumes the camp and targets Sasagawara parallels the gossip that surrounded the Japanese community before the time of their internment. Her accusers, thus, resemble those who provided only circumstantial evidence against the Japanese; that is, Yamamoto's short story asks readers to examine and reexamine the names leveled against Miss Sasagawara, markers that exact a continuance of gender bias. This continuance has been culturally, politically, and socially examined by other literary artists such as Charlotte Perkins Gilman (author of "The Yellow Wallpaper"), Kate Chopin (*The Awakening*), and others such as Adrienne Rich, Alice Walker, Toni Morrison, and Gloria Anzaldua.

The resolution of "The Legend of Miss Sasagawara" is fixed with polar oppositions yet a fragmented sense of peace echoes by the close of the narrative; the once demonized Miss Sasagawara has become a poet and her text about a man who achieves Nirvana, who rids himself of all "earthly desires," is prescribed as "mad" because he does not relinquish his pursuit of the eightfold path. Those who follow the eightfold path search for a virtuous avenue, which includes right speech, right action, and right thought—to many it refers to a transcendentalist ideology. Within this ideology, there is no basic concept of good or evil, there is only a search for higher understanding, a comprehension of oneself that is not readily likened to the black-and-white rhetoric embedded within institutions like the United States military. So the duality that exists for an Asian American, a Japanese American, is not a fixed or static dichotomy in which one feels as though he/she can choose a position easily. The fictional depiction of Miss Sasagawara contextualizes how some of the actual women in internment camps had to justify their "madness." Here again, Cheung (1993) argues that justice was an illusion, perhaps transmuted in order for the United States to soften the angles of their political alignment:

> In the face of the triple occlusion of Miss Sasagawara—as a daughter by her father, as a single woman by the community, and as a member of a persecuted people by the government—she exhibits perhaps the only appropriate response to the situation; her "madness" is also a flight from the crazy circumstances. Miss Sasagawara's poem, which challenges our earlier perceptions of madness and saintliness, aberration and innocence, should also make us wonder who was the guilty party. (1993:69)

In Gilbert and Gubar's *The Madwoman in the Attic* (1984), the symbolism of the female cave can be likened to the allegorical story of Miss Sasagawara and the two women discussed in this paper. A central question the authors raise is applicable to feminist writing aiming to reconfigure the cave, to illuminate literary discussions, and to complicate the diagnosis of madwoman: "how does such a woman distinguish what she is from what she sees, her real creative essence from the unreal cut paper shadows the cavern-master claims as reality?" (95). The conception, the aesthetic work that the fictional character of Miss Sasagawara and Haruko Takahashi conceive or undertake, hold no material value in a society that depends on production or finite results. In the transcripts that follow, the "cavern-masters" solidify the campaigns against women who trace lines that fall outside of patriarchal patterns or who follow a different interstice.

Transcripts of official hearings held for Haruko Takahashi, the woman rendered as "a problem" by government officials, underscore the bias, innuendo, and discriminatory language markers that led to her internment. On March 9, 1944, (Takahashi 1945) the Military Governor's Review Board decided to prolong Takahashi's imprisonment based on the following:

> The board, which reheard her case, questioned her extensively regarding her loyalty. At that time she stated that she felt the same towards the United States and Japan; that she would be unable to obey a United States order to harm Japan; and does not know what she would do at such a time. Throughout her rehearing she gave indefinite middle-of-the-road answers always careful not to give direct replies.

Using circular reasoning instead of linear answers is a reflection of cultural context—to answer indirectly, at times, subsumes an air of humility or diplomatic tact. The US government required Takahashi and other Japanese females to don two conflicting roles: one of gendered deference and one of standardized practice; namely, to use American speech or rhetoric by answering definitively but remaining polite or discrete. Rather than citing the difficulty of her honest response, the lack of understanding by the board and their ignorance of a different culture cost Takahashi more time in the internment camp. More significantly, she lost social, political, and narrative capital despite her numerous attempts to reestablish her civil rights. Iris Marion Young (2000) defines democracy according to pluralistic involvement from all sides, not simply an approach that privileges those who hold positions of authority. She contends that social justice must employ an exposé of power and a foundational knowledge regarding how it functions within a civil society:

> [T]he freedom of civic activity arguably makes more possible such moral appeals than political action under the constraints of bureaucratic or profit-oriented imperative. Sometimes the force of public moral appeals made by otherwise powerless people effects a change of policy because the powerful agents have been successfully *shamed*. (2000:175)

Because those who were interned felt "shamed" and held little hegemonic power, they were unable to act with any semblance of resistance; they held little agency to directly question what was happening to them, especially within the moment that it was taking place. Here, the "it" symbolizes the act and the questioning, the violation that took place the moment they were asked to choose Japan or the United States. Young's work further contextualizes how power works through the subject versus object position; here, the object position is Takahashi as she is reduced (in description and name) by offering "middle-of-the-road" answers. Young's use of the word "shamed," that those in power should embody this idea, has not materialized; and after more than 70 years since the attack on Pearl Harbor, it is paradoxically problematic that the interned continue to feel ashamed to share their narratives. Taking this further, one can interpret Takahashi's "middle" answers as a self-conscious action; in this context, Takahashi resists the demand for linear answers, exhibits a sense of voice, but is punished for her responses.

The men who comprised the Board of Officers and Civilians were as follows: Lieutenant Colonel Edward K. Massee, president; Mr. Joseph J. Kelley; and Major Robert I. Freund. During Takahashi's rehearing, there was no attorney present but an interpreter was available, though, at this writing, his/her identity remains unknown. Some of the facts about Takahashi include her study to become a Shintō priestess at Konkōkyō Church, that she was born in Kohala, on the Big Island of Hawai'i, and that she held dual citizenship. Also, at the beginning of her rehearing, "evidence" of her initial hearing was brought to the attention of the board. Though she was a resident and citizen of Hawai'i, her single trip to Japan within 33 years was a primary reason she was held prisoner beginning December 14, 1941. Some of the more disturbing notes during her rehearing include items such as:

> [I]n spite of her residence and education in this country, Subject speaks very little English. The three primary motives provided for her internment were: 1) "That the Internee, HARUKO TAKAHASHI, is a dual citizen, being a citizen of both Japan and the United States"; 2) "That she is disloyal to the United States"; 3) "That she is engaged in subversive activities, spreading the Japanese propaganda." (Takahashi 1945)

The conclusion of the board offered the following: "In view of her activities as a Shintō priestess and her apparent loyalty to Japan, Subject, in the opinion of this office is dangerous to the public peace, safety, and internal security of this country" (Takahashi 1945). The case was considered closed after this statement. In reviewing some of the questions Takahashi was subjected to (during her rehearing) to determine if she merited parole, some of the most problematic include the following: "How much English schooling did you have here in Hawai'i"? As linguist Charlene Sato argues in articles about Hawaiian

Creole English, language bias is an embedded tool used against those who do not assimilate to hegemonic English.[2] Because language acquisition is "twin skin" to one's identity, the question posed is based on a one-sided loyalty assessment and presumes that if one does not speak English fluently, one cannot be a patriot, a "loyal" US citizen.[3] At a time when racial profiling becomes exceedingly complex but consistently conflated because ideas of nationalism, borders, and "enemy alien" are still marketed and reproduced according to those who hold power, revisiting a time in history when the US government created an "other" or used the word "subject" in hearings to describe American citizens seems particularly timely.

What follows is part of the transcript for her rehearing and though the rhetoric she uses is fluid and circular, her inquisitors demand linear answers.

A: We believe in following our God and doing right daily from our soul and to give thanks to the God of Heaven and Earth. We believe in practicing wisdom and thank to the God economy in all things and brotherly love.

Q: Next to the Ten Chi, the God of Heaven and Earth, who comes after that, the Emperor?

A: No, we don't pray to the Emperor.

Q: Do you consider him next to your God?

A: I don't think the Emperor is a God.

Q: No, but is he next to the God? Did he come down from the Gods or the Sun Goddess?

A: Well, I don't know a great deal about Japanese history. I know very little about that, and I don't think the Emperor is a God.

Q: But is he the representative on earth of the God?

A: I know nothing about that. (Takahashi 1945)

The coercive line of questioning continues for several pages, all of which would strike most reasonable citizens as nebulous. At this time, based on transcripts for both the hearing and rehearing, it is apparent that Takahashi was given numerous non sequiturs and simplistic binarisms to address, and her character was questioned based on the practice of her religion, not due to suspicious actions. Perhaps what is most disturbing is the method in which the men on the board highlight her unfamiliarity of the Constitution of the United States and repeatedly attempt to define her loyalty according to the either/or binarism:

"Suppose the United States Government says you cannot stay in the center. You must choose. You must either give up your American citizenship or your Japanese citizenship" (Takahashi 1945). Her response conveys the complexity of choosing and instead of recognizing that she is Japanese American, a hedged or hybrid term that academics continue to discuss, they declare she is disloyal, nullifying the right for an American to methodically take her time when making a significant decision. When Takahashi states that she wants to remain in the "center," her response resonates ideals of democracy. That is, she may have identified as Japanese due to her family structure but she also identifies as American due to her upbringing in Hawaiʻi. This duality, the point of double consciousness as discussed by various scholars such as W.E.B. Du Bois, Gloria Anzaldua, Henry Louis Gates, and others constitute a "center" that resists the either/or binarism.[4]

The reference to Takahashi as "subject" becomes interchangeable with the word "object" (in this context) for she is neither American nor citizen, she has become an entity, a "subject" studied and interrogated but never treated as a human being. The government collapsed a complex identity by referring to this Japanese American woman as "subject." Like the No-No Boys who had to answer a questionnaire that left them no choice but to serve in the US military or be declared traitor to one's country, the question and the answer, whether affirmative or negative, leaves one stifled, and the government feels justified in creating one's identity based on what they believe is patriotic rhetoric (Okada 1957). Like the other Japanese women who were interned at Honouliuli, there was no justifiable reason to imprison Haruko Takahashi. The subsequent paragraph illustrates this point:

> The Board was unable to get any clear-cut idea of all that went on in her institution. She insisted most emphatically that they did not believe that the Emperor was a God and that they did not pray to the Emperor, but at times there would be Shinto priests at the ceremony. It seems inconceivable to the Board that there could be such connection with the Shinto Church and she being entirely ignorant of the Shinto home, a Shinto shrine in the Church, but they never talk loyalty to the Emperor and that there was no picture of the Emperor in either her home or the Church. She stated that she would bow to the picture of the Emperor as a great man as she would bow to the picture of the President. (Takahashi 1945)

The result of this treatment, of being rendered as defiant or disloyal, continued during Takahashi's time at Honouliuli. In letters she writes to officials, she laments her imprisonment and asks for release; one could argue she is also a poet, not asking directly for her release and never making demands of those who caused her suffering and injustice. Instead, the words in her letters, like the responses she gave government officials during her hearing and rehearing, reflect an active and engaged persona, symbolized through a Western lens as "indirect thought" and/or language. Many narratives have been written about the effects of ill treatment during the time of internment; as Takahashi repeatedly asked for release but was met with resistance, her narrative has strong parallels to the short story written by Hisaye Yamamoto. As a woman, as a Japanese American woman, Takahashi was regarded with disdain and belittled according to a Westernized, myopic lens.

Although the board notes Takahashi as deranged and "pathological," there are documents that assert a sensitive temperance and a poetic ideology that denies anger or retribution toward the US government. The following illustrates her melancholy as she struggled to accept her fate:

> We came into this concentration camp for what reason.
> It is just like dew on the ground.
> We are stepped on.
> We can't take our head up.
> There are thousands of things to be recalled in our memory.
> Months and days spins like the trade-winds.
> Even when we sing our song does not sing like a melody.
> Thus clothes can be dyed, for instance, yellow could be dyed
> To brown, white, into red, but our heart cannot be pounding if we are aim-
> ing for Japan, we can't think about America.
> We are born into this.
> The room which we are in is just cold at night,
> We dream of our home, also homeland.
> Even in the moonlight we can't walk.
> What fun we're going to have.
> It is just like a trade-wind, always going around.
> When we wear our shoes and walk on the street.
> We came here but don't sit here like a dummy.
> Think fast like an arrow, but don't think what they say.
> Think that what you have been taught, but don't cry, be strong.
> You will obey orders, but obey the right ones. (Takahashi 1945)

This poem echoes what Takahashi's accusers were not able to recognize: Japanese American citizens did not "sit like dummies," rather they were aware of the injustice imposed upon them, and Takahashi's intelligence is symbolized throughout the poem. The lines, "if we are aiming for Japan, we can't think about America" and "We are born into this" capture the conflicted identity Takahashi and many other Japanese Americans endured. The point of being immobilized, of not being able to walk or move, to turn a corner, is made apparent by not being able to walk "even in moonlight." The feeling of being under surveillance is made clear whether one attempts to assert oneself in daylight or in the moonlight. Takahashi also seemed acutely aware of taking directive points by the government and attempting to closely comprehend what the consequences were if she did not follow the "right orders." Takahashi knew and said outright that Japanese Americans "[were] being stepped on" and she was also aware of the nebulous manner in which the United States interned specific groups of people; within the last few lines of the poem, she comments that they do not sit like ignorant people and that they must demonstrate restraint in terms of what they can and cannot articulate. Thus, she demonstrated a tactile insight that goes against the grain of the government's perception. Despite the fact that she was an English as a second language (ESL) speaker, her command and comprehension of English is articulated and well documented. In terms of social justice, we see in this particular poem that institutionalized oppression stripped away not only basic civil rights but the structure of the phantasm, as noted by Jacqueline Rose in *Why War* (1993) is constructed by those who wield power. In the historical and cultural consciousness of the US government, their sense of the perceived enemy is an entity they construct; unfortunately, for those who suffered from incarceration, articulating and knowing how they have been oppressed becomes highly difficult. As noted by organizations such as TACS that work toward bringing awareness about institutional oppression,

> established laws, customs, and practices systematically reflect and produce inequities based on one's membership in targeted social identity groups. If oppressive consequences accrue to institutional laws, customs, or practices, the institution is oppressive whether or not the individuals maintaining those practices have oppressive intentions. Institutional Oppression creates a system of invisible barriers limiting people based on their membership in unfavored social identity groups. The barriers are only invisible to those "seemingly" unaffected by it. (Cheney, LaFrance, and Quinteros 2006:2)

This definition ties into hegemonic practices in the United States when "invisible barriers" create a fictionalized account that includes, but is not limited to, producing a phantasm, a projected enemy, for the convenience of capitalism benefitting those in privileged and entitled positions. The primary character in "The Legend of Miss Sasagawara" is a former dancer who possesses an eccentricity that sets her apart from the other internees,

> nor did she ever willingly use the shower room, just off the latrine, when anyone else was there. Once, when I was up past midnight writing letters and went for my shower, I came upon her under the full needling force of a steamy spray. (2001:22)

Yamamoto presents Sasagawara as a perceptive person, someone whom the rest of the internees cognitively elect to alienate and treat as a social pariah. The text also serves as a form of protest but one in which the prose and characters focus on their capabilities as individuals as they maintain a sense of grace in spite of vitriolic behavior and speech. I argue here that eccentricity is likened to individuality, an attribute that was historically associated with American ideology.

In one exchange in which Miss Sasagawara attempts to escape, the narrative displays the contemptuous manner in which she is treated:

> And this morning, just now, she ran out of the ward in just a hospital night-gown and the orderlies chased after her and caught her and brought her back. Oh, she was just fighting them. But once they got her back to bed, she calmed down right away, and Miss Morris asked her what was the big idea, you know, and do you know what she said? She said she didn't want any more of those doctors pawing her. *Pawing*, her, imagine! (Yamamoto 2001:26)

The character has often been described as an example of female hysterics or, as King-Kok Cheung notes, that Yamamoto's work is a "haunting story of a Nisei woman driven insane by the combined pressures exerted upon her as an 'other'" (1993:54). After she's sent away and returns, she is treated with disdain, not unlike the way in which internees were treated after their return to "normal" life:

> It must have been several months, and when, towards late autumn, she returned at last from the sanitorium in Phoenix, everyone in Block 33 was amazed at the change. She said hello and how are you as often and easily as the next person, although many of those she greeted were surprised and suspicious, remembering the earlier rebuffs. There were some who never did get used to Miss Sasagawara as a friendly being. (Yamamoto 2001:28)

Monica Chiu (2009) argues that "The Legend" connects race and gender as Mari Sasagawara's "flighty female behavior" (2009:32) is consistently named by those who regard her with suspicion. Whether it is her colorful clothing or dancing through the camp, the internee's discriminating attitude against Sa-sagawara reflects the patriarchal internalization of the inhabitants. The contrast between Sasagawara and her father is stark and necessary and he is depicted as a community leader in the camp, aloof and indifferent of her achievements as dancer and teacher. In many contexts, Yamamoto illustrates Sasagawara as a forward-moving feminist metaphorically using her body to resist the treacherous effects of internment. As Chiu argues, "her body becomes a yardstick by which to measure their own angst over being female, elevating Sasagawara to the status of a respected woman at the same time that she is both a 'decorative ingredient' to camp experience and a seemingly naive child" (2009:33). It is questionable as to how or who respects Sasagawara; only toward the end of the narrative, as she takes on a new role of author, does the text imply a new status within the community. Indeed, those who live in the camp use Sasaga-wara as a way to measure their own perceptions and self-perceptions, and she becomes a double negative, a woman and a woman of Japanese ancestry who does not conform to expected norms. Chiu contextualizes this point further:

> in the end, Mari represents the catalyst by which her fellow internees protested their treatment in the only way they could: censuring their own peers, especially a female peer. The internees' diagnosis of her illness served to displace the pathology of their identities as Japanese Americans in a nation seeking to extricate its own misdiagnosed cancerous population. (2009:35)

Chiu's reading of Yamamoto's allegory underscores the point that the US government needed to produce an "enemy," and, as a result, the consciousness of the nation became infected. Chiu complicates her argument in stating that Sasagawara's fellow internees need to "displace the pathology" (2009:35) and that an illness plagues the entire nation. The maladies that infused America, that continue to infuse how we direct our discriminatory consciousness have been examined and discussed by scholars such as Noam Chomsky, Cornel West, Michael Omi, Jacqueline Rose, and many others who continue to request that we contemplate how we commit acts of injustice. The internment of Japanese Americans has been studied across many different disciplines, but we are only now beginning to share individual narratives and considering how powers of horror impacted several generations.[5]

When initially researching the Japanese women who were interned, the similarity among them was the practice of the Shintō religion. It became apparent that a leader among the women interned at Honouliuli was Ryuto Tsuda, and in several documents her name is mentioned in the context of community services, prayers, study, and healing. On her "Individual Internee's Record" card (Tsuda 1945) Tsuda is described as an American civilian and the "Date of internment or capture" is June 18, 1942. She was held at the Sand Island Detention Camp before being moved to Honouliuli and like the other American civilians who were unjustly interned, the point of loyalty, or an attempt to define the word "loyal" served as the primary reason for imprisonment. I offer here a few conclusions from her rehearing held on May 17, 1944; it was decided by the board that her internment would continue. The board was comprised of Joseph J. Kelley; Lieutenant Colonel Edward K. Massee, president; Mark A. Robinson; and Major Robert I. Freund, CAC, AUS. They are all presumably tied to the US government and/or had a link to the commerce community in Hawai'i and on the continent. Throughout her rehearing, Tsuda was described in terms related to "ancestor worship, healing the sick, and assisting the troubled through prayer" (Tsuda 1945). As a dual citizen, it is noted that she did not surrender her Japanese citizenship and under finding or reason number two, the board typifies her as "not truly loyal to the United States" and "she was engaged in activities that verge closely upon being subversive" (Tsuda 1945). The word subversive has been used repeatedly in reference to Japanese nationals and Japanese Americans, the racial connotation implicates one as stealthily plotting or evading. In this particular context, "evidence" against Tsuda (comprised of approximately three pages of single-spaced prose) includes innocuous letters she wrote to other Japanese civilian internees as well as other vague reasons.

Here again, there is a construction of the phantasm as the basis for internment in an imagined community: In one letter the Internee referred to the flag of the rising sun and stated that it really was a Buddhist expression and meant the glory "of the sunrise." This explanation the board does not believe. She also referred to "the country" and stated that meant both countries. This the board does not believe (Tsuda 1945). I use the term "imagined community" to demonstrate how a group in power constructs those who have no power and are able to create, fantasize, or impose a value system onto the targeted group of people or culture.[6] The remainder of the board's findings consistently mentions Tsuda's involvement in the temple and in one paragraph, there is notation of how she offered prayers to "boys who entered the United States military service" (Tsuda 1945). Creating in their imagination, a woman who held "subversive" capital within her community and might be influencing military men, the board decided to restrain and imprison her, in effect attempting to silence her. If "she," she being in the object position and regulated to an "other," is described as an alien life force, as offering prayer that lies outside of the heteronormative expectation, "she" is creating evil. In the final paragraph of this rehearing, Tsuda is described in a similar manner to Haruko Takahashi:

> This woman is in many ways bright, sharp, and shrewd, but cares little for orders or instructions if she desires to disobey and sustain a reason which satisfies her for doing so; would not hesitate to twist meanings or give false information if she deemed it to her advantage. She is believed a religious woman of the fanatical type, probably made so by lack of deep religious training and overstressing of form and repetitious ceremonies, and accentuated by frequent fasts. She insists she wants to be left in the Camp unless a house can be found for her to conduct her services again, but at the same time insists she is disgraced by being there. Whether or not she is a pathological case the Board is not prepared to state. In conclusion the Board believes that she is dangerous to the public peace, safety, and internal security of the United States. (Tsuda 1945)

The linear line of questioning and subsequent conclusions provide no internal gaze on the part of the US government, and there is no self-reflection about their actions or pronouncements; this is illustrated as they are unable to reconcile Tsuda's desire for a home outside of the internment camp. Particularly puzzling is their inability to grasp the point or idea of being shamed through incarceration and "arrest."

The initial hearing of Tsuda in 1943 offers a more layered context for comprehending the rhetoric used by the United States to intern Japanese Shintō priestesses. What follows is merely one passage taken from Tsuda's hearing:

> You have received four years of education in Japan and you were ordained at the Todai Temple in Nara, Japan, in 1941. You have criticized the Americanization of American-born Japanese. You claim to have supernatural powers. You have made no attempt to Americanize yourself or assume the duties and obligations of American citizenship. You admit that you are as loyal to Japan as you are to the United States. You have indicated a desire to return to Japan. You have not cooperated with the Internment Camp authorities. (Tsuda 1945)

The indictment of the board cites Tsuda's disloyalty as rituals of praying, of keeping a shrine in her home, and of not choosing either America or Japan as a "home base." Here again, as in the case of many internees, there is no substantive reasoning as to why Tsuda was interned and remained interned for several years. Another supposed reason for internment was the government's ideology of the phrase "supernatural powers." In English, this has negative connotations, contexts that relate to the occult but Tsuda (and others who knew her) describe her practices as a healer. A specific example is cited in a letter written by a Fred Patterson who states that "[he] also heard of others who also benefited by these consultations, and I have never heard from any of them that she ever tried to influence them in such a way that it would lead them to believe that she was an enemy of the United States, or was in any way trying to assist Japan in the present war" (Tsuda 1945). The consultations Tsuda held allowed people like Fred Patterson to pray in a religious and spiritual manner, and there is no reference that she misled anyone who sought her expertise. Despite this, Tsuda was considered an "enemy" capable of inflicting tremendous damage against American citizens.

In Jacqueline Rose's (1993) *Why War*, the ideology of war is presented as an abstraction or distortion of truth and Rose implies that the primary reason we engage in war is due to paranoia, a threat, a fear instilled in our consciousness. She uses the word "phantasm" as a fantastical category embedded within and constructed through propaganda, by those who hold situated stations of power, and by scientific reasoning that aims to classify and create a perceived reality. Part of her argument includes:

> [R]eality is unable to secure the political distinctions or effects it is being required to perform. One could in fact say that, instead of a just appreciation of reality being the means whereby one cures the individual and the culture of its propensity to war, it is war which, in this argument, has the victory, by undermining the undiluted appeal to reality which is meant to bring it to an end. The distinction between fantasy and reality cannot withstand, or is revealed in its most difficult relation under, the impact of war. We can never finally be sure whether we are projecting or not, if what we legitimately fear may be in part the effect of our own projection. (1993:29)

The testimonies, letters, and line of questioning for both Takahashi and Tsuda reveal the preoccupation of the US government to obviate both women while accusing them of treacherous powers. On one hand, they were belittled and dismissed as ill, pathological, and subversive; on the other hand, as women who spoke English as a second language, they were rendered unclear and confusing. Like many tactics related to imperialism and colonialism, the desire to create an enemy transpires through not only what the "enemy" says but also the type of information the inquisitor seeks—the rhetoric used by those who aim to persecute. In this case, the internment of the Japanese was based on inaccurate data and assumptions grounded in propaganda, in innuendo and gossip. The "reality" that was constructed and implemented was based on what Rose refers to as "limited resources of the real world" (1993:30) and this precipitates a reality enmeshed in declaring that "there has never been enough for all and we have lived by competition" (1993:30). The structure of capitalism, of democracy itself, demands that we adhere to a competitive lifestyle, altering ethics and truth to fit a system that makes "sacrifices," a means to justify the capitalistic choices we make. The choice to intern the Japanese was made to appear justifiable, as a method to protect all involved; however, the language used to indict the two women I have discussed throughout this paper was based on the phantasmic structure that man has utilized to justify war. ❖

Notes

1. See Roger Daniels's "The Decision for Mass Evacuation" (2000) for a discussion regarding use of the terms internment and concentration.

2. See Charlene Sato's discussion of Hawaiian Creole English (1985). Sato was a sociolinguist who compared Pidgin to other Creole languages.

3. Gloria Anzaldua's "How to Tame a Wild Tongue" (1999) chronicles her experiences as a bilingual speaker forced to learn hegemonic English and to think/speak in ways that conform to a problematic identity. Her argument entails citing how one's natural tongue is "tied down" in various situations and contexts and that language is an integral part of one's cultural identity.

4. Resisting the either/or binarism used to incite multiple wars is discussed by various scholars and academics and they argue that the construction of an enemy begins by coercive manipulations, forcing people to choose one side over another.

5. See Julia Kristeva's *Powers of Horror* (1982) for a discussion of the subject, object, and abject positions. The abject is defined as a form of narcissism.

6. Benedict Anderson argues that the concepts of nation and nationalism are imagined or imaginary since one can never know all the members of their community. It is only in one's mind that a community exists. Communities, he states, "are to be distinguished, not by their falsity/sincerity, but by the style in which they are imagined" (1992:6). Therefore, the idea of community is based on the cultural and political institutions of a given period, as well as in the political and cultural resistances to power.

References

Anderson, Benedict. 1992. *Imagined Communities: Reflections on the Origin and Spread of Nationalism*. London: New Left Books.

Anzaldua, Gloria. 1999. *Lafrontera/Borderlands*. Chicago: Aunt Lute Books.

Cheney, Carol, Jeannie LaFrance, and Terrie Quinteros. 2006. "Institutional Oppression." *Tools for Diversity*. TACS.

Cheung, King-Kok. 1993. *Articulate Silences*. Ithaca: Cornell University Press.

Chiu, Monica. 2009. "Japanese American Internment, National Pathology, and Intra-Racial Strife in Hisaye Yamamoto's *The Legend of Miss Sasagawara*," *Notes on Contemporary Literature* 12(2):29–41, September.

Daniels, Roger. 2000. "The Decision for Mass Evacuation." Pp. 29–63 in *What Did The Internment of Japanese Americans Mean?*, edited by Alice Yang Murray. Boston: Bedford St. Martin's Press.

Gilbert, Sandra M., and Susan Gubar. 1984. *The Madwoman in the Attic: The Woman Writer and the Nineteenth-Century Literary Imagination*. New Haven: Yale University Press.

Kristevera, Julie. 1982. *Powers of Horror: An Essay on Abjection*. New York: Columbia University Press.

Murray, Alice Yang. 2000. *What Did the Internment of Japanese Americans Mean?* Boston: Bedford St. Martin's Press.

Okada, John. 1957. *No-No Boy*. Rutland, VT: Charles E. Tuttle.

Rose, Jacqueline. 1993. *Why War*. London: Wiley-Blackwell Press.

Sato, Charlene. 1985. *Language of Inequality*, edited by Nessa Wolfson and Joan Manes. Berlin: Walter de Gruyter.

Takahashi, Haruko. 1945. Record Group 489, Entry (A1) 19 Alien Processing Center, 1941–45, Box 97, Takahashi, Haruko. National Archives and Records Administration II, College Park, Maryland.

Tsuda, Kiyome. 1945. Record Group 489, Entry (A1) 19 Alien Processing Center, 1941–45, Box 105, Tsuda, Kiyome (alias Ryuto). National Archives and Records Administration II, College Park, Maryland.

Yamamoto, Hisaye. 2001. "The Legend of Miss Sasagawara." Pp. 20–34 in *Seventeen Syllables and Other Stories*. New Jersey: Rutgers University Press.

Young, Iris Marion. 2000. *Inclusion and Democracy*. Oxford: Oxford University Press.

The Effect of Internment on Children and Families: Honouliuli and Manzanar

Susan Matoba Adler

ABSTRACT

The effect of internment in Hawai'i on children and families is considerably different from the mainland where families were interned together and camps provided schools, activities, and resources for internees. At Honouliuli, only a few children were interned with their parents, and there is limited information on their experiences in camp. The more compelling stories come from the few adults I interviewed who, as children, lived outside of camp under martial law in Hawai'i and visited their fathers and mothers in camp. This qualitative study contrasts interview data and literature on experiences of Nisei, who were teens in Manzanar, with adults of Japanese and German heritage, who were children with one or both parents interned at Honouliuli. Findings indicate that the participant groups share displacement in a time of political turmoil, weakening of the nuclear family unit, and changing women's roles as a result of internment. The foundation of family cohesion was crumbling under martial law in Hawai'i and incarceration on the mainland.

Research on children and families of internment is both a professional inquiry and a personal journey into my family history. As an Early Childhood teacher educator and a researcher of Asian American families in the Midwest, I never expected that my move to Hawai'i would provide me the wonderful opportunity to work with an interdisciplinary team investi-

Susan Matoba Adler, Professor of Education, University of Hawai'i–West O'ahu, 91-1001 Farrington Highway, Kapolei, HI 96707. This material is based upon work assisted by a grant from the Department of the Interior, National Park Service. Any opinions, findings, and conclusions or recommendations expressed in this material are those of the author and do not necessarily reflect the views of the Department of the Interior. The author may be reached at adlers@hawaii.edu.

gating different aspects of Honouliuli, the Hawai‘i internment and prisoner of war site. My family left Manzanar and settled in Wisconsin where I was born in 1947. My mother was a teenager in camp, and my father was a young journalism student who worked at the *Free Press*, Manzanar's camp newspaper. The *Free Press* was the official publication of the Manzanar Relocation Center administration and of the Manzanar Cooperative Enterprises under the editorial leadership of Roy Takeno (Adams 1944). My father, Kishio Matoba, is photographed in Ansel Adams's (1944) book, *Born Free and Equal: The Story of Loyal Japanese Americans*,[1] while my mother is featured in several sports events in her high school yearbook, *Our World 1943–1944 Manzanar High School*[2] (Manzanar 1944). The recently published book, *Children of Manzanar*, by Heather Lindquist (2012) included a variety of quotes from my mother, Chiyeko "Chickie" Hiraoka Matoba. She described camp schools where children sat on the cold linoleum floor while the few available desks were for the teachers. She also commented on how things became more "normal" later on as schools acquired needed educational supplies. I wonder how one comes to judge "normality" when you are removed from your community, rounded up with folks that look like you racially, and relocated to a desert. I wonder if those austere camp experiences helped my parents and grandmother acclimate from sunny California to a cold, unfamiliar postwar life in Wisconsin. I wonder how I ever gained a sense of my own racial, ethnic, and cultural identity growing up in the Midwest with little Japanese community and with the expectation to assimilate and be 100 percent American.

In this article, I contrast the effect of internment on children, left at home in Hawai‘i when their parents (mostly fathers for Japanese Americans, but both fathers and mothers for German Americans) were interned at Honouliuli with the experiences of my mother and her octogenarian classmates, who lived in the camp and graduated from Manzanar High School in 1944. These internment sites differed greatly in terms of context as indicated by Burton et al. (2014):

> The first key distinction between the mainland and Hawai‘i is that the Hawaiian internment was authorized by martial law, rather than Executive Order 9066. Martial law left little imprint on the landscape, so Honouliuli is a rare physical manifestation of those numerous wartime restrictions, which had a profound effect on all the citizens of Hawai‘i.... Unlike the mainland, where the vast majority of internees were of Japanese ancestry, the heritage of Hawaiian civilian internees included Japanese, Okinawan, German, Italian, Austrian, Norwegian, Danish, Russian, Lithuanian, Swedish, Finnish,

Irish, and British. While 100 percent of Nikkei (Japanese who have located overseas on a permanent basis, as well as their descendents) living on the mainland's west coast were interned, less than 2 percent of the Hawaiian Nikkei were interned.

In Manzanar, the internees were predominantly Issei (first generation Japanese immigrants), Nisei (their American born children), and Kibei (second generation Japanese Americans who were educated in Japan). Falgout (2014) described how Honouliuli also housed more than 4,000 POWs from a variety of ethnic backgrounds including Japanese, Okinawans, Koreans, and Filipinos sent from various locations in the Pacific Theater, plus Italians picked up from the Atlantic Theater. The camp also served as a transition point for those POWs sent to destinations on the US mainland.

Regarding the Hawai'i context, I examine several key questions. How did traditional Japanese American and German American mothers and other family members for European internees, raise children in an atmosphere of fear and military presence, with no male head of household present? Where did families of Hawai'i internees get resources to live in their communities? How did they help their children gain a sense of "normality" during visitations to the internment camp? What happened to the children when their schools were taken over by the military leaving little space for children to congregate, socialize, or just play together with their friends?

This article is organized by emergent themes from my qualitative study described by and experienced differently by Nisei adults who were children at Manzanar in contrast to Hawai'i adults who had one or both parents in Honouliuli. Emergent themes from both sets of interviews include: the shock of Pearl Harbor, trying to comprehend displacement, the weakened nuclear family unit, and changing women's roles. Some themes will not be comparative, such as children in Honouliuli, visitations to Honouliuli, and support for families of Hawai'i internees.

The Shock of Pearl Harbor

By 11:30 a.m. on December 7, 1941, Governor Poindexter announced that martial law had been declared and the Territory of Hawai'i was under military control. Three hundred forty-five Japanese aliens, 74 German aliens, and 11 Italian aliens were taken into custody by the night of December 8, 1941 (Rosenfeld 2014).

One father who was interned in Hawai'i expressed fear and concern about his family members living outside of camp in an atmosphere of scarcity and martial law. After being taken to Sand Island Camp, Ozaki recalled:

> Explosions reverberate against a sky dotted with flickering early morning starts, while at Pearl Harbor the dissipating black smoke reveals the sight of military ships. My thoughts suddenly turn to my family. Worried and anxious—fearful even of the sound of the wind—families no doubt pray for the safe return of their husbands and fathers, their breadwinners and heads of households. (Honda 2012:44)

Ron Tsuchiya, who was four years old, shared his story of that day:

> At the time of the attack, he [his Dad] and his friends were up at the Moanalua Mountains and they saw the planes, and he said he thought it was a maneuver.... Then they heard that there was an attack, so he ended up driving back and coming home to Liliha, where my mom had already heard on the radio about the bomb, the attack. So she took me under the house—I remember that vividly, that we went under the house, and we just stayed there and waited until my father came back. And when my father returned he said that it was an attack from Japan. (Tsuchiya 2011)

Elaine Fukada, who was 14 years old at the time, described her experience of December 7:

> Oh, the Pearl Harbor day was an exciting thing! I was up on the roof of our two story warehouse. We had the shoyu factory.... I was hanging the Sunday wash.... I could see perfectly, we were in Kapalama, that's where we lived. And I could see all the black smoke coming up out of those big boats. And coming up over from the back of the mountain was one of them [a Japanese plane] so low I could even see the pilot. And then, I can't remember for sure, but I think I saw a red *hinomaru*, "sun disc," used to refer to the flag of Japan.... I saw all that going on.... [T]hey had maneuvers all the time. And so here I was watching and saying, "Wow they're doing the real thing today." And my sister downstairs [was] yelling at me, "Come down, come down." (Fukada 2010)

The response of her older sister indicated the seriousness of the situation.

In contrast, two Manzanar internees, who were 15 years old on December 7, recalled hearing about Pearl Harbor in Hawai'i being bombed by the Japanese military from their neighbors (they both lived in predominantly white areas of California). Seigo Yoshinaga was out playing ball with his childhood friends while my mother, "Chickie" Matoba, was at home with her family. It was Sunday, a workday for the farmers as they were preparing to take their produce to market. A Caucasian neighbor, who Matoba had been babysitting for, came over to their house and asked if they were listening to the radio: They were not, but when they did turn it on, they heard about the attack. Both remember being assured by their Caucasian friends that they would be supported and even protected by them from those who were anti-Japanese "if anyone tries to harass you, just let me know" Matoba was told by that neighbor (Matoba 2012).

A more introspective response documented by Lindquist (2012:10) was from their Manzanar classmate, Sam Ono:

> We heard the news on the radio and naturally we thought it was a very terrible thing. I kind of felt ashamed because we were Japanese, and Japan would have the audacity to invade American soil. A lot of my classmates were afraid to go to school the following Monday for fear of reprisals, but I didn't feel that way. I really didn't feel Japanese, if that makes any sense, because the only connection I had was that my [ethnicity] was Japanese.

These 15-year-old Nisei were American citizens, American teenagers.

Chiyeko Hiraoka Matoba, Seigo Yoshinaga, and Sam Ono at 2007 Manzanar Reunion. Courtesy of Seigo Yoshinaga.

When considering both contexts, Hawai'i and California, children faced uncertainty knowing that their ethnic heritage (which the military lumped together under the designations of "Japanese," "German," and "Italian") matched that of enemies of the United States. War had become a reality, though still incomprehensible. Their family life would change drastically and they had no control over what would happen to them and their families after the attack on Pearl Harbor. Irrational fear was rampant. Matoba recalled that the father of her best friend was told by his Caucasian buddy that the government would gather up all of the Japanese, incarcerate them, and open a dam flooding the desert killing all the Japanese people. The father, fearful of what might happen, became distraught and drank himself to death. This death affected the entire community by instilling trepidation, followed by the arrest of the Japanese schoolteacher, who was taken the next day. Matoba and her friends began writing letters to their teacher, unaware that everyone would be evacuated (Matoba 2012).

Trying to Comprehend Displacement

Trying to understand why her parents were being questioned and taken away in Hawai'i, Doris Berg Nye, who was 11 years old at the time her parents were interned, shared her constant fear that her parents were no longer alive. As a youngster, she did not consider her German ethnicity as a problem or

Doris Berg shortly before her parents were taken away. Courtesy of Doris Berg Nye.

perceived her family as being the German "enemies." In her words, "You see, I heard about the Nazi in Germany at that time, but my parents were not bad. I did not know who they were, or what they were, (or) why they were picked up. I didn't know anything about that" (Nye 2009).

I asked Nye whether accommodations were made for children after parents were taken away. She replied, "No, they [the soldiers] were very hard-nosed.... [E]very kid had to take care of themselves" (Nye 2009). She recalled a soldier with "kind eyes" who probably went against orders to allow her older sister, who was in Moloka'i, to call and check on them. She believed he "could not stand the fact that we were left, screaming little kids..." (Nye 2009). According to Nye, there were orphanages and she felt the soldier in charge wanted the children to be taken there, but allowed the older adult sister to make arrangements instead.

As a young child of four, life changed for Ron Tsuchiya when his father was taken away and he went to live with his aunt. Tsuchiya did not remember much about that day, but he did recall when his mother was hospitalized dying of cancer, and when his father was taken away after her funeral. He remembered how he felt:

> I recall that the military people [were] there, and ... I cried because I remember that my dad was going to be taken away, and my mom had just passed away ... I was so upset that I kind of ran, just kind of sat down and hid and cried by the house.... And I remember sitting down and crying because my mom had already passed away, and then my dad was being taken away. (Tsuchiya 2011)

This was raw emotion of a small child expressing incomprehensible loss.

Lindquist's (2012) book, *Children of Manzanar*, describes children in camp as not really understanding the enormity of what was happening, fearful about where they were going based on rumors of desert scorpions and snakes, and feeling sadness about leaving their belongings and friends. In the book, Sam Ono explained the major loss of displacement that many Japanese families experienced:

> I think the most difficult things to leave behind were memorabilia of family.... Apparently there were some unscrupulous people that backed up a van (up to the community center where we stored our things), and they just loaded the van up and took off.... Everything of my childhood memory went with them. It was of no value to them, so I presume it's probably buried in some dumpsite now. (Lindquist 2012:13)

It was clear that children of internment experienced loss in many different ways. There was change in family caregiving, uncertainty about their daily life, and physical displacement, whether by relocation to camp or by changes in living arrangements outside of camp. But perhaps, most devastating was the fear of not knowing what would happen to them and to their family members. As Nye explained, she did not know whether her parents were dead or alive once taken away so abruptly.

Children in Honouliuli

US National Archives II, College Park, Maryland, records indicate 10 names of children at Honouliuli. In a memo from John A. Fitzgerald (1944), 1st lieutenant to provost marshal, the daily report of internees and detainees from July 12 to July 13, 1944, includes 163 men internees, 4 women internees, 0 internees admitted during the past 24 hours, *and* 10 children totaling 177 internees. This is only one of many daily reports so it is unclear when the 10 children arrived, whether they were family members of the 4 women, or when they left. The children ranged from 2 to 14 years old. There appear to be five surnames so I am assuming they were siblings. The following table provides information on the children taken from several daily logs and daily physical checklists; therefore, there are different spellings of names and different ages for some children. Citations on the geographic locations of the families have been lost.

The two Yoshida children's parents were in Japan and they were under the care of Tomi Naha, ISN-HJ-981-CI (Memo 1944). In addition, at 14 years old, Hisako Yamamoto was listed with a camp ID, ISN-HJ-994-CI (Fitzgerald 1944). It appears that after age 14 ID numbers were assigned since in other accounts Hisako is listed at 13 years with no ID number. Also, an older sister Umeko Yamamoto, sent from Saipan, had been listed with a camp ID as 25 years old (Fitzgerald 1944). The Sakamoto parents, Ryohei (father) and Kii (mother) along with the children were brought to Honouliuli from Saipan, Mariana Islands. The family unit was listed in a letter to the Swedish vice consul, dated February 5, 1945, requesting repatriation to Japan.

A memo from 1st Lieutenant John Fitzgerald to his commanding officer indicated that clothing, shoes, and diapers (cloth diapers, I assume) were needed for children of these women in the camp. An interesting note on this request states that a Captain Reilert suggests that ten [diapers] (for Sakamoto) and 15 [diapers] (for Naha) for their one-year-old babies be allotted since the babies were "partly broken" (Morning Report 1944). From a parenting or early childhood perspective, this terminology I assume, is code for "potty trained."

My research notes from National Archives and Records Administration II included a variety of information on families and children, but unfortunately, I do not have the specific citations. I share the general information without details to identify areas of further study. In examining some of the Military ID pictures I noticed that the teenaged girls had shaved heads. In discussing this with my fellow researchers, one possibility emerged as a rationale; prevention against an infestation of lice. I also found an account of caregiving of children while parents were interned. One letter from a Japanese woman to parents in camp promised to care for their children until they were released.

Table 1
Children at Honouliuli

Name	Gender	Age	Address	Other Information
HANASHIRO, Masako	Female	13	Rota, Marianas Island	
SAKAMOTO, Fumiko	Female	2	Ishikawa Prefecture, Japan	Ryohei Sakamoto (father) and Kii Sakamoto (mother)
SAKAMOTO, Nobuko	Female	10	Ishikawa Prefecture, Japan	Ryohei Sakamoto (father) and Kii Sakamoto (mother)
SAKAMOTO, Shozo	Male	7	Ishikawa Prefecture, Japan	Ryohei Sakamoto (father) and Kii Sakamoto (mother)
SAKAMOTO, Ioshio (Yoshio)	Male	5	Ishikawa Prefecture, Japan	Ryohei Sakamoto (father) and Kii Sakamoto (mother)
YAMAMOTO, Hisae (Fusaye)	Female	13	Saipan, Marianas Island	Umeko Yamamoto (25 years) older sister
YAMAMOTO, Hisake (Hisako) (ISN-HJ-994-CI)	Female	14	Saipan, Marianas Island (25 years) older sister	Umeko Yamamoto
YATSU (Tanizu), Makio	Male	9 (7)		
YOSHIDA, Kimiko	Female	2	Shizuoka, Japan	Tomi Naha, caregiver
YOSHIDA, Takashi (Takahashi)	Male	4	Shizuoka, Japan	Tomi Naha, caregiver

Source: Morning Report (1944).

Likewise, there was one account from an extended family member of a soldier stationed in Hawai'i promising to care for his children on the mainland because the military zone under martial law was too dangerous. Pearl Harbor had been bombed and therefore Hawai'i was no place for children to grow up. Unfortunately I have not been able to find any records of policies regarding children at Honouliuli.

Children Visiting Parents at Honouliuli

Several study participants described their visits to Honouliuli, although there was not a lot of detail about their experiences. Elaine Fukada described her visit in the following way:

> The bus would be at the Kamehameha statue where the old post office and federal building was. I guess any member of the family [could go]. I can't remember whether there were military restrictions for the number of people going. My mother, myself, and my kid brother would go. Of course my sister had to stay back to run the store. It was Sunday and the store got busy on Sundays.... Just getting into the camp was quite a drive too. There were so many guard gates. Soldiers would come on the bus and check everybody's name.... It was frightening when you are on military grounds. (Fukada 2010)

Even though there was a military presence in all of O'ahu, the procedures for getting into Honouliuli required many clearances. I imagine the tension was great for all visiting family members.

Ron Tsuchiya recalled visiting his father in a tent where the families sat at a table across from the internee and there was no partition. He described the interaction as "structured" and devoid of social interaction. "I don't think I ever remember him hold me, or hug me, or love me. It was like my dad was on that side. You know like you go to prison ... they're on one side of the table and you're on the other side" (Tsuchiya 2011).

On some of her visits to Honouliuli to see her parents, Doris Berg Nye noticed that another German American couple had a three-and-a-half-year-old son, Kurt Moderow Jr., with them in camp since they did not have relatives in Hawai'i to care for their child. Apparently he was given permission to stay with his mother, though he was not officially registered as an internee (Nye 2009; Rosenfeld 2014). Nye also recalled that the German section at Honouliuli was smaller and there was less for a young teenager to do while there. She enjoyed visiting the Japanese section of the internment camp because there was a store and it was more developed (Nye 2009). I have wondered where the Jaspanese children were housed in Honouliuli since there was a men's section and a women's section, and separate accommodations for POWs. It was unclear how this German American family and those Japanese families from Micronesia were accommodated within Honouliuli.

Support for Families of Hawai'i Internees

Official Government Policy

In a draft document dated March 31,1942, entitled, "Statement of Procedure in Connection with the Providing of Welfare Service to the Dependents of Internees and Detained Persons," the major objectives for the mobilization of community resources were "to prevent suffering and want among such families and or dependents through sympathetic consideration of their needs, and to build a morale of these persons to help them maintain a useful place in the civilian community" (Statement of Procedure 1942). It is unclear how the second objective on morale and citizenship would be facilitated. This document clearly states "It is therefore recognized that the American Red Cross will act as the official liaison organization between the Military Government and the community agencies in connection with the provision of assistance for the dependents of internees" (Statement of Procedure 1942). The Red Cross Home Services Department played the major role for meeting most needs except financial assistance, which was referred to the Territorial Department of Public Welfare.

Hawai'i's Red Cross

My research of Hawai'i Red Cross documents at the National Archives II in College Park, Maryland, also found that their wartime purpose was to assist families of service personnel and internees with household needs in Hawai'i and to assist in uniting families. Most relocating families needed supplies like clothing for colder climates and some needed diapers for infants. Red Cross volunteers were recruited to be nannies or nurses traveling with women who had young children or for larger families.

Red Cross personnel often traveled with wives who had young children, on ships to the mainland to join their interned husbands. For example, one description indicated that: "Mrs. Yamada and her children have been living on savings ... they do not need relief ... they are looking toward a relocation center on the mainland" (Red Cross 1942). General statistics on relocation from Hawai'i indicated that, "Nearly all citizens, composing 416 family units were evacuated to mainland relocation camps between Nov. 1942 to Mar. 1943" (General Statistics on Relocation 1943).

Office of the Swedish Vice Consul in Hawai'i

I had the privilege of interviewing a 94-year-old Japanese American woman, Shim Kanazawa (2010), who became the executive secretary of the Swedish vice consul in Hawai'i. Kanazawa's responsibilities included assisting Japanese American wives whose husbands had been interned. She described her job during World War II as the liaison between the Japanese population in Hawai'i and the military government. Some of the women needed income so she facilitated jobs such as sewing, doing "piece work" for a shirt factory to earn some money for their children. She spoke of women crying on her shoulder everyday since many did not have the skills to work outside the home. Kanazawa explained, "Sometimes I wanted them to go to the depart-ment of social services to get help, but the Issei women did not want help." With a sense of humor, Kanazawa concluded that some of them were "hard headed" (Kanazawa 2010). This attitude could have been caused by a sense of *haji* (Japanese shame) that caused the women to avoid official assistance.

Kanazawa also taught skills like check writing and helped the wives secure financial resources since some family bank accounts were frozen during the war. There was a time when Kanazawa had to transport a six-month-old baby to its grandmother and she had no idea how to provide for it. Even though Kanazawa got advice from a doctor friend on how to care for the child, she remembered that it cried all the way. Her job also took her on board a ship carrying Japanese prisoners of war to make sure the Geneva Convention rules were being implemented.

One of the fascinating pieces of information Kanazawa shared was that some of the women whose husbands had been taken away by the military police were ostracized by neighbors. There was irrational fear that if any neighbor associated with those wives, the same fate would come to their husbands. It was sad to hear that when the wives of internees encountered neighbors, the women crossed the street to avoid interaction, making the wives feel socially isolated, unable to talk with anyone. There was too much fear for others to offer compassion and support. This kind of negative social treatment may have caused some of the wives to volunteer to join their husbands in mainland internment camps. Facing the challenge of traveling to the mainland with their young children was preferable to being socially isolated in their own community.

In her capacity to assist the wives of internees who had been sent to the mainland, Kanazawa knew when the ships were sailing, which was classified information; therefore, she could not inform her own family when she was to leave to accompany these wives. On a trip to the internment site at Crystal City, Texas, she did not tell her mother where she was going, realizing that her phone was tapped. Kanazawa explained,

> So, I didn't tell my mother anything, but somehow [through] mental te-
> lepathy she sent me $5,000 of the hard earned money she earned selling
> vegetables to the Marines. So, that was my extra money that I had to (use)
> because every time these families had to stay over for a few days, or a week...
> they had to go to a cold country, they don't have clothes. I had to use my
> money—my personal money—to buy them clothes...and food for them
> to stay with me. That's the kind of thing I did without anybody knowing
> about it. (Kanazawa 2010)

As the wives who were helped returned to the community where Kanazawa lived, some stopped by to thank her mother for her gift (for "what your daughter did").

It was also interesting that in her official capacity representing the Swedish vice consul of Hawai'i, Kanazawa could accompany the wives to the internment camp but was not allowed to enter the camp. For her efforts, Kanazawa was rewarded with a trip through 37 states in three months. She was also counseled to wear a Red Cross uniform so she would not be harassed as a Japanese woman, a sign of the postwar racist American landscape.

The Weakened Nuclear Family Unit

In Manzanar, where Japanese American families were interned together, "communal living weakened family ties and undermined parental authority" (Lindquist 2012:25). My mother, Chickie Matoba, is quoted as saying, "As children we all ate separately with our friends.... My older brother worked in the mess hall. My younger brother worked as a dishwasher someplace, so our family never ate together. That was a sad, sad thing about that" (Lindquist 2012:25). Along with these daily changes of life in Manzanar, "they [the chil-dren] saw their parents become powerless, witnessed systemic injustice, and faced an uncertain future" (Lindquist 2012:25–26). Other accounts concur that, "Parental discipline tends to break down in the centers; the family, as such, is robbed of its traditional function" (Adams 1944).

Issei fathers were no longer breadwinners and saw their sons and daughters employed in camp since they were American citizens, not aliens, like themselves. Lindquist (2012:26) adds: "Once respected patriarchs, many Japanese and Japanese American men saw their roles as provider and authority figures usurped by the government, camp administrators, and WRA rules and regulations." My mother, Chickie Matoba, shared her analysis, "It ruined the family structure. Parents were no longer in charge of their children.... There was no more family feeling anymore," (Lindquist 2012:26). This is particularly sad for me since both of my grandfathers died of cancer in camp, about a week apart. I suspect that it was more than the physical disease that ended their lives. These proud Issei men had been denied their traditional Japanese male roles and responsibilities.

Issei mothers in Manzanar also found their traditional maternal role weakening as their teenaged children ate with their friends, rather than family, and had their own school activities and social events. I recall my mother's story of my maternal grandmother standing in line to eat by herself, then returning to the line to get her sick husband's dinner to take back to their barracks (Matoba 2012). Certainly sharing living quarters with other families, having communal bathrooms (with no stall partitions), and having free time to socialize with other Issei women changed the dynamics of the Japanese family in camp.

Japanese American and German American families in Hawai'i who were physically separated from their interned loved ones, living without a male "head of household," also experienced a weakening of the nuclear American family. Extended family members had to fill the parental gap and families of internees in Hawai'i often had to move in with relatives to survive. German American study participant, Doris Berg Nye described the fear she and her younger sister shared when their parents were taken away. They wondered when their older sister, who lived on Moloka'i, could come and care for them. In this case, there was no nuclear family left so the children had to fend for themselves, as well as maintain the family boarding house (Nye 2009).

Wives chose to unite with their husbands in mainland internment camps for a variety of reasons, including inability to financially support the family in Hawai'i, lack of extended family to live with and for support, and decisions to repatriate to Japan with their spouse. Travel to the mainland provided hope of strengthening the nuclear family but was a difficult transition. "The transfer of Hawai'i internees to mainland camps started in February 1942. Over 1,000 wives and children did just that [reunited with spouses and fathers], many of them ending up in camp in Crystal City, Texas, while others ended up in War Relocation Authority administered camps in Tule Lake, California or Jerome, Arkansas" (Niiya 2010:3).

In Hawai'i, as family members who remained outside the camp tried to survive in an environment of martial law, there was growing concern about delinquency of the children in the community. Without strong parental discipline, living in multifamily households, there was concern about the social well-being of children in Hawai'i. Letters from community leaders reported that child delinquency was reaching an alarming degree due to lack of recreational facilities, working parents, and limited playground space. There was overcrowding in the Damon Tract housing area possibly due to additional children from the military base and the army was taking space for a garden and bomb shelter. The response to these letters was that the Automatic Weapons Battalion Headquarters needed the land (Huffman 1945). Children and families were subject to military priorities. It is possible that as families of internees moved in with relatives, children spent more time unsupervised on the streets or at the playgrounds.

One well-documented account regarding a Japanese internee held briefly at Kīlauea Military Camp, Honolulu Immigration Station, and Sand Island Detention Camp and then sent to several mainland camps, illustrates the trauma of separation and desire for family unification (Honda 2012). Initially wives and families had little information about their interned husbands and fathers. But communication between Ozaki and his wife indicated constant fear and uncertainty as they tried to become united as a family. Letters included information about family members' well-being, as well as the activities of the children as they developed and grew throughout the years of separation.

Repatriation to Japan was an issue in which Ozaki, who was a Japanese language teacher and "one of several individuals who functioned as agents for the Japanese Consulate in Hilo to service Japanese friends and neighbors," wished to return to Japan while his wife, a Kibei, born in the United States but educated in Japan, preferred to settle in Hawai'i after the war (Honda 2012:xviii).

Changing Japanese Women's Roles

As described in previous sections of this article, Japanese wives in Hawai'i whose spouses were interned had to learn new skills, assume leadership roles, maintain child-care responsibilities, and even in some cases, become employed to provide income for the family. As difficult as it may have been, they had to assure the well-being of their children by creating a stable environment in a time of turmoil. Nishigaya and Oshiro (2014) describe how wives of Buddhist priests in Hawai'i took over practices once their husbands were interned. When the Reverend Komagata was interned he left a newly constructed temple on the edge of downtown Honolulu with a congregation of several hundred followers. In his absence, his wife oversaw the temple and conducted Buddhist services (wedding and funeral) as did the Reverend Kodo Fujitani's wife.

Another example of the changing roles of Hawai'i women was when the daughter of an interned *shōyu* factory owner tried to get her father released to save the family business. Hatsuko Terada, older sister of study participant Elaine Fukada, took over the family business and appealed to have their father, Kyuzo Terada, furloughed because of his expertise to brew *shōyu*. Her request was denied because, according to authorities, it would require three furloughs of a month's duration, the process could be taken over by another company (which was untrue since other competitors in the *shōyu* business were unwilling to assist), and another case of release to attend to property matters had been denied (Fukada 2010). This is an example of the responsibility adult children of internees had to assume due to internment of one or both parents.

In the mainland camps, Issei women's roles changed considerably especially for those who came from rural areas and who had had heavy duties with child rearing, cooking, and working in the fields with their husbands. Once in camp, they did not need to cook (everyone ate in the mess halls) or work outside the home (Issei were aliens, not citizens like their Nisei children who could work) and enjoyed the social company of other Issei women. In Manzanar, where my grandmothers were interned, social connections between Issei women grew as they had more leisure time to play cards and share stories of their families and life in Japan. In fact, my paternal grandmother connected with a woman from Wakayama, the same prefecture in Japan where her family resided, and our families became lifetime friends, across generations. As a picture bride of a tenant farmer in northern California, my grandmother had no female friends in her daily life. Farmwork and child care had dominated her prewar life so internment brought relief from a life of daily toil and isolation. I believe this life path made her decide not to go to work outside the home during the postwar years, when she was still in her fifties. Instead, she chose to be the matriarch in her firstborn son's home causing generational conflict in our Midwestern Japanese American household.

Concluding Remarks

Only recently since Lindquist (2012) wrote *Children of Manzanar,* highlighting the voices and perspectives of children and families on internment, have there been specific accounts of how internment affected the lives of children, both inside and outside of camp. Many internees never spoke about their experiences in camp, or of their family relationships as a result of incarceration. Current support for qualitative research and oral histories of internees has raised awareness of the lived experiences of internees across all internment sites. In Hawai'i, oral histories recorded by the Japanese Cultural Center of Hawai'i contributed to the documentary *The Untold Story: Internment of Japanese Americans in Hawai'i.* In addition, oral history researchers, Warren and Michiko Nishimoto at the University of Hawai'i at Mānoa, along with our University of Hawai'i–West O'ahu Multidisciplinary Honouliuli research team are actively creating a rich mosaic of voices and perspectives on internment and imprisonment.

Differing accounts and interpretations of internment develop as researchers, historians, journalists, artists, and political activists tell varied stories in print and media. One controversial representation of internment is the recent musical *Allegiance* produced by George Takei (actor of *Star Trek* fame), which depicts a political and activist interpretation of internment, portraying the role of the Japanese American Citizens League (JACL), and its leader Mike Masaoka, at the time of Executive Order 9066, requiring the evacuation of 120,000 Japanese Americans on the mainland. *Allegiance* won the Outstanding New Musical 2012 Craig Noel Award (Takei 2012). I mention this because my California study participants Yoshinaga and Matoba mentioned their distaste for an activist interpretation of internment, indicating that as teenagers in camp, they recall a positive, joyful time of growing up with dances, sports, and peers. Takei was four years old in camp and now tells a political story with his musical, while these Nisei octogenarians were teenagers and social interactions in their camp high school dominated their fond memories. There are many lenses by which internment can be viewed.

Another creative play on internment, *Shikataganai (It Can't Be Helped)* by playwright and activist Kendra Arimoto, depicted the life of families as they encountered cramped living arrangements in camp barracks and adjusted to life behind barbed wire. Each character portrayed a personal context of internment often shared among others (Arimoto 2010). The play, performed as live theater, was presented at the 2011 Hawai'i International Conference on Arts and Humanities and received the 2010 James Baldwin Fund Prize for Multi-cultural Playwriting.

There are so many lenses we can take as we listen to the voices of diverse internees, with generational, regional, educational, military, and religious differences. Hawai'i under martial law and mainland incarceration from major cities in California to rural communities across the West Coast contributed to a collage of rich experiences and diverse interpretations of internment during World War II. I am attempting to capture the stories through the eyes of children, reflected upon years later as adults.

In summarizing my study findings, it is clear that the two participant groups experienced displacement in a time of political turmoil, a weakening of the nuclear family, and changing women's roles as a result of internment. For the Manzanar teens in my study, displacement meant relocation into internment camps with their families, while displacement for Hawai'i participants meant the dismantling of the nuclear family with parents, for Japanese mostly fathers, in camp and the rest of the family left to survive under martial law. Some moved to live with relatives, but all faced a hostile environment in which there was an implicit perception of wrongdoing if the head-of-household was arrested, detained, and interned. Everyone lived in fear and uncertainty in a society of which they had no control.

My research on the effect of internment on children and families in Hawai'i will continue as I attempt to find out more about the 10 children who were at Honouliuli. In addition, more research needs to be done on the life of all children in Hawai'i under martial law. How did parents of Japanese, German, and Italian heritage explain internment to their children? How did military personnel explain martial law to their children? How was parenting impacted by the war? How did families affected by internment rebuild their lives once the internees returned? And, importantly, were parents' voices silenced as they tried to rebuild their communities and their lives? There are many questions for future studies. ❖

Notes

1. The original 1944 Ansel Adams photo journal, *Born Free and Equal*, was edited by Wynne Benti and published by US Camera. Adams was friends with Manzanar Camp Director Ralph Merritt and was invited to document the internees and life at camp between 1943 and 1944. The original collection of photos was considered controversial (he photographed the guard towers) and in 1965 Adams donated his camp photos to the Library of Congress where they languished for years. In 2001 Spotted Dog Press in Bishop, California, redesigned and republished *Born Free and Equal* and in 2002 produced it in hardcover.

2. The camp yearbook, *Our World 1943: 1944 Manzanar High,* was published in 1944 under editor-in-chief Reggie Shikami. Reggie is a retired former CEO of a manufacturing company, resides in the Chicago area, and maintains contact with his 1944 classmates, including two of my study participants, Chickie Matoba and Seigo Yoshinaga. Chiyeko Hiraoka Matoba passed away February 17, 2014.

References

Adams, Ansel. 1944. *Born Free and Equal: The Story of Loyal Japanese Americans.* New York: US Camera. Reprinted by Spotted Dog Press, Inc., 2002.

Arimoto, Kendra. 2010. Shikataganai. Retrieved December 31, 2012 (www.kendraarimoto.com).

Burton, Jeff, Mary Farrell, Lisa Kaneko, Linda Maldonato, and Kelly Altenhofen. 2014. "Hell Valley: Uncovering a Prison Camp in Paradise." In this issue.

Falgout, Suzanne. 2014. "Honouliuli's POWs: Making Connections, Generating Changes." In this issue.

Fitzgerald, John A. (1st lieutenant). 1944. Memo to Provost Marshal on the Daily Report of Internees and Detainees between July 12th to July 13th, 1944. Record Group 494, Entry 25, Box 335. National Archives and Records Administration II, College Park, Maryland.

Fukada, Elaine. 2010. Interview by Susan Matoba Adler, Kailua, HI, September 26.

General Statistics on Relocation from Hawaii between Nov. 1942 to Mar. 1943. 1943. Record Group 494, Entry 11, Box 45, 1942–1945. National Archives and Records Administration II, College Park, Maryland.

Honda, Gail. 2012. *Family Torn Apart: The Internment Story of the Otokichi Muin Ozaki Family.* Honolulu: Japanese Cultural Center of Hawai'i.

Huffman, C. E. 1945. Box 46. Letter to Otto Hays Regarding Child Delinquency at Kaloaloa District (Damon Tract), February 12. Record Group 494, Entry 11, 1942–1945. National Archives and Records Administration II, College Park, Maryland.

Kanazawa, Shim. 2010. Interview by Susan Matoba Adler, Ernest Oshiro, and Amy Nishimura, Honolulu, July 28.

Lindquist, Heather C. 2012. *Children of Manzanar*. Berkeley: Manzanar History Association.

Manzanar High School. 1944. *Our World: Manzanar, California*. Manzanar, CA. Reprinted by Diane Yotsuya Honda, ed. Logan, UT: Herff Jones Yearbook Company, 1998.

Matoba, Chiyeko (Chickie). 2012. Personal phone communication with Susan Matoba Adler, December 24.

Memo Indicating that the Two Yoshida Children's Parents Were in Japan and They Were under the Care of Tomi Naha. 1944. Record Group 494, Entry 19, Box 320, 1942–1944. National Archives and Records Administration II, College Park, Maryland.

Morning Report. 1944. November 16. Record Group 494, Entry A1 22, Box 172, O-P. "Orders" 1942–1946. National Archives and Records Administration II, College Park, Maryland.

Niiya, Brian. 2010. "World War II Internment in Hawaii." Online resource for students and instructors. Retrieved December 17, 2012 (www.hawaiiinternment.org/history-of-internment).

Nishigaya, Linda, and Ernest Oshiro. 2014. "Reviving the Lotus: Japanese Buddhism and World War II Internment." In this issue.

Nye, Doris Berg. 2009. Interview by Susan Matoba Adler, Kapolei, HI, December 5.

Red Cross. 1942. Letter from Red Cross Regarding Mrs. Yamada and Her Family Survival in Hawaii, Nov. 30. Record Group 494, Entry 19, Box 313, 1942–1944. National Archives and Records Administration II, College Park, Maryland.

Rosenfeld, Alan. 2014. "Neither Aliens nor Enemies: The Hearings of 'German' and 'Italian' Internees in Wartime Hawai'i." In this issue.

Statement of Procedure in Connection with the Providing of Welfare Service to the Dependents of Internees and Detained Persons. 1942. Draft Document, File 36, March 31. Hawai'i War Records Depository, University of Hawai'i at Mānoa, Hamilton Library, Honolulu, Hawai'i.

Takei, George. 2012. *Allegiance*. Retrieved June 5, 2013 (www.allegiancemusical.com).

Tsuchiya, Ronald. 2011. Interview by Susan Matoba Adler, Kapolei, HI, August 2.

Psychic Wounds from the Past:
Investigating Intergenerational Trauma in the Families of Japanese Americans Interned in the Honouliuli Internment and POW Camp

GARYN K. TSURU

ABSTRACT

The Japanese Americans hold a distinct place in the pages of US history. Many immigrated to the United States from Japan in search of prosperity and a better future for their families. Enduring years of hard work and living in hostile conditions, the Japanese Americans who chose to remain in the United States put their trust in the democratic system of this country. Following the attack on Pearl Harbor this trust was shattered, as the Japanese Americans suffered from not only a loss of their constitutional rights, but one of the worst crimes against civil liberties in the history of the United States. More than 120,000 Japanese Americans were ordered to leave their home and relocate to internment camps under armed guard. The psychological

Garyn K. Tsuru, University of Hawai'i–West O'ahu, 91-1001 Farrington Highway, Kapolei HI 96707. The material is based upon work assisted by a grant from the Department of Interior, National Park Service. Any opinions, findings, and conclusions or recommendations expressed in this material are those of the author and do not necessarily reflect the views of the Department of the Interior. The author would like to thank Kristen Miyamoto for the transcription services she provided. The author can be reached at garynt@hawaii.edu.

effects of the internment have been well documented, with the impact of the trauma generated by the event affecting generations of Japanese Americans.

This paper examines the intergenerational effects of trauma, through the lens of the historical trauma theory, on three families who had a family member that was interned at the Honouliuli Camp during World War II. Their experiences were compared and contrasted to what has been written about families who were interned in camps on the continental United States. The Honouliuli Camp provides a unique opportunity to investigate the psychological sequelae resulting from interning a small fraction of the total Japanese American population in Hawai'i, and provides more insight into the deleterious effects of civil injustice.

Introduction

On February 19, 1942, President Franklin D. Roosevelt signed Executive Order 9066, authorizing the forced relocation and incarceration of more than 120,000 Japanese Americans living on the West Coast of the United States. Many had less than a week to evacuate their homes before being escorted under armed guard to internment camps located in the most remote and desolate areas of the United States. A reaction to the Japanese attack on Pearl Harbor, the Japanese American internment was deemed necessary to preserve the national security of the United States, and protect the country from espionage and insurrection from within.

Thousands of miles away in the US Territory of Hawai'i, processes that closely paralleled, yet were distinctly different from what was happening on the continental United States, were underway. Rosenfeld (2014) had pointed out in this volume that rather than a directive driven by Executive Order 9066, the internment in Hawai'i was authorized by martial law. As a result, less than 1 percent of the 159,000 ethnic Japanese civilians living in Hawai'i were subjected to any form of confinement (Niiya 2010). Two reasons have been given for this more "moderate" approach to the internment of Japanese Americans living in Hawai'i. First, martial law afforded the Hawai'i wartime military government greater control over the entire population, circumventing the need for a wide-scale internment of the Japanese Americans living in Hawai'i (Rosenfeld 2014). Second, since a large proportion of laborers in Hawai'i were ethnically Japanese, the Japanese Americans played a vital role in Hawai'i's agrarian economy (Kashima 2003).

By the evening of December 8, 1941, 430 local civilians, including individuals who were part of a short list of "potentially dangerous individuals" to US interests in Hawai'i (such as male Japanese schoolteachers, community leaders, Buddhist and Shinto priests as well as 85 individuals classified as German and Italian) were quickly rounded up and placed in detention centers across the islands (Kashima 2003; Rosenfeld 2014). Many where held for a few days to even months before being transferred to the Sand Island Internment Station on the island of O'ahu where they would receive further hearings from Hawai'i's wartime government (Kashima 2003; Rosenfeld 2014). In the days following the attack, the list of names and number of internees grew. According to Nishimura (2014) and Rosenfeld's (2014) contributions to this volume, unlike the internment sites on the continental United States, which were comprised primarily of Japanese Americans, the civilian internees in Hawai'i were more diverse, including men and women from German, Italian, Austrian, Norwegian, Danish, Russian, Lithuanian, Swedish, Finnish, Irish, British, and Jewish European ethnic ancestries. In February of 1942, some of the internees were transferred to internment camps on the continental United States, such as Crystal City in Texas, Tule Lake in California, and Jerome in Arkansas (Niiya 2010). On March 1, 1943, the Sand Island Internment Station was closed, and the remaining internees were transferred to the Honouliuli Internment and POW Camp on the island of O'ahu, and were confined there until the end of the war. Although the camp was built to hold 3,000 people, at any one time it held no more than 320 civilian internees (Niiya 2010). In contrast, the Honouliuli Camp was one of Hawai'i's largest POW camps, housing as many as 4,000 or more Japanese, Okinawan, Korean, Filipino, and Italian POWs (Falgout 2014).

Nearly forty years later, a governmental investigation of the circumstances surrounding the internment failed to find a single documented act of disloyalty by any Japanese American during World War II (Commission on Wartime Relocation and Internment of Civilians [hereafter CWRIC] 1997). The CWRIC (1997) had concluded that the internment of the Japanese Americans was a "grave injustice" and a harrowing reminder of the great infraction committed against their civil liberties. Unfortunately, the damage had already been done. The internment literally uprooted these people from their homes and businesses, incurring anywhere from $810 million to $2 billion (calculated at the value of the 1983 US dollar) in lost revenues, but more insidious were the psychological scars that would never truly heal.

The psychological effects the internment had on Japanese American internees have been well documented, and it is suggested that nearly every internee was affected by the trauma of being interned (Mass 1986; Nagata 1993). Even more deplorable were the intergenerational consequences of the internment, a cruel legacy of the social injustices meted out to internees that had a profound impact on subsequent generations (Nagata 1990). Much of the literature on the intergenerational impact of internment trauma on children of internees has focused on camps located on the continental United States. Little, if anything has been written about the internment experience in Hawai'i. It is important to note that the social and political climate of Hawai'i during World War II offered a unique internment experience that was different from what had been experienced on the continental United States (Kashima 2003). As previously noted, Hawai'i was placed under martial law and only a small fraction of the Japanese American population was interned. Furthermore, rather than the wholesale internment of entire families, and the seizure of their land and businesses by the US government, the Japanese Americans interned in Hawai'i consisted primarily of Issei (first-generation) males. These differences may have affected the psychological sequelae of internment-related trauma, and how this trauma was expressed by those incarcerated in the Honouliuli Camp and received by their children.

The following paper focuses on the Japanese American civilian internees, and examines the interviews conducted on three families who had a close relative interned in the Honouliuli Camp during World War II. Each interview was approximately 45 minutes in length, and took place during the fall of 2012. In order to maintain anonymity and protect the privacy of those interviewed, the author identifies each interviewee by the initials of their names. The interviews include: (1) the ES family—three daughters of a local tailor (consisting of the eldest child ES and her two younger sisters—middle born GF and youngest sister DH); (2) the grandson of a Buddhist bishop who was sent to Hawai'i from Japan to be raised by his grandparents (SK, now a bishop himself); and (3) the son of a farmer who later went on to serve in the US military (RH). Their experiences were evaluated in context to the historical trauma theory for themes suggesting the intergenerational transmission of trauma related to the internment. Their experiences were also compared and contrasted to what has been recorded in the existing literature on the Japanese American internment in order to find differences between those family members who were interned in Hawai'i versus the continental United States, and how these differences impacted their lives.

Historical Trauma Theory

Historical trauma is defined as "the cumulative emotional and psychological wounding across generations, including the life span, which emanates from massive group trauma" (Brave Heart-Jordan, Chase, Elkins, and Altschul 2011:283). The term was first introduced by social work researcher Maria Yellow Horse Brave Heart-Jordan in her work on American Indians (Brave Heart-Jordan and DeBruyn 1995). Since the inception of this theory, a resurgence of interest in the study of intergenerational trauma has led to a small but growing corpus of work outlining the physical and psychological consequences of intergenerational trauma. Unlike post-traumatic stress disorder, which focuses on the individual's stress response to a traumatic event, researchers in the emerging field of historical trauma study the historical and social events that lead to intergenerational stress responses in groups.

In her work, Sotero (2006) provided a conceptual model of historical trauma which included the following stages: (1) The subjugation of a "minority" group by the dominant group through segregation/displacement, physical/psychological violence, economic destruction, or cultural dispossession; (2) the primary or first generation's exposure to this subjugation; (3) a physical, psychological, or social response to this trauma (the response may include any or all three factors), and (4) the intergenerational transmission of this trauma to subsequent generations.

Much of the theoretical underpinnings for the historical trauma model come from studies on the survivors of the World War II Jewish Holocaust and their offspring (Barocas and Barocas 1973; Nadler, Kav-Vaenaki, and Gleitman 1985; Prince 1985; Solkoff 1981). Interviews conducted on survivors who experienced the horrors of the Holocaust firsthand uncovered a constellation of similar reactions to this very traumatic experience (Barocas 1975). Researchers have coined this traumatic reaction as "survivor syndrome," which includes symptoms like denial, depersonalization, isolation, somatization, memory loss, agitation, anxiety, depression, intrusive thoughts, nightmares, psychic numbing, and survivor guilt (Barocas 1975; Neiderland 1968). Shackled with emotional distress stemming from their traumatic experience, the literature suggests that the parental effectiveness of Holocaust survivors may have been compromised thereby resulting in symptomatic first generation offspring (Danieli 1982).

Studies outlining the cross-generational effects of the Jewish Holocaust suggest that the traumatic nature of the event had a significant impact on some first generation offspring of survivors (Barocas and Barocas 1980; Nadler et al. 1985; Prince 1985). Interviews conducted on first generation offspring of survivors taken from clinical populations have uncovered evidence of a myriad of post-traumatic symptoms such as depression, difficulty with expressing emotions, overdependence, and experiencing themselves as different or damaged due to their parents' status as Holocaust survivors (Kestenberg 1980; Prince 1985). When compared to individuals whose parents had not experienced the Holocaust, even some nonclinical (i.e., individuals not exhibiting symptoms of a psychological/emotional disorder) offspring of survivors exhibited a heightened sensitivity to culture and ancestry, as well as an emphasis on the primacy of ethnic survival (Heller 1981). The trauma of the Holocaust coupled with the rich historical legacy of Jewish culture, their religious ideology, and the emphasis on family and community were a catalyst for these individuals to focus on their ethnic heritage. In the end, there is little doubt that the stress generated by the Holocaust had to have a profound effect on the survivors, which in turn greatly influenced the way their children perceived the world around them.

Japanese American Internment on the Continental United States

Before any discussion of the Japanese American internment can begin, it is important to acknowledge the multiple factors that distinguish the Jewish Holocaust from the Japanese American internment. First and foremost, governmental documents purport that the Japanese Americans were incarcerated in order to maintain national security in the United States during World War II (CWRIC 1997). In contrast, the Nazi regime intended to ethnically cleanse Europe of anyone of Jewish ancestry, and set up death camps to implement this heinous initiative. Second, Japanese Americans confined in internment camps were granted some civil liberties, while the Holocaust camps granted none. Finally, Japanese Americans where able to create a greater sense of community within the internment camps through organizations like schools and sports teams, and were eventually allowed to serve in the US military. Comparing and contrasting the Holocaust and the Japanese American internment is an exercise in futility, as the two events are inherently different. Despite these differences, when you evaluate the two events through the lens of the historical trauma theory, it is evident that in both cases one group of individuals (the dominant group) subjugated another group of individuals (the minority group). Although the Japanese Americans did not experience the same level of physical violence and despair as those who survived the Holocaust, the

Japanese American internment was undoubtedly a traumatizing experience, and the impact of the trauma affected subsequent generations (Mass 1986).

During this dark chapter of US history, over 90 percent of all Japanese Americans living on the continental United States were incarcerated in internment camps for an average of two to three years (Nagata 1993). Many were whisked away individually or as families during the middle of the night. Confused and frightened, they were herded onto "evacuation trains" that had their windows drawn and had absolutely no knowledge as to where they were going. Some even believed they were going to be taken to remote locations to be executed. Back at home heirlooms and cultural icons were either confiscated by the military or destroyed by family members fearing they would be seen as symbols of disloyalty (Nagata 1998).

The internment camps themselves were located in the most inhospitable areas of the United States (Mass 1986). Supposedly built to keep Japanese Americans "safe" during the war, the camps were surrounded by barbed wire and imposing guard towers, which made it impossible to mistake the sites for anything other than prisons. Internees faced sweltering heat during the summer, bitter cold during the winter, and flooding during the rainy seasons. The camp accommodations were horrendous, with multiple families sharing cramped quarters in hastily built shacks. Such living conditions challenged the Japanese cultural beliefs regarding family solidarity and harmony, shattered any longtime traditions, and compromised many parents' ability to discipline their children (Morishima 1973).

The Japanese Americans already faced anti-Asian sentiment through prewar laws enacted to exclude and marginalize this population (Park 2008). Based on xenophobic reactions to the burgeoning population of Asians in the United States, the Immigration Act of 1924 not only rendered Asian American immigrants ineligible for naturalization, but also barred any Asians from entering the country. As a result, the internment only served to compound the bitter feelings and resentment Japanese Americans had toward the US government (Mass 1986). Upon release from the internment camps, many families returned to find their homes and businesses in ruin, or even seized by the government. Although the majority of internees went on to lead successful lives, many suffered from a loss of self-esteem, shame, self-consciousness, and a cynical attitude toward democracy (Mass 1986; Morishima 1973; Nagata 1998). In order to cope with the internment experience, internees resorted to using defense mechanisms such as repression, denial, rationalization, and identification with the aggressor (Mass 1986). For example, some developed a greater mistrust of European Americans and associated only with Japanese Americans, while others avoided any contact with other Japanese Americans.

With regard to their child-rearing practices, some internees made a conscious effort to raise their children to be as "American" as possible, while others made efforts to make sure their children remained inconspicuous in society (Kitano and Kikumura 1976; Morishima 1973). Some even refused to discuss anything about their internment experience with family members (Daniels 1986). In her study on the cross-generational consequences of the Japanese American Internment, Nagata (1993) found that children whose parents were both interned had a greater attitudinal preference for Japanese Americans. Furthermore, children of former internees also reported feeling less secure about their status and rights in the United States than children whose parents were not interned. In conclusion, the extant literature underscores the magnitude of the trauma caused by the internment, and the cross-generational effects of this trauma.

The Honouliuli Internment and POW Camp Experience

The story behind the Honouliuli Camp diverges slightly from its continental US counterparts due to the social, economic, and political climate of Hawai'i during the 1940s. By the beginning of World War II, Japanese Americans made up 37.3 percent of Hawai'i's total population (Kashima 2003). Initially, some members in the US government supported the idea of interning all individuals of Japanese ancestry living in Hawai'i. When the government evaluated this proposed policy more carefully, it became glaringly apparent that this would not be an economically viable option. A large proportion of sugarcane workers were ethnically Japanese American, and the wholesale imprisonment of these workers would bring Hawai'i's economy to a screeching halt. In addition to this, martial law was declared in Hawai'i, which in effect allowed the Hawai'i wartime military government even greater control over the entire population in comparison to the widespread internment of the Japanese Americans (Rosenfeld 2014). As a result, only a small percentage of Japanese Americans living in Hawai'i were actually interned. Furthermore, the conditions of the Japanese American internment in Hawai'i directly affected the composition of the internees in the Honouliuli Camp, which consisted primarily of Issei (or first generation Japanese American) males.

The Honouliuli Internment and POW Camp was opened in March 1943 to house the internees who were confined in the Sand Island Internment Station, and who were not transferred to an internment camp on the continental United States (Kashima 2003). In a similar vein to what was occurring on the continental United States, the Japanese Americans that were eventually interned in the Honouliuli Camp and their families also faced the anxiety of an uncertain future. By the evening of December 7, 1941, following the Japanese attack on Pearl Harbor, FBI agents and the army were mobilized to round up individuals on the custodial detention list (i.e., the list of individuals deemed as potentially dangerous to US government interests) (Kashima 2003). Just as on the continental United States, individuals on the list were seized from their homes without reason or warning. As traumatic as the internment was for the internees, the children of the internees faced similar traumatic experiences themselves. ES, the eldest daughter of a tailor who was interned in Honouliuli recalls the day her father was taken away, feeling as if he simply vanished:

> Well, to me he disappeared. There were some men who came and after their talk he went with them, and I never saw him for a while after that.... I was confused. I thought "what's happening here?" and before that too, you know, war had broken out and that's traumatic in itself. I mean I didn't connect it to my dad, but the fact that he was taken away really impacted me. All of us, I think. (ES Family 2012:3)

RH, the son of a farmer who was interned in Honouliuli recounted a similar experience:

> I was still in high school and after school I went home and my mother was crying out in the garage and I said "Mom what's going on? Why you crying for?" She says, "[S]omebody took papa away...2 FBI agents they carried sidearms," and we didn't see him for a whole year.... No communicating.... You couldn't go to Fort Shafter and say, "[W]here's my dad?" (RH 2012:2)

Both families expressed intense concern about the whereabouts of their fathers. Absconded from their homes without so much as an explanation, the children began to fear for the worst. One member even experienced posttraumatic stress disorder symptoms. DH, the youngest sister from ES's family reported recurring dreams that her father was home, only to awaken to the reality of the situation (ES Family 2012). The idea of not knowing what happened to their father, or whether their father would ever return home weighed heavily on their minds.

Inside and Outside of Honouliuli

The Honouliuli Internment and POW Camp was located on 160 acres of arid land in Central O'ahu. Like the internment camps on the continental United States, armed guards patrolled an encampment that was surrounded by barbed wire and watchtowers. The internment camp proved to be a foreboding sight to families of internees. In her interview, ES elaborated, "We didn't know what it was.... [W]e didn't know why it was there.... [A]ll I knew was that as we go down to the camp, I would look up and we would see guards with machine guns.... [M]y gosh what's happening...?" (ES Family 2012:13)

Internees were housed in prefabricated sixteen-man demountable barracks (Burton et al. 2014). The living conditions of the internment camp, with the sweltering heat and swarms of mosquitoes, were horrible enough to earn it the moniker Jigoku Dani, or Hell Valley (Japanese Cultural Center of Hawai'i n.d.). Days would drag on, and internees found themselves hard-pressed to find activities to pass the time.

Back at home the family of the internees struggled to make ends meet. ES's family relied on their father's tailoring business to generate income for their family. Without their father, their mother and grandfather were forced to shoulder the responsibility of caring for six children. ES recalls how her mother and her family had to make living adjustments in order to survive:

> Well, we [had] to make adjustments in our living too, everything had to be blacked out, and they had a shop [that] was kind of important [to] have transportation, and [my father] was the driver. My mom didn't drive, that put a lot of pressure on her too.... My father was very articulate, [he talked] to everybody; not my mother. And so when it came for her to collect I was thinking "[H]ow's she gonna do it?" But I guess she did.... [It] was really hard for her. (ES Family 2012:3–5)

RH experienced the same struggles, with his mother stricken with grief over the loss of their father, and his brother having to make career adjustments in order to support his family:

> So my brother had to quit school, he had to go to work right? Back then we had no welfare system; you were on your own. My mother [was] crying all the time "[W]here's daddy, where's papa?" She was always crying. I told mommy, "[W]e don't know...." Mother cried every night. And I felt so sorry because you know it's hard to lose your husband after living together for so long. (RH 2012:3)

The families also had to deal with the stigma of having their fathers interned, and the fear and shame that came with this stigma. Since they could not communicate their distress to anyone, they were unable to turn to their neighbors for support, and in some cases did not even divulge this information to their own siblings:

> I knew but my mother told us—my sister and me—not to tell them, the younger ones. Well, my father didn't want them to [know] ... especially her (referring to her youngest sister DN).... So my sister and I knew.... I don't know whether my brother knew. My brother must've known. But from GF (her younger sister) on, I don't think they had too much knowledge on what happened. (ES Family 2012:5)

ES's father gave her explicit instructions to tell her brother and sisters that he went to the mountains to hunt pigs. The family had to also deal with the feelings of being alone and isolated during this trying time. ES recounted that, "... hardly anybody came around, so they must've known. They were kind of afraid to come around," (ES Family 2012:6). RH faced similar circumstances:

> [T]he thing is that nobody in high school knew that my father was interned. I didn't tell anybody, because anybody interned, they'd think he was a spy.... [M]ost [thought] my father was working all day long, so nobody knew where he was anyway, you know, but I didn't tell anybody my father was interned. (RH 2012:3)

The veil of secrecy only added to the stress each family was experiencing. Both ES and RH's families believed that their friends and neighbors may have known about their fathers, but did not come around for fear of associating with a family declared as an enemy to the United States. Regardless of if this was true or not, little help or consolation was offered to these families.

Life after Honouliuli: Strength and Resiliency in Japanese Americans

The Honouliuli Internment and POW Camp officially closed in late 1945 (Kashima 2003). Life seemed to return back to normal for the families of the three internees. ES vividly recalled seeing her father one day, "I remember ... you know we had a tailor shop right? [My father] used to wear shorts after he came back and he would mop the floor, and I'm going, 'Oh Pop? Mopping the floor?' And he was like [a] king.... [H]e was really happy..." (ES Family 2012:8). Despite the trials he endured, what little ES's father had to say about his internment experience was far from negative. This in turn seemed to help his children cope with their own experience:

> The thing is he never said anything bad about the government, so that kind of helped us too in a way. Yeah because there was no negative thoughts just that you do whatever you need to do.... Maybe that's the reason why we didn't have any kind of [negative] feelings because maybe we got to see [him] once in three months, but we saw him and he was always happy. (ES Family 2012:9)

Her father even went on to tell her that he was grateful for earning 10 cents an hour for doing tailor work while he was interned. Bishop SK, whose grandfather (a Buddhist bishop himself) was interned in Honouliuli, also had a similar experience:

> He didn't say anything negative, that he was so bitter or anything like that. No. He [said] he was well fed; of course it's not the kind of food that he liked to eat but well fed and he [said] there was no physical or form of torture or anything like that and he said on top of that he got paid. (SK 2012:4)

RH's father was more reticent when questioned about his experience:

> I asked him a lot of questions.... How'd they treat you? He didn't say anything. Whatever he said, he felt it might hurt him later I think, but he didn't say nothing negative about the camp. My father is the type that he doesn't talk—he doesn't want to upset anybody; very quiet, very considerate and he wasn't the type that [would] say anything bad about anybody, yeah, especially the camp. (RH 2012:10)

Despite the circumstances, RH's father supported RH's enlistment into the US Army. RH reported that his father "wasn't happy in the camp, no, but when he came out, he was happy that I got my draft. I told my dad, 'Hey I got drafted,' you know, and good he told me, 'yeah ... this is your country, do it'" (RH 2012:10). Rather than dwell on the past, the three former internees seemed to look toward the future. The positive front each of them showed their children seemed to help their families make the necessary postwar adjustments.

Hawai'i and the United States: The Intergenerational Impact of the Internment

To reiterate once more, there is little doubt that the magnitude of the trauma created by the Japanese American internment affected almost every internee. Long after World War II ended, some of the former internees from continental US camps still suffered from post-traumatic stress disorder symptoms such as recurring distressing dreams, avoiding talking about the internment, and hypervigilance (Mass 1986; Nagata 1993). Recommendations from the War Relocation Authority warning former internees against congregating in large groups in public spaces and from living next door to another Japanese American only served to compound their anxieties (CWRIC 1997). For the individuals living on the continental United States, the internment had intergenerational consequences as well. In her seminal work, Nagata (1993) suggested a link between the struggle some children of internees had with issues relating to self-confidence, a lack of self-esteem, and difficulty asserting themselves and with their parent's wartime incarceration. Some first generation offspring of internees also exhibited a preference for associating with Japanese Americans over Caucasian Americans (suggesting avoidant behavior) if both their parents were interned, and feeling less secure about their rights in the United States (Nagata 1990).

Surprisingly, on face value the families interviewed for this paper appeared to be relatively unscathed by their experience. It is important to note that their present-day views should not detract from how serious their situation was during World War II, as each of the families dealt with their own struggles with having a member of their family interned. Despite these circumstances, all three families went on to live successful lives, and their own children seemed to follow in their paths. For example, RH took delight in talking about his own military career and how proud he was of his children and grandchildren. A good portion of his interview time was spent looking through picture albums. ES's family was very open about marrying outside of their own ethnic group, and over the years developed a multiethnic family of their own. Bishop SK followed in his grandfather's footsteps and became the bishop of his Buddhist sect. His own children carried on this tradition and took the vows of priesthood themselves.

Several factors may have played a role in mitigating the intergenerational effects of trauma on the children of internees in Hawai'i. First, was the actual demographic composition of the Honouliuli Camp. Unlike the internment camps on the continental United States, the majority of the internees that occupied the Honouliuli Camp were male Issei. For the most part, their families were allowed to remain at home and keep their land and businesses. In fact, all three of the families expressed how fortunate they and their family members were not to have been interned in one of the camps on the continental United States. As result, the former internees were more easily able to return to the role of providing for their families, free from the shame of having their entire family uprooted from their homes and shackled with the anxiety of having their businesses and possessions seized. Second, unlike the internment camps on the continental United States, the rules in the Honouliuli Camp appeared to have been more lax (Kashima 2003). Internees were free to speak in Japanese, and to practice Japanese religions. Probably the most important difference was how the Honouliuli internees were allowed visitation rights. Both ES and RH's family described their visits to see their fathers as taking on a picnic-like ambiance. RH's mother would splurge to make Japanese delicacies (such as pickled vegetables) and fried chicken to take to their father and the other internees. RH recalled how happy his father was to see his family:

> We were able to see our dad twice a month mostly Sundays and we enjoyed taking bento lunches to my dad because he was happy to see us and camp food is different from what we can prepare, like sushi…. [Y]ou know, they [didn't] serve rice in the camp; the army didn't have rice at that time anyway. And they were happy they could [eat rice]. (RH 2012:4)

After long months of not knowing what happened to their father, during their first visit, ES recalled, "We just sat there side by side. I don't think we sat across, but I can't remember. It was good just to be by him. And I remember we always used to buy a pack of gum …" (ES Family 2012:7). Gift exchanging was also allowed. ES and her family accumulated beautiful trinkets and jewelry that were crafted from seashells, plastic toothbrushes, and whatever material was on hand to the internees.

Third, was the spirit of the Japanese culture and the observance of two philosophical approaches to life: *gaman* and *shikataganai*. *Ga-man* means to persevere or endure, and to internalize emotions, and *shi-ka-ta-ga-nai* loosely translate into "It cannot be helped" (Kitano 1969). This fatalistic attitude about the forces outside of one's control promotes forward thinking in Japanese, and also cautions against dwelling on one's past. It was this cultural belief that allowed the Japanese Americans who were interned on the continental United States to persevere as well (Kitano 1969; Morishima 1973; Nagata 1993). As a result, the internees in the Honouliuli Camp tried to make the best of their situation. In his interview, Bishop SK even mentioned how his grandfather volunteered to clean the camp toilets as an extension of his Buddhist practice in the camp:

> [S]o living with the spirit of being a Soto Zen priest, to clean your own surrounding starting with the toilet is the first thing you do when you're going to the monastery. It used to show that you can become a humble person. And to clean the toilet is to help cleanse yourself… physical cleaning is a form of mental therapy to cleanse [himself] of all the negative karma that he had. (SK 2012:3)

It is likely that some or a combination of all these factors helped the internees and their families to cope with their experiences and to thrive in their post-internment lives.

What the Honouliuli Camp and continental US camps both had in common was a general lack of communication regarding internment-related experiences. All three interviewees had asked their family members about the internment, but little if anything was said. More surprising was the internees almost never had anything negative to say about their internment experience or the US government. There are several theories that could explain this phenomenon. First, as Nagata (1990) had proposed in her study on the third-generation Japanese American children of internees, the lack of communication and general silence around internment issues may have been part of an effort to avoid thoughts and feeling associated with the trauma. Avoidance of anything, be it a thought, person, or place associated with a traumatic experience is one of the symptoms of post-traumatic stress disorder (American Psychiatric Association 2013) and an indication of psychological trauma. Furthermore, the internee's positive spin on their internment experiences may have been a form of psychological denial to protect internees from having to deal with the reality of the situation (such as being considered a foreign enemy by their own country), their true feelings about the internment, and how traumatic the internment really was. Second, the Japanese attitude of *shikataganai* and to not dwell on the past may have acted as a vehicle to help internees focus on regaining their lives back after they were released. Third, the actual existence of the Honouliuli Camp seems to have been shrouded in secrecy. After it closed in 1945, the military tried to keep any information about the camp from the public through the use of military-security classification (Kashima 2003). In an interesting but related story, the 94-year-old grandmother of the author of this paper, who lived her whole life in Hawai'i, did not know there was an internment camp on the Hawaiian Island of O'ahu. A longtime family friend of Bishop SK's grandfather, she was very surprised to hear that he was interned in the Honouliuli Camp. Despite seeing him on a daily basis (as Bishop SK's grandfather used to frequent her family's Japanese-style bath), she believed he went back to Japan rather than being incarcerated. The stigma of having a family member interned also contributed to this veil of secrecy, as both families of the former internees did not want to be branded as traitors, and consequently neighbors and friends did not want to be seen associating with possible enemies of the United States during World War II.

Conclusion

The present study investigated the intergenerational consequences of the World War II Japanese American internment in Hawai'i. Before any concluding remarks can be made, it is important to note the limitations of this study. The material used to support the theories proposed in this paper was extrapolated from the interviews conducted on the family members of three former internees. Since this represents only a small fraction of the total number of internees incarcerated in the Honouliuli Camp, their views may not be an accurate reflection of the general views and opinions of the population from which they were drawn. Nevertheless, their stories stand as important contributions to the Japanese Americans internment literature, as they are representative of a population that is fast dwindling and whose stories and history are in jeopardy of being lost forever. It is also important to note that the interviewees were asked to recount information about events that had transpired over 60 years ago. As a result, the accuracy of the information should be interpreted with caution.

In contrast to families of internees who were incarcerated in continental US internment camps, the families of the Honouliuli Camp internees seemed to have adjusted better to their post-internment lives. This remained true despite the fact that the internment experience in Hawai'i was very similar to what happened in the continental United States (e.g., family members being seized without reason or warning, the anxiety of not knowing if loved ones were okay, and forced incarceration). Several factors may have helped to mitigate the more deleterious effects of the internment and the traumatic sequelae seen on the continental United States. Since only a small portion of the total Japanese American population was interned, the families of Hawai'i internees seemed to have lost less than their continental US counterparts. For example, family units were generally left intact and unbroken. As a result, family members who were not incarcerated were able to tend to their homes and continue to operate family businesses. One of the most important differences between the continental US camps and Honouliuli was the more relaxed visitation rights that the Honouliuli internees were allowed. Despite the ominous guard towers, machine-gun nests, and barbed wire, trips to see family members interned in the Honouliuli Camp took on a level of gaiety that was not seen in any other camp. Family members were allowed to converse in Japanese with internees, and even participate in a limited amount of gift exchange.

On the other hand, there was an unnerving amount of silence around the internment. The veil of silence and secrecy was thickened by a lack of communication about the Honouliuli Camp. In a way, the topic of the internment became a taboo subject. Stigma and shame plagued family members of internees that were further exacerbated by wartime fear and hysteria. Friends and neighbors seemed to limit their contact with some of these families for fear of being associated with a family who had a member "branded" as an enemy of the United States. Although the families interviewed in this study seemed relatively happy and untouched by their experience, a faint shadow cast by the internment seemed to color their own worldviews. For example, RH and ES expressed a great distaste for war, and were hypervigilant about not having any group of people experience what they had experienced during World War II. For RH, the aftermath of the September 11, 2001, terrorist attacks and the events that had transpired in the Guantanamo Bay Detention Camp seemed to echo what happened to the Japanese Americans during World War II. RH was adamant in his views when he said, "So I don't want these things, what happened to me, [to] my family, to happen to anybody here whether it's Filipino, Chinese, Korean, whatever, you know, that's my thing.... [I]t's going to happen, look what happened to [the] Muslims!" (RH 2012:6)

All three families were also ineligible to receive the monies distributed by the Civil Liberties Act of 1988, authorizing the payment of $20,000 to each surviving internee, because their family members had long passed. RH, who more strongly felt the sharp bite of civil injustice, expressed disappointment in the government. Both RH and ES remarked that more than the monetary compensation, they would have liked some kind of apology from the government. In a way the feelings of disrespect cast a specter of doubt on the authenticity of democracy and the government for these individuals.

Over the years, dense jungle has threatened to swallow up not only the remains but also the history behind the Honouliuli Internment and POW Camp. Like the Jewish Holocaust (Danieli 1985), the trauma of the Japanese American internment has created a heterogeneous group of responses and reactions in the internees and their families. The Honouliuli Camp offers us a look into the effects of the government's decision to use a different set of procedures to intern the Japanese Americans living in Hawai'i. Finally, it offers an important piece to the Japanese American internment history, and underscores the inimical effects of civil injustice. ❖

References

American Psychiatric Association. 2013. *Diagnostic and Statistical Manual of Mental Health Disorders: DSM-5.* 5th ed. Washington, DC: American Psychiatric Publishing.

Barocas, Harvey. 1975. "Children of Purgatory: Reflections on the Concentration Camp Survival Syndrome." *International Journal of Social Psychiatry* 21:87–92.

Barocas, Harvey, and Carol Barocas. 1973. "Manifestations of Concentration Camp Effects on the Second Generation." *American Journal of Psychiatry* 130:820–821.

———. 1980. "Separation and Individuation Conflict in Children of Holocaust Survivors." *Journal of Contemporary Psychotherapy* 11:6–14.

Brave Heart-Jordan, Maria Yellow Horse, Josephine Chase, Jennifer Elkins, and Deborah B. Altschul. 2011. "Historical Trauma among Indigenous Peoples of the Americas: Concepts, Research, and Clinical Considerations." *Journal of Psychoactive Drugs* 43(4):282–290.

Brave Heart-Jordan, Maria Yellow Horse and Lemyra M. DeBruyn. 1995. "So She May Walk in Balance: Integrating the Impact of Historical Trauma in the Treatment of Native American Indian Women." Pp. 345–368 in *Racism in the Lives of Women: Testimony Theory and Guides to Anti-Racist Practice*, edited by J. Adleman and G. Enquidanos. New York: Haworth Press.

Burton, Jeff, Mary Farrell, Lisa Kaneko, Linda Maldonato, and Kelly Altenhofen. 2014. "Hell Valley: Uncovering a Prison Camp in Paradise." In this issue.

Commission on Wartime Relocation and Internment of Civilians (CWRIC). 1997. *Personal Justice Denied.* Seattle, WA: University of Washington Press.

Danieli, Yael. 1982. "Families of Survivors and the Nazi Holocaust: Some Short and Long-Term Effects." Pp. 405–423 in *Stress and Anxiety.* Vol. 8, edited by D. Spielberger, I. G. Sarason, and N. Milgram. Washington, DC: Hemisphere.

———. 1985. "The Treatment and Prevention of Long-Term Effects and Intergenerational Transmission of Victimization: A Lesson from Holocaust Survivors and their Children." Pp. 295–313 in *Trauma and Its Wake: The Study and Treatment of Post-Traumatic Stress Disorder*, edited by C. R. Figley. New York: Brunner/Mazel.

Daniels, Roger. 1986. "Relocation, Redress, and the Report: A Historical Appraisal." Pp. 3–9 in *Japanese Americans: From Relocation to Redress*, edited by R. Daniels, S. C. Taylor, and H. H. L. Kitano. Salt Lake City: University of Utah Press.

ES Family. 2012. Interview by Garyn Tsuru, Wahiawa, HI, October 5, 2012.

Falgout, Suzanne. 2014. "Honouliuli's POWs: Making Connections, Generating Changes." In this issue.

Heller, David. 1981. "Themes of Culture and Ancestry among Children of Concentration Camp Survivors." *Psychia* 45:247–261.

Japanese Cultural Center of Hawai'i. N.d. "Honouliuli: The Story of the WWII Internment of Japanese Americans living in Hawai'i." Japanese Cultural Center of Hawai'i. Unpublished manuscript.

Kashima, Tetsuden. 2003. *Judgment Without Trial: Japanese American Imprisonment during World War II.* Seattle: University of Washington Press.

Kestenberg, Judith. 1980. "Psychoanalysis of Children of Survivors from the Holocaust: Case Presentations and Assessment." Pp. 137–158 in *Generations of Holocaust,* edited by M. Bergmann and M. Jucovy. New York: Basic Books.

Kitano, Harry H. L., and Akemi Kikumura. 1976. "The Japanese American Family." Pp. 41–61 in *Ethnic Families in America,* edited by C. Mindel and R. W. Habenstein. New York: Elsevier.

Mass, Amy I. 1986. "Psychological Effects of the Camps on the Japanese Americans." Pp. 159–162 in *Japanese Americans: From Relocation to Redress,* edited by R. Daniels, H. H. L. Kitano, and S. Taylor. Salt Lake City: University of Utah Press.

Morishima, James K. 1973. "The Evacuation: Impact on the Family." Pp. 13–19 in *Asian Americans: Psychological Perspective,* edited by S. Sue and N. N. Wagner. Palo Alto: Science and Behavior Books.

Nadler, Arie, Sophie Kav-Venaki, and Beny Gleitman. 1985. "Transgenerational Effects of the Holocaust: Externalization of Aggression in Second Generation of Holocaust Survivors." *Journal of Clinical and Consulting Psychology* 53:365–369.

Nagata, Donna K. 1990. "The Japanese American Internment: Exploring the Transgenerational Consequences of Traumatic Stress." *Journal of Traumatic Stress* 3:47–69.

———. 1993. *Legacy of Injustice: Exploring the Cross-Generational Impact of the Japanese American Internment.* New York: Plenum Press.

———. 1998. "Intergenerational Effects of the Japanese American Internment." Pp. 125–139 in *International Handbook of Multigenerational Legacies of Trauma,* edited by Y. Danieli. New York: Plenum Press.

Neiderland, William G. 1968. "Clinical Observations on the 'Survivor Syndrome.'" *International Journal of Psychoanalysis* 49:313–315.

Niiya, Brian. 2010. "World War II Internment in Hawaii." Online resource for students and instructors. Retrieved October 30, 2013 (http://www.hawaiiinternment.org/history-of-internment).

Nishimura, Amy. 2014. "From Priestesses and Disciples to Witches and Traitors: Internment of Japanese Women at Honouliuli and Narratives of 'Madwomen.'" In this issue.

Park, Yoosun. 2008. "Facilitating Injustice: Tracing the Role of Social Workers in the World War II Internment of Japanese Americans." *Social Service Review* 82(3):447–484.

Prince, Robert M. 1985. "Second Generation Effects of Historical Trauma." *The Psychoanalytic Review* 72(1):9–21.

RH. 2012. Interview by Garyn Tsuru, Honolulu, September 21.

Rosenfeld, Alan. 2014. "Neither Aliens nor Enemies: The Hearings of 'German' and 'Italian' Internees in Wartime Hawai'i." In this issue.

SK. 2012. Interview by Garyn Tsuru, Honolulu, September 21.

Solkoff, Norman. 1981. "Children of Survivors of the Holocaust: A Critical Review of the Literature." *American Journal of Orthopsychiatry* 51:29–41.

Sotero, Michelle M. 2006. "A Conceptual Model of Historical Trauma: Implications for Public Health Practice and Research." *Journal of Health Disparities Research and Practice* 1(1):93–108.

Contributors

Susan Matoba Adler is Professor of Early Childhood Education at the University of Hawai'i–West O'ahu. Her research on Asian American families began as a PhD student at the University of Wisconsin–Madison, led to her book, *Mothering, Education, and Ethnicity: The Transformation of Japanese American Culture* (1998) and continued as a faculty member at the University of Michigan and the University of Illinois at Urbana–Champaign. She has also published on Hmong teachers and families and on racial/ethnic identity of Asian American children.

Kelly Altenhofen, a veteran of the US Armed Forces, was a student in the first University of Hawai'i–West O'ahu field class at Honouliuli, and has worked as a Biological Science Technician at Jean Lafitte National Historical Park and Preserve for the National Park Service.

Leilani Basham is an Associate Professor at UH–West O'ahu where she teaches Hawaiian language and Hawaiian studies courses. Her educational background is interdisciplinary, including Hawaiian Studies (BA, UH–Mānoa, 1992), Hawaiian Language (Certificate, UH–Mānoa, 1993), History (MA, UH–Mānoa, 2002), and Political Science (PhD, UH–Mānoa, 2007). Her research interests focus on the convergence of these disciplines, and include topics such as wahi pana (traditional place-names), mele lāhui (nationalist poetry), Hawaiian sexuality, and second language curriculum development. She is also the kumu hula of Hālau Kupukupu Ke Aloha, a small hālau hula focusing on educating her students on the contents and contexts of the dances and chants taught.

Jeff Burton is the Cultural Resources manager for Manzanar National Historic Site in California. He received his MA in Anthropology from the University of Arizona in 1990. Although he has published reports on topics ranging from Archaic-period pithouses to eighteenth-century Spanish missions, his greatest passion is the archaeology of World War II Japanese American internment sites.

Joyce N. Chinen is a Professor of Sociology at the University of Hawai'i–West O'ahu. She received her PhD in Sociology from the University of Hawai'i at

Mānoa in 1989. Her research has focused on the intersection of race, class, and gender in "work," Okinawans in Hawai'i's Labor Movement, transnational identity, social movements, and the Okinawan diaspora.

Suzanne Falgout is a Professor of Anthropology at University of Hawai'i–West O'ahu. She received her PhD in Anthropology from University of Oregon in 1984. Her research has focused on Micronesia, especially the island of Pohnpei, and has covered topics ranging from archaeology and oral traditions, indigenous epistemology, women, ethnohistory, and World War II from indigenous perspectives, to Micronesian diaspora to Hawai'i.

Mary Farrell is the director of Trans-Sierran Archaeological Research, a small consulting firm in eastern California. She received her MA in Anthropology from the University of Arizona in 1991. Retired from a long career as a US Forest Service archaeologist, her work has focused on cultural resources management, historic preservation, and public interpretation.

Lisa Kaneko received her BA in Anthropology from the University of Nevada, Las Vegas in 2011. She is currently pursuing a Certificate in Applied Forensic Anthropology through the University of Hawai'i–West O'ahu while continuing her education in Forensic Science at Chaminade University of Honolulu.

Jane Kurahara is a staff associate at the Japanese Cultural Center of Hawai'i and co-chair of the Hawai'i Confinement Sites Committee since its inception in 2005. A retired school librarian, she has been a volunteer at the cultural center for nearly two decades. In that time, she has taken the lead in many aspects of the center's work on the Hawai'i internees' story including outreach, archaeology, and internment-related collections, exhibitions, and education.

Linda Maldonato received her BA in Social Sciences with a concentration in Anthropology from the University of Hawai'i–West O'ahu in 2013. She also completed a certification in Applied Forensic Anthropology through the University and the Joint POW/MIA Accounting Command. While in school she was an Oak Ridge Institute of Science and Technology fellow and is planning to continue her education in Anthropology at the University of New Orleans.

Brian Niiya is the content director for Denshō: The Japanese American Legacy Project and editor of the *Denshō Encyclopedia*. A public historian specializing in Japanese American history and culture, he has held senior positions at the Japanese American National Museum and Japanese Cultural Center of Hawai'i and has written, produced, or curated numerous projects in a variety of media including print, museum exhibitions, videos, and websites.

Linda Nishigaya is a retired Professor of Sociology at the University of Hawaiʻi–West Oʻahu. Her areas of specialization are in Social Psychology, Race and Ethnic Relations, and Social Stratification. Her research interests have focused on community-based human services targeting minority groups and institutional research related to curriculum and teaching.

Amy Nishimura is an Associate Professor of English at the University of Hawaiʻi–West Oʻahu. She teaches classes on Gender and Sexuality, Postcolonial Literature, and Feminist Literary Theory. Her research interests includes Literature of Hawaiʻi and Postcolonial Literature. She continues to engage in research about local, female immigrant writers of Hawaiʻi and the Japanese American women interned at Honouliuli.

Gary Y. Okihiro is Professor of International and Public Affairs at Columbia University. His latest publications are *Island World: A History of Hawaiʻi and the United States* and *Pineapple Culture: A History of the Tropical and Temperate Zones.*

Ernest Oshiro is a retired Professor of Economics at University of Hawaiʻi–West Oʻahu. He received his PhD in Agricultural Economics from the University of Hawaiʻi at Mānoa in 1978. His research and teaching focused on microeconomics, statistics, and educational assessment. Since retiring in 2010, he has been studying Japanese culture, language, and religion, especially Shin Buddhism.

Toni Han Palermo is the Program Specialist at the King Kamehameha V Judiciary History Center located in Aliʻiōlani Hale, the home of the Hawaiʻi State Supreme Court. She received a degree in anthropology with an emphasis in archaeology from the University of Hawaiʻi, Mānoa in 1974. For many years, Toni conducted archaeological research in French Polynesia and in Hawaiʻi. At the judiciary, she conducts research on Hawaiian kingdom related court documents and history as well as coordinating programs that meld the historical with contemporary legal history.

Alan Rosenfeld is an Associate Professor of History at University of Hawaiʻi–West Oʻahu. He received his PhD in History from the University of California–Irvine in 2008. Although his research endeavors have operated on two separate planes, he is particularly interested in the dynamic of state power and resistance. In addition to investigating public and state reactions to left-wing extremist violence in the Federal Republic of Germany, he has explored the topic of martial law and the internment of civilians in wartime Hawai'i.

Garyn K. Tsuru is an Assistant Professor of Psychology at the University of Hawai'i–West O'ahu. He received his PhD in Clinical Psychology from the University of Michigan, Ann Arbor in 2010. He currently directs the Psychotherapy Process and Treatment Outcome Lab at the University of Hawai'i–West O'ahu.

Betsy Young is a staff associate at the Japanese Cultural Center of Hawai'i. An award-winning public school teacher with language arts, children's literature, reading, and special education curriculum specialties, and, as a school librarian, she has dedicated much of her retirement to volunteering at the cultural center where her main focus has been on developing curriculum on Japanese American internment for Hawai'i's schools. She has facilitated numerous Honouliuli internment site tours and has conducted countless outreach presentations to community groups and schools.

Social Process in Hawai'i

SELECTED ISSUES

Social Process in Hawai'i
Editorial Policy

Social Process in Hawai'i is a journal published by the University of Hawai'i at Mānoa Department of Sociology with the objective of disseminating to scholars, students, and the community the results of outstanding social science research on the people and institutions of Hawai'i.

Since this journal's inception, the Department of Sociology has taken the view that the communities in Hawai'i offer a rich and varied opportunity for observing the interplay of social processes which maintain stability and provoke social change. It is our hope that the journal might stimulate social research in Hawai'i, provide materials for instruction of students, and enhance the understanding of the community among those who live and work here.

With the support of the Andrew W. Lind *Social Process in Hawai'i* Fund, we welcome suggestions and submissions for special issues (thematic edited works, small monographs) in addition to occasional issues of a more general character. Contributions are encouraged from University faculty, graduate and undergraduate students in Sociology and other disciplines as well as other knowledgeable persons in the community. Preference will be given to research based upon sound methodologies and systematic evidence. Articles should employ a mid-level of writing and minimize technical terms. The presentation of complex statistical techniques should be kept to a minimum, and where used, should be accompanied by a clear textual description of the technique and its results.

Manuscripts are evaluated by the editors and other referees. Editors may occasionally solicit manuscripts, but in general most selections will be from among unsolicited manuscripts.

Authors interested in submitting manuscripts for consideration should send three copies to SOCIAL PROCESS IN HAWAI'I, Department of Sociology, Saunders Hall 247, University of Hawai'i at Mānoa, Honolulu, HI 96822. The following guidelines should be observed in preparation of the manuscript:

1. Due to space limitations, short articles are preferred. Manuscripts should not exceed 15 double-spaced pages. Photographs, charts and graphs are welcome.

2. Preparation of copy and the format for references should follow the guidelines of the AMERICAN SOCIOLOGICAL REVIEW. In case of unusual problems, consult the Editor.

3. Manuscripts submitted to the journal should be of final draft quality; the editor reserves the right to make minor editorial changes.

4. The University of Hawai'i guidelines for allocating credit for research and writing should be observed.